Freeman's
California

Previous Issues

Freeman's
California

Est. 2015

Edited by

John Freeman

Grove Press UK

First published in the United States of America in 2019 by Grove/Atlantic Inc.

First published in Great Britain in 2019 by Grove Press UK, an imprint of Grove/Atlantic Inc.

Assistant Editor: Dhyana Taylor
Managing Editor: Julia Berner-Tobin
Copy Editor: Kirsten Giebutowski

1 3 5 7 9 8 6 4 2

A CIP record for this book is available from the British Library.

Grove Press, UK
Ormond House
26–27 Boswell Street
London
WC1N 3JZ

www.groveatlantic.com

Trade paperback ISBN 978 1 61185 473 2
Ebook ISBN 978 1 61185 906 5

Printed in Great Britain by Bell and Bain Ltd, Glasgow

Contents

CONTENTS

Introduction

JOHN FREEMAN

H e didn't tell us where we were going.
This was not unusual. My father loved pointless drives.
He'd hustle us into the car and then we'd tool across town. No
destination. Sometimes these drives went on for fifteen minutes.
Sometimes several hours.

We'd meander home from church the long way, stopping at open
houses. *Are we going to live here?* No, let's just look, he'd reply.

Do I need to say all the homes we ogled were much bigger
than ours?

And so I grew up in the multiverse. Have you heard of this
term? The theory that reality is simply a series of stacked ver-
sions of itself.

This idea—that something else was always simultaneously
happening elsewhere—called to my father, and so that Christmas
night in 1985 my mother, my brothers, and I—there are three of
us—knew we could have been going anywhere.

We passed the malls, then the turnoff to the adjacent suburbs.
Then it seemed clear we were going to downtown Sacramento.
Our hearts sank.

My father ran a family service agency in the city that provided
health and human services. They did things the government gave

up on. Meals on Wheels programs, counseled people getting on or off welfare.

The office was a big old home with sticky floors and it smelled of Tab cola. Most of the time he stashed us in a room with no toys and we were told to wait.

The whole place had the low, quiet ache of disappointment.

And looking back I suppose it should have . . . that's what the agency dealt in, how to cope with disappointment.

It was dark now and we had sailed right past his work; none of the streets were looking familiar. My mother was talking quietly to my father as they drove.

Where are we?

We're here. Come on, help me with this.

My father opened the back of our banana-colored station wagon and yanked out several wrapped presents.

Come on guys.

We followed him and my mother to the door. All of us had paper routes, and though we lacked any kind of social IQ, we were experts in front doors.

This was the kind of metal that would bang if you tried to one-hop the paper to the porch and hit the door by accident.

My dad rapped it loudly. RAP RAP RAP. A light turned on. The metal door opened and a woman appeared. She was dressed for work in the kind of outfit Lucy wore in *I Love Lucy*. She looked confused but friendly.

Hi we're your neighbors from United Way, and we just wanted to say Merry Christmas.

By this point, my brothers and I were holding the presents.

We still didn't know what we were doing there, but the woman behind the door, she had figured out why. Her eyes softened, and then she put on the face you make when you have another face you need to cover up.

Oh you are so kind. Thank you . . . !

A child our age appeared behind the woman.

This is my daughter . . .

There we stood on the other side of the door. Two families. Ours, the five of us, and theirs, the two of them.

That's when the girl our age burst into tears and ran back into the house.

We have been talking a lot in recent years about privilege. White privilege, male privilege, straight privilege. I know I have benefited from all these things, but when I have to identify a period where I understood—before I could articulate—what any of these things meant, I think of that night.

We use a horrible phrase to describe such incidents: teachable moments. But who are they teaching? And what? At age eleven the lesson, for me, was too complex. What was supposed to be an objective demonstration in generosity—giving is good—turned into a tutorial in the invisibility of power. That it takes power to give, and power to create moments for learning, rather than have them thrust upon you. The woman's daughter had decoded all of it in under a second and it made her feel ashamed.

It took me years to understand that, because as a middle-class striver, I had other teachable lessons I was paying attention to—mostly in books. You read the books, you followed the plan, you took the classes, you did the right activities, you got into the schools that enlarged your life progressively, sequentially, logically, coherently.

But of course, we often learn the most from what we see. It sits inside us like a spinning top, moving of its own accord, until we grab it.

That Christmas set one such dynamo in motion.

Here is another one.

All those nights I stayed up late as a teenager, reading books, doing my homework, determined to get into college, I often shared the dining room table with my mother, who was a social worker in Sacramento, like my father—a professional listener. Most of her patients were in hospice, and this was the 1980s, so they were cancer patients, Alzheimer patients, and early AIDS patients, dying in terror. Lonely and afraid, angry, bewildered. *Why has this happened to me?* She once told me they said this a lot.

While I dutifully extracted the teachable lessons from the core curricula of the San Joaquin Unified School District, she wrote notes of her visits to patients in Vacaville, Sonora, Placer County.

I see her in memory's lamp, bent over her notebook transcribing their stories, and I now know there was something holy in what she was doing. While I was racing to turn myself into an excavator for meaning, she had turned herself into an abacus for pain. Recording and measuring and holding what was often seen, but remained invisible—the stories of people who were suffering.

I tell you this now because eventually the meaning of these stories caught up with me—because life did. I did get into the good school, I did move to New York, which is where you went to work in the storytelling business. I did get a job in publishing and did turn myself into a freelance writer. I spent a decade reviewing books full-time, and became an editor of a literary magazine, and did all the things a striver in my field with a passion for literature might try to do because I genuinely loved it—I loved the possibilities of literature. What it was and what it stood for. I believed in all of it.

All these things are true.

But here's another story from the multiverse. What if I told you that if I had to construct a reunion of this gift exchange, say, fifteen years after the fact, just two members of my family would be standing on that West Sacramento porch? My older brother would be homeless, living out of a van on a construction site in Oregon, sometimes wrestling his 120-pound malamute in the dark so she knew he was top dog; my younger brother would be under full restraint at a psychiatric ward, in the throes of a schizophrenic breakdown. My mother would already be in the steep decline of a frontal lobe dementia. And come to think of it, my father, who took care of her through this illness—the one that garbled her speech, then stumbled her legs, then sat her down, and then turned her into just her ability to smile, before clicking off the lamp behind her eyes—he wouldn't be there on that reunion porch either. No, he'd be waiting for a social worker to come to his door to listen to him talk about his unbelievable problem.

California has for a long time been seen as the Valhalla of far-flung dreams. The far shore. It's why my family moved back there in 1984. The place of starting over. The end of the horizon, as Joan Didion famously wrote.

California is also, however, the site of real people's homes. Real people's lives. Real lives begun as dreams and perhaps dribbled into boredom. Or unraveled into nightmares. Or fabulously, miraculously achieved. This schism—between what California represents in popular imagination and what it is, what it means to live there, to be from there—means Californians collide constantly with the rupture of existence.

How to dream the life we are already living.

One of the best definitions of literature I ever heard was uttered by a California writer, T. C. Boyle. Literature, he said, is how we dream in story. One of the best definitions of immigration was also told to me by a Californian—Natalie Diaz. Immigration, she said, is dreaming with the body. You imagine a better future somewhere else, because you must, and so you move—you move your body into a dream.

L iterature from California is among the most alive in the world, in part because it is being driven by these questions. California has more immigrants than any other state in the U.S.— nearly a quarter of the immigrant population. Nearly a third of the state is foreign-born. In a world in the throes of a massive global migration, this makes California the most literary state of an increasingly unliterate nation.

A state built with, stolen, and powered by immigrants is an army of living untold dreams. So here are some of them, dreams lived, deferred, daydreamed, nightmare-dreamt. This special issue of *Freeman's* is an attempt to celebrate these stories, these writers, and to follow the fog lamp of their imagination into the other issues California faces, which, in fact, mirror some of the most important issues of our time—from global climate change, to the radical and pernicious stockpiling of wealth in one minuscule group of individuals.

If our civilization is ever going to reckon with these realities, it is going to have to dream better in story. Californians do not, most of them, have the luxury to postpone such dreams. The state is literally on fire.

D riving down 1-280 in his opening piece, Jaime Cortez stops at a rest stop in the Central Valley and sees what he thinks is a collection of people living out of their cars. Instead he discovers it packed with escapees from the recent Paradise Fire.

William T. Vollmann dons a protective mask and drives up into the foothills outside Sacramento with the photographer Greg Roden to witness the Carr Fire, and finds a world in which the supposed future of climate disaster is now. In her short story, Karen Tei Yamashita chronicles the aftermath of World War II as it plays out in the lives of a widowed Japanese woman and her Japanese-American husband's relations.

Motion is a big part of these pieces, clocking the emotional doppler effect of migration. In Javier Zamora's poem he remembers how hard it was to relearn beauty in a new language. Reyna Grande tells of her mother, the half of her family who didn't become the immigrant success story, and the vertigo she experiences when she grapples with that—a feeling that turns into a ghost story in Oscar Villalon's tale of his father being visited by a spectre on his porch growing up in Mexico.

How to live with such hauntings—there's no other word for them. In Manuel Muñoz's tale, a Mexican man turns up half buried in the fields, like an ostrich. None of the white people in town know who he is. Are such visions projections of guilt or something else Rabih Alameddine asks, as he recounts his brief detour as a bartender, when many of his friends were dying of AIDS, and he found in a gang of regulars an unlikely form of fellowship. In a state tilted forward into dreams of the future, the past can become kitsch, or worse, capitalist marketing material, as D. A. Powell writes in his poem about the gay pride parade. In her essay, Heather Smith wonders if the bison brought to Golden Gate Park knew this all along.

The land in California was twice stolen from the peoples who lived there. Growing up on it, Natalie Diaz learns to make her body a tool, an offensive weapon, essentially putting on hold some of the issues she would eventually have to deal with as a queer Native woman with Mexican heritage. Is there a way to stopper this process? The narrator of Tommy Orange's story is so exhausted by the mental work of asserting his existence he falls into a thought pattern: maybe ending his life is the only legitimate route?

There's a quiet surrealism to some of these tales. In Xuan Juliana Wang's memoir, a simple avocado takes on magical powers when seen through the eyes of a culture that was forcibly starved. Shobha Rao's short story revolves around a family of immigrants who turn up in California in time to watch the Space Shuttle Challenger explode. Anthony Marra notes how the Italians in San Francisco's North Beach immortalize their journey in food that's so tasty, when they ask if you like it, it isn't a question.

Some of the writers here are in the process of re-narrating the stories that disguised their part in California's history. Lauren Markham describes how four generations of her family have occupied and told the tale of their possession of a dry as hell part of the state, where water and land is everything, and most of it has been taken by white families, like hers. Frank Bidart recalls driving across the Mojave on the way to Bakersfield to visit his grandfather in an envelope of protection so great it had kept his father out of World War II. "The government didn't draft—even / refused to enlist—rich / farmers," he writes.

Sometimes simply acknowledging reality has a powerful effect. It has the sonic boom of truth. Yiyun Li describes the strange brittle friendliness of neighbors in Oakland who turn mean when they can't sell you anything. Elaine Castillo goes to visit a loved one in prison and turns the essay form inside out. Héctor Tobar depicts the inner life of a latchkey boy whose mother has to leave him home all day, proving the immortal stories of James

Joyce could have just as easily taken root in the dry southern part of California.

Piece by piece, these writers reassert what is possible to see clearly when you press down on language with enough care and force. Matt Sumell describes his relationship with the man who sleeps in a cardboard box outside his window in L.A. in a way that pays equal attention to the man as it does Sumell's proximity to his circumstances. Mai Der Vang honors the beauty of the state's most iconic tree—the redwood—in a poem so tightly wound it feels like seeing one for the first time. In his latest poem, former California and U.S. poet laureate Juan Felipe Herrera shows how everyday laborers turned fantastic with a change of clothes in his part of the state, some years ago.

Is it any wonder, given these juxtapositions, that California is a state full of dream machines—from the internet to drugs to cars. Rachel Kushner describes all the fabulous vehicles she's owned and the peculiar world in which cars are more vivid than people. Geoff Dyer describes why it's no longer fun to get high in California. In Namwali Serpell's story, a homeless teenager gets invited to a free-love party in the Berkeley hills, powered by drugs and a fantasy of benevolent togetherness.

Even as a fourteen-year-old, Jennifer Egan knew this world— this hippy world—was powered by significant oversights, and danger. Just as Catherine Barnett was aware that driving home with her father when he was drunk wasn't safe, and Maggie Millner worried there were parts of Monterey that might blow her illusions away if she stayed too long. This layering—of dreams with dreams within nightmares—is one of the ways California writing distinguishes itself. It takes looking back, sometimes, as Robin Coste Lewis does in her poem about going to the movies with her family, to see its lack of perfection is what makes it paradise.

As I write this, I am getting on a plane to go home to California to celebrate my father's eightieth birthday in Los Angeles. The number eighty, once so ancient sounding, now hardly feels miraculous, the closer we get to it. His father lived to be ninety-seven, so there is that, too, but packing for the trip I couldn't help but think of my father's father, who died much younger, penniless, and of the generations before, like my great-great-great grandfather, who came to Grass Valley in the late 1800s, also broke, married to his brother's widow, as one did more often then. The journey from Canada must have been difficult and long; there were no trains upon which one could travel it. So it would have been completed by foot and by horse. We have almost no records of him, until one day he emerges in county records, renting a storefront to a baker.

Later this week as I meet my father and hug him, a part of his body will call back from that storefront, a very long time ago. I wish my mother could be there, but she will be only in the stories we tell. My brothers will be there, my older brother, no longer in his van, and my younger one, resettled in Texas and very much well. Deadpanning his acute observations of the absurdities of our lives. How the earth falls through space. I am already thinking of the multiverse questions I want to ask my father, his life a record of events created by choices or events even he couldn't imagine had quantum implications. Each day a new stack of realities. As our literature can be, as it ought to be, as California literature is in its finest moments. Hold it close and you will hear it singing of its incredible journeys, of what it dreams possible.

Seven Shorts

FIRE NOTES: NOVEMBER 2018

My evening commute takes me north on Highway 280 towards San Francisco. One hundred and fifty miles to the east, Paradise is burning at the heart of the largest wildfires in California's long and storied history of fires. The thick smoke, which blankets the entire region for hundreds of miles, contains the particulate remains of Paradise. It occurs to me that in unison, millions of us are inhaling the sofas and ottomans of Paradise, the cars and gas stations of it, the trees and lawns, the clothes and detergent, the wedding pictures and divorce papers, the cadavers. This thought comforts and discomforts me as I drive through the evening traffic.

I need to use the bathroom, so I pull over at the Crystal Springs Highway Rest Area. The rest stop used to be notoriously cruisy, drawing gay and temporarily gay men from around the region with the promise of nocturnal sex in the bathroom stalls, in the cars, or on the trail that winds up the scrubby adjacent hillside. Increased surveillance of the rest stop, and finally a mini police station planted near the bathrooms, put an end to the nightlife.

The now-chaste rest stop is packed. Its parking lot is sizeable, with room for thirty or forty cars, but every parking spot is occupied. I find a patch of roadside and improvise one. I walk to the bathroom, and there is not one person in there.

Hmmm . . .

The whole rest stop is jammed full of cars, but no one is using the bathrooms. "But it's a rest stop," I think. "It's all about bathrooms, isn't it?" Evidently not. On my way out, I see through the open door that no one seems to be using the women's bathroom either.

I walk back to my car slowly, and I notice now that one car after another is packed to bursting with stuff. There are pickups with their beds stacked high with blankets, bicycles, boxes, and chairs, Beverly Hillbillies–style.

My nosiness is piqued. I slow my walk to a near shuffle and assess each car. I see a woman in an old Civic bundled up in the fully reclined passenger seat. She is turning about in her blankets, trying to find a comfortable position to settle in for the night. She sees me looking fixedly, and I feel a small wave of shame rise and break in my chest. I have been busted being morbidly nosey. I witnessed this act of settling in, this act that is normally so intimate, to be seen only by the eyes of your kin or your lover.

Next door, in a little red pickup with a rusted hood and bumper, I see someone's hands adjusting a metallic folding windshield sun screen for privacy. The overhead LED lights shine through the windshield, reflecting off the silver screen, and the hands seem those of a deft puppeteer in a sad, surreal cabaret.

I see a bearded man with a steaming paper cup of something sitting on his car hood and chatting with a second man in the passenger seat of the neighboring car. I eavesdrop. Their chatter is a bit of nothing about the brisk weather, the smoke. Backlit by lights from the rest stop map kiosk, their words exit their warm bodies and become delicate vapor genies that dissipate into the darkness.

Shit. I finally understand. The parking lot is either a longtime encampment for car-dwelling folk, or an ad hoc way station for refugees from the epic fires engulfing Paradise and the neighboring areas of Butte County.

Or both.

I stand there for a moment, and take in a big breath of smoke-tinged air, and I am stunned by how deeply dystopian this scene is. The dirty twilight air. The car people battered by inequity and priced out of proper shelter. The people who gazed into the burning eye of climate change and fled for their lives.

We did not ask for this, but we chose this. Through our action and inaction, we chose those fires, that smoke, and this displacement. We are all paying for it, though these people are paying more dearly than the rest of us. Of course I am complicit in this, just like everyone else. Of course I can do better. Of course. Of course.

I feel a dull, leaden weight on my shoulders. I turn my face towards the hillside. The gate to the uphill trail is locked for the night, but I mentally vault over it and take the short hike up to the vista point, where a hulking statue of the eighteenth-century Franciscan monk Junipero Serra awaits. Serra is bowed down on one knee, but the statue of the colonial missionary is still of heroic scale, perhaps twenty or more feet in height. His right arm is raised. His forefinger is pointed towards a polluted sunset of such lurid and awful beauty that gazing upon it gives me the dread of a marooned astronaut, emerging from his smoking capsule and pondering the heavy descent of the first, unknowable night.

—Jaime Cortez

GHOST STORY NO. 2

The dead come to you, but not to everyone. I have yet to see them—those who were here but left us, never to return. Yet there they are, at the end of a hall terminating at the closed door of a bathroom, or standing outside a living room window, looking down upon you as you watch cartoons on TV. Night or day, it doesn't matter. They try to announce themselves, waiting for you to see them.

This happened to my father when he was very young. He would've been in his early teens. He was on the small, covered patio in front of my grandmother's house. It was late. It was dark. My grandmother may or may not have given me the specifics on what my father was doing on the patio (these things are impossible to recall perfectly), but let's say he was in a rocking chair. Or he may have been sleeping out there, lying atop a couple of thick blankets, folded double for a cushion against the tile floor. But there he was, in the evening, nothing but quiet around him, the stars all easily visible as they are in that part of Mexico in that time some sixty or so years ago. Then my grandmother heard a crash (a rocking chair bowled over? A shoulder slammed into the closed front door before a hand could turn the knob all the way?), and then she saw her son in the sala, babbling and crying, his face drained of color.

I spent nights—scores of them—on that same patio. I was just a boy. Eleven, twelve, then thirteen, then once more when I was in high school, and not again till I was a junior in college, and nevermore since. (At first, the circumstances of work and life kept me from returning; then the evil of the drug war, which envenomed my father's hometown, extended that absence and does so to this day.) Stretches of summer were spent penduluming on a rocking chair, reading a novel, a Robert Ludlum or a Stephen King, doing "nothing." Between the time my father had to leave home, barely out of his teens, and when his sons roamed around his mother's house, bored and homesick, the view from that roofed patio had changed little if at all. Set into the foot of a hill, my grandmother's house slightly rises above a rocky dirt road. Below that road is an asphalt one leading, eventually, to the town's main plaza, and in between them is a steep wedge of tangled and desiccated greenery. Look into the horizon and there are rows after rows of flat rooftops, and mint and rose and lavender facades receding all the way to another set of hills in the distance, a gleaming reservoir smeared across its base. When the deep darkness falls, the tops of the streetlamps—ten-foot-tall, creosote-coated logs rigged with powerful light bulbs and metal shades—mark the distance like glowing buoys. But way back then, those streetlamps might not have been there, especially not the one some yards to the left of the patio that allowed us to make out each other's faces and bodies as we stretched out on thick cobijas, trying to fall asleep on hot nights, desperate for the air to finally cool. The darkness would have been near perfect. Yet my father could make out his grandfather. He could see him as if illuminated. And he could somehow hear him. And my great-grandfather spoke to him urgently, with terrible news, and that's what my father was trying to heave out, beyond "I have seen my grandfather!" He was trying to convey to his mother a message freighted with the authority of the dead returned among the living. Is it any wonder he was overwhelmed? To cry and to lose language is the purest response to witnessing a breach between the mortal and the immortal. It is awful. It is awesome. It is the stuff of myth.

Parents tell their children complicating facts in dribs and drabs, if at all. Sometimes, they do so judiciously, meaning

5

they're ready for the ensuing questions a disquieting bit of family history will stir. More often, they do so unthinkingly, meaning they hope the child will not think too hard about the peculiar revelation, maybe just offer a "really?" and leave it at that. The hope is the child won't exacerbate a father's recklessness: thinking aloud. Once we were driving in northern San Diego County (I think we were on the 5 or the 76), about twenty miles from home. My dad gestured to the landscape beyond the driver's window and said something like, your grandfather nearly died around here. He'd been hit by a car. Or was he thrown from one? I don't remember clearly. But that it was a car-related accident I do recall. I had tried writing about it when I was in college—a fiction redolent with descriptions of an unnamed character lying by the side of the road, legs ruined, the sun burning his face, his eyes closed and teary as car after car zooms past him, their black-and-yellow license plates rattling in their wash. My father's father could pass for Anglo, meaning he looked plenty American, and would cross the border as often as he pleased, working in the States, making his nut and bringing it back home, sometimes promptly blowing it. He came home once with a brand-new pickup, a treasure that made his oldest kids beam. It augured better things to come; no more wanting, a lot less suffering. Days later he lost it in a coin toss. Flipped a thick peso, and it came up wrong. Handed over the keys and that was that.

My grandfather woke up in a hospital in Oceanside. This would have been in the fifties. I can't help but think that his being tall and fair-skinned, with light-colored hair and eyes, may have had something to do with his being plucked from the road and placed in a bed. (Because being Mexican in San Diego has never been an easy thing. In 1983 Tom Metzger founded the White Aryan Resistance in Fallbrook in northern San Diego County. And the first successful school desegregation case in U.S. history—in

1931, Roberto Alvarez vs. the Board of Trustees of the Lemon Grove School District—ruled that Mexican kids in San Diego didn't have to keep going to separate schools; tellingly, it's a proud civic moment you might never hear about there.) My father tells me my grandfather was in the hospital for a while. Tells me one day my grandmother received a postcard from the hospital letting her know her husband was recuperating there, a way, I presume, of telling the family not to worry that they hadn't heard from him for so long. I strongly suspect my grandfather never kept his wife and children in the loop about anything, so his long silence wouldn't have meant much. Still, the postcard came as a relief. For now they knew my grandfather was out of danger. They had been anxious about his well-being since the night my great-grandfather appeared on the patio with the news that his son—my grandfather—was dying.

What a strange world. You're in a beat-up white van with your son, still a child but barely, driving by the place where your father was laid up so many years ago. And now you live near there, getting up at 4 a.m. to push a broom. Dinner for your family is sometimes eggs, or two frozen pizzas for ninety-nine cents a box. What do you have to show for your life? You're raising your kids in government housing. There are things you see in the neighborhood that you can't do anything about. You might as well be a ghost. But yet, the dead have come to you. And they do not come to everybody.

—Oscar Villalon

EVERY AVOCADO

I saw my first avocado when I was five years old, in the winter of 1990. My mom smuggled it back in her suitcase after her first trip to America. Its name, I was told, was butter fruit. Since this is the stuff of memory, I remember the room was very dark, almost as if our only sources of light were candles and the moon. The avocado emerged from her suitcase and my family gathered around it, passing it from hand to hand. Nobody had ever seen such a thing before. Then I believe my dad sliced it with his pocketknife, and my mom broke it in half and cut each half into slices the width of my thumb. We ate it like a watermelon, with the dark skin still attached. Since it wasn't ripe, I remember distinctly that it had a rubbery texture and tasted like a pencil eraser. The flavor of that first avocado stayed with me for days afterward.

After our family immigrated to California I stayed away from avocados. It wasn't until my parents purchased their first house, and we met our neighbors, that I was reunited with this strange fruit. With great pride, the neighbors showed us their avocado tree, recalling a recent burglary where thieves jumped into their yard and harvested every single avocado of the season. That's how I discovered these things were precious. They gifted us with two avocados and told my parents to prepare them for me at home with spoonfuls of sugar or soy sauce.

But our new home wasn't ready for us to live in yet. Ours was still the infamous abandoned house on the street, the only one we could afford. All the mirrors were smashed. The toilets had been ripped from the ground, shattered. One day as my parents were working on the house, this same neighbor knocked on our door and gave my dad an avocado sapling, sprouted from their tree. "You won't be able to get any fruit from it for many years.

The tree will grow and grow but the fruit will not be edible. It will be ready, well, about the time your daughter's married," he said. I remember it well because he said it in front of me.

In middle school I learned about guacamole. What is this? What do you do with it? The first bite and it blew wind through my hair. My mom and dad both loved it. They called guacamole, avocado. And avocados, guacamoles. By the time my *lau lau* and *lau ye* came to live with us, my grandmother had no teeth left in her mouth. I served her avocados mashed up with big spoonfuls of sugar mixed in. She said, "Ah, this is good, this is good" while staring straight ahead at the Peking opera at full volume on satellite television.

In college I meet some Chileans who became dear to me. Their mothers traveled from their land of sunshine to stay with us, and prepared grilled meats that were always accompanied with avocado and tomato salad. I was in awe of these mothers, who behaved like no mothers I'd ever seen before. I loved the way they laughed freely in colorful dresses, how flowers blossomed from their hands as they spoke, and how they hugged and kissed all of us. I learned the Chilean way of dressing the avocados—creamy mayo, lemons, and garlic—and I took that recipe with me all the way back to China, where I moved after graduating from college.

In Beijing it was no longer so unusual to eat avocados. But they were rare and expensive. At Western restaurants, waitresses made guacamole tableside with half an avocado and enormous theatricality while my friends and I watched. In those years, I craved avocados more than ever; I wanted to eat them all the time. Their name was now oily pear or alligator pear and I loved asking for them, letting the strange words lope around my mouth. At the party of an American expat, the host had bought more than a dozen avocados and I was in charge of making the guacamole.

The Chinese guests watched me with fascination. They examined the avocados, gently pressing with their fingertips. Many of them were rotten. They were from Mexico. Almost from home.

The avocado tree in my parents' backyard was growing fruit by then. Not a lot. Not enough. Each year my dad waited for more. Perhaps it was because I was still not married.

In my *nai nai*'s house in south China, she planted an avocado with a seed we smuggled in our care package. Ten years later it has been growing and growing but never bore any fruit until last year. Then, during monsoon season, all the tiny avocados fell off the branches in the rain. My aunt showed them to me through the camera on her computer screen. Each and every single one. She held them in her palms like the eggs of a mystical bird.

I don't know when I started to associate avocados with wealth and perfection. Each time I cut into one, I make a little wish, that this one will be immaculate as the morning sun. My *nai nai* never neglects to water her avocado trees. My parents split up but my dad kept the house with our original sapling, even after he married again and a new daughter and mother-in-law moved in. When I bring my *lau lau* and *lau ye* avocados to eat at their nursing home, my grandmother still says, "Ahh, this is good, this is good." I spoon the softened sweet pulp into their open mouths, even on days when they don't recognize me.

When my boyfriend and I visited my family together for the first time, I knew he was the man I was going to marry because I could picture moving back to California with him. At the time I tried to entice him with avocados. Look at them, I said, holding out to him the objects of desire. Here in California they are plentiful and perfect. They are creamier here than anywhere else on earth.

I made something with avocados at every meal, fanning out slices on white porcelain plates to show off their svelte necks, their full bellies. Each time the avocados held up their end of the bargain: they were divine. As I set them down in front of him I hoped he would fall deeper in love with the sunshine that made them grow, with the air that smelled like the sea, with those strange fruits, with me.

—Xuan Juliana Wang

BOXES

To be clear it's not literally a coffin, but it is literally coffin-shaped, as in hexagonal, as opposed to the cushier rectangle of a casket. Mike's is built of broke-open Intercept Free Nitrile Glove boxes, the logos along their lengths lending this the look of a corporate sponsored funeral, only Mike's not dead, which I can tell because he pops his hand through and waves hello in the half-second lag between the headlight switch and my halogens fading out. He rarely if ever gophers his head up anymore—I'm guessing because by now he recognizes the particular whine of an old Jeep transmission and because I'm the only asshole who overnight parks there—but occasionally, after the thunk and click of my driver's side door, he'll ask how I'm doing. I don't ask how he's doing because I know how he's doing. He's doing homeless in Los Angeles for five years. He's doing sleeping in a box. Instead I ask if he needs anything—a blanket, food, money. There's always a pause before he tells me he's fine. I ask if he's sure and he assures me he's sure, and then me and this packaged voice in the dark wish each other goodnight.

This is the unglamorous side of Hollywood, the only side of Hollywood for me. Maybe I'm biased. Maybe just poor. I've lived here a decade, in an exposed brick studio between an elementary school and a fire station and directly above a horn shop, as in musical horns, with a problematic pocket pit bull with a cleft-face—Tink has teeth in her nose which connects to her mouth, kind of like a sea lamprey—who the day after I signed the adoption papers decided to become vocal, so now she barks at every recess announcement and wee-yoo and lonely flute through the floor, and at the voices of people smoking or arguing or shooting up or grunting out a shit in the alley below the window by my bed, which happens more than you might think, because it's Hollywood, and because the L.A. homeless population has surged from roughly 32,000 to roughlier 57,000 in just the last six years, and the city's attempts to deal with it have led to roving encampments and outbreaks of hepatitis and typhus and topless guys and one bucket bongo busker who accused Tink of being a water buffalo before assaulting the entire Blackwood Coffee Bar. Not the people, the furniture. The walls. The *Us Weeklys*.

Apparently, some of the Skid Rowers pushed out of a gentrifying downtown went westward, to Echo Park and to Culver City and to the lot my low beams light up every night along with the abandoned building behind it, its busted-up numbers first and its glass entryway leading to an off-white partition and a bathroom door the color of Chef Boyardee spaghetti sauce second. The floor inside is polished concrete, bare but for a crumpled strip of turf putting green the former tenants left behind with a tipped over wire wastebasket and two golf balls adjacent as testicles. Third or eighth, depending what you count, is a reflective Unauthorized Vehicles Will Be yabba blabba sign mounted halfway up the exterior wall that catches half-a-headlight and half-zings it back at me, its shine voltaic and scattershot, illuminating, just a little, Mike's setup.

It's not until six-thirty the next morning that I actually see him through the window nearest my table, where I sit with a cup of Kroger coffee and every few sips tell Tink to shush the fuck up and stop staring at me, Daddy's busy watching this bro blink at the front end of my car for like the last ten minutes. Eventually Mike pulls his winter cap off and runs a comb through his hair ten times, puts his hat back on and pulls it low, like right over his eyebrows low, like even his forehead is cold low, then folds and slides his blanket into a black backpack and gets weird with the zippers. He's very particular about those. I've seen him lean to look at them from different angles, then hold the bag up in front of his face and rotate it, making sure they're zipped to where he wants them zipped—up top and centered—and when he's satisfied he places the bag behind him against the wall. He puts his right shoe on before his left, methodically folds and stacks his boxes, then tucks them out of the way between a concrete safety bollard and the adjacent fence. Dude is diagnosably neat. Even if I don't see him I can tell if he's been there by how clean that corner of the lot is.

On the mornings Tink barks enough and stares enough to guilt me enough to get me outside early enough, we catch Mike midroutine or en route to the bus stop. Up close and in the low light of predawn or just-dawn, when the diesel diffused sun hasn't burned through yet, he looks a bit like the actor Michael Shannon, or like Michael Shannon's second cousin from Burbank, maybe, or maybe it's better to say what the two really share is that unsettling alchemy of vulnerable and terrifying. His eyes are LSD spooky—wide-set, wide-open, uneasy. Most of the time you can see the whites all the way around his irises. People are scared of him, but to me he seems more imposed on than imposing. Intelligence can do that. Trauma. Mental illness. Maybe they're the same thing. Maybe they're all folded into each other. Maybe that's what bad luck is.

While it's a bit too on the nose I can't help but think of Shannon's turn in *Take Shelter*, both for the physical likeness and because he depicts a man struggling with hallucinations and voices in his head, voices he's not sure he can trust. The fact that Mike sleeps on the street is reason enough to wonder, as even the most conservative estimates put serious mental illness among the homeless somewhere between twenty and twenty-five percent. That number goes way up in "unsheltered individuals." Then there's the zipper thing, the obsessive neatness, the fact that he once turned down my offer to buy him breakfast because he needed to brush his teeth. Mostly, though, it's not his answers that worry me but the pauses before them. His responses to even the most basic questions are sometimes so considered I wonder what the argument in his head is.

A few weeks ago we had a cold snap and—in the middle of telling Tink that my putting forks in a drawer not only shouldn't concern her, it's also none of her fucking business—I glanced up to see Mike dracula his way to seated and blow breath into his hands, so I poured a second cup of shitty coffee because, I figured, even if he doesn't like it he can at least hold it. I don't know what he thought of the weak and creamerless but he for sure appreciated Tink handstand-style pissing on my car—it's like a parkour trick she does—and it was the first time I saw Mike smile in the year or so he's been sleeping there. The second came a minute later when she jumped in his box and sat next to him. He scratched her head and asked how old she was, and I told him I wasn't sure, that someone found her wandering the streets of Vegas half-starved with a prolapsed vagina, cystic nipples, ear and eye and respiratory infections, mange, the cleft face, and necrotic box-cutter-cropped forever open ears—but based on her teeth I'm guessing around four. He nodded and looked at her, and she looked at him, and I sipped my coffee and learned he splits his days between the So-Cal Storage off Franklin and the library on Ivar, has a brother he doesn't talk to because he doesn't want to be a burden to him anymore, is fascinated by Charles Manson and the Straight Satans, and that I was right about the voices.

"What do they say?"

The pause was a good four Mississippis.

"I've heard like uh, like, like, 'He doesn't like you,'" he said. "'She's mine,' stuff like that. Just like personal . . . just . . . 'What are you looking at? What the fuck did you just say?' It's like a . . . it's like a fight that never ends."

"Huh," I said, surprised and disappointed that his crazy is as boring and antagonistic as mine, just louder. I guess everything is when your walls are made of paper. "The voice in my head doesn't sound all that different."

And while I haven't always ignored it, I can usually tell what's in my head and what's outside of it, which voice in the dark is imagined and which is real, but why I'm in here and he's out there, I'm not sure I can tell. Why my box is bigger than his.

—Matt Sumell

FLOWER CHILDREN

After a day of walking barefoot in San Francisco, the soles of my feet looked like shoes. It was a city, after all, even in the late 1970s; the streets were made of concrete. It's hard for me to believe, looking back, that I really went barefoot as a teenager— Would my fastidious mother have allowed it, or did I do it without her knowing? Would I have been permitted on city busses, my chief mode of transport? The biggest question, of course, is why

15

I would want to go barefoot at all. But I think I know: Feeling the city's texture against my skin was a way of owning it.

To be a teenager in San Francisco in the 1970s was to be plagued by a sense of catastrophic failure in timing. The ringing aftermath of the summers of love still tingled through the city. At times it was possible for my high school friends and me to forget we'd missed that golden age: listening to drumming in Golden Gate Park, for example, surrounded by the reek of pot (much of it generated by ourselves). That smell was as much a part of San Francisco's atmosphere as the cold white fog that gushed over the hilltops at the end of each day.

In truth, the 1960s had barely passed. But in the mind of a fourteen-year-old, ten years was forever. The city abounded with suggestive artifacts: the old guy selling psychedelic concert posters in North Beach; the Magic Eye occult shop on Broadway, where a wild-haired lady hocked bright, mysterious powders and books on witchcraft. And there were plenty of diehards, now a decade older, sometimes derelict. They loitered in places like Union Square, where they bought and sold hard drugs and searched the shrubbery for smokable cigarette butts. Often they were barefoot, too. To me, they were refugees from a reality so piercing it had maimed them. Their company brought me nearer an intensity I craved, though I never would have had the courage to seek them out by myself. I was a follower, tagging along with bolder kids whose rebellion was more overt than mine.

I felt closest to the 1960s when I lay on the fuzzy white rug in my best friend's apartment, smoking pot (or sometimes tripping), listening to Pink Floyd and Patti Smith while a foggy breeze poured in through the window. Outside, San Francisco shimmered and hummed. Who knew what decade it was?

Looking back, I wonder whether that hum I detected was the roar of technology pullulating just to the south. I had never heard of Silicon Valley. Our family trips always took us north of San Francisco, to Mendocino, perched alongside a tempestuous patch of Pacific and populated by hippies who showed Chaplin films in a café on Saturday nights and made sculptures out of driftwood. Inland, there were dense redwood forests. Through their towering silence we paddled in a rented canoe—my mother, stepfather, little brother, and I—on a river so cold that it stopped your breath if you dared to jump in.

It seems to me now that I grew up in the last calm moments before an explosion. San Francisco's modest downtown, then presided over by I. Magnin and Joseph Magnin, local department stores now long defunct, has become a glittering international metropolis. The technology story we all know. Lately I've had an urge to return to Mendocino with my husband and kids, to see what it's like nowadays, but I always end up nixing it. Are the hippies still there? Have other hippies replaced them? Is there—God forbid—a Starbucks? How many of those redwoods survived the recent apocalyptic fires? For the moment, I'm holding fast to my old version: when everyone I loved was still alive, and the city was mine.

—Jennifer Egan

O THE GOLDEN SUNSET OF CALIFORNIA

A few years ago, I visited an MFA program. A student turned in the first chapter of a novel, opening with the narrator standing next to a window, in Carmel, California, watching the sunset and the Monterey cypresses bathed in the golden evening light. I complained about the clichés. Afterward, the student said to me, "That moment of watching the trees in the evening light—that was me, watching. And that sunset, it only happens in California. I can't believe that you told me to take the golden evening light out."

"Because nobody but you would be able to see that light," I said. "Trust me, I know the Californian sunset."

At the time we lived in Oakland, up in the hills, and from the top of our driveway we could watch the sunset, just as the student described, our neighbors' Monterey cypresses bathed in golden light. But these words mean nothing. People who have not seen the Californian sunset will not understand the goldenness of the light, just as a reader reading the description of a woman's red golden curls will never get to touch them and see the hue change between caressing fingers.

When we first moved into our house, everyone in the street came to us with stories of the previous owner, a man named George. George was an architect. He had remodeled the house we purchased and built another house nearby. He was said to have become an eccentric after his children grew up and moved away and his wife died. He kept his blinds shut. He did not greet the neighbors. He refused to sign a petition that every family had signed to save a nearby creek. He sold the house to us and moved to South Dakota, where he bought a piece of land to build a house for himself.

Two weeks after we moved in, Deb, a woman who lived down the road from us (it was her Monterey cypresses I enjoyed when they were bathed in the evening sunlight), knocked on our door at eight o'clock on a Saturday morning. I was the only one in the family who was up, and I was in my pajamas.

Deb chitchatted. I was conscious of not wanting to be a bad neighbor like George. She then asked if she could send "a young friend of mine" over to practice his presentation skills. "We live in a friendly community. I try to help people when I can," she said. "And you, we heard you're an author and a professor, so any feedback from you will be good for him."

The young friend knocked on my door a few days later. He was at least six feet tall, muscular, and he came with a bag of cooking knives of all sizes. We sat down at our dinner table, and he demonstrated how sharp each knife was, with the props of an apple, a carrot, other materials like leather and cloth and cardboard.

After he went over his presentation, which lasted forty minutes, he passed me a form and said the company recommended the whole set, with a market value of eight thousand dollars, but he could give me a discount, and I could own the set for two thousand.

I gaped. I gasped. "I don't need knives. We have good knives already."

"Can you show me yours, ma'am?" the young man said.

I took out a chopper I had brought from China and had used for almost twenty years. He tested it on the leather and cloth and cardboard and gave the verdict that mine was of inferior quality.

"It's good enough for me," I said.

The young man persisted. He kept slicing a piece of leather with a knife while going over the presentation from the opening line. The knife was good, slicing the leather like tofu.

I bought a chopper for eight hundred dollars, and vowed to myself that I would never spend another cent when someone knocked on our door. This promise was hard to keep. In the next nine years we had all sorts of people knocking, selling all sorts of things for the welfare of the mother earth and its various groups of children. The knockers always came in the late afternoon or early evening, some more persistent than others. Once a young man signed a receipt for my check and told me to keep the signature,

19

as one day he would be famous. Once a young woman asked to microwave her burger and eat at my kitchen counter so she could give me more time to decide on which magazine to subscribe to.

Shortly before we moved away from California, I was out of town, and I was on the phone with my husband, checking in about the various appointments he had to drive the children to, their school projects, and a thousand other things that parents have to deal with on a normal evening. Then the doorbell rang. I heard my husband apologize to the visitor, saying he could not buy anything at the moment, as he was busy with feeding his children and talking with his wife.

"What do you mean you don't have time?" the young woman said (part of the conversation I overheard, part was reproduced by my husband and my elder son later).

"You see, my wife is calling long-distance from Russia and I have two boys who are hungry," my husband said.

"Don't you lie to me," the young woman said, pointing from the door to the dinner table. Our elder son, who was fifteen, was sitting with his back to the door. He had long black hair. I always admired how shiny his hair was. "Isn't that your wife there?"

"That's not my wife," my husband said. "He's my son."

"Your son?" the young woman said. "Your son has long hair like that?"

"Why can't my son have long hair like that?" said my husband.

At this moment our elder son turned to watch the drama from the dinner table. At fifteen he had an androgynous look.

"Sir, if your wife, like you say, is out of town," the young woman said, "I think you owe her some explanation. You're not only lying to my face but also cheating on her with a woman half your age."

The encounter left two people indignant. No, three, including the young woman, and it made me laugh. I couldn't help but

20

imagine her walking up our driveway, seeing the same Californian sunset, golden over the cypresses.

Perhaps I was wrong to tell the student to take the golden sunshine out of his novel. He was right. At least we have that in California, and it's poetic.

I have never used the chopper but have kept it as a souvenir of my dislike of my neighbor, Deb. It wasn't fair, I know, as it was her trees and the golden sunlight over her house I enjoyed in the evenings. Soon after we moved, when a contractor repainted our house for sale, Deb went to our realtors' office and had a huge argument with them. The fresh paint, she said, was hurting her eyes when the evening sun shone on our house and reflected back to her windows.

—Yiyun Li

LITTLE LIBRARY

When I moved to California for the second time, I spent several weeks with my aunt Margie—technically, my mom's first cousin—who lived in the East Bay neighborhood of Pleasant Hill. While making lunch one day, I found a rusty butcher's knife in Margie's knife drawer. It was over a foot long and looked like it belonged to a horror movie clown.

"Oh, that'll be Bill's," Margie said, smiling. Bill, Margie's husband, had worked as a teamster delivering papers for the *Oakland Tribune*. Early one morning in the mid-eighties, Bill was dropping off papers down by Lake Merritt when a man tried to kill him. It was winter. He was wearing leather gloves. He grabbed the knife and twisted it from the other man's grip. The other man ran away and Bill stood there holding the butcher's knife by the blade while geese beat their wings around him. He kept it as a trophy and lucky charm. Margie, who tolerates no clutter, told him that knives go in the knife drawer.

Bill was a big guy, always halfway into a story, a dapper dresser who could describe a pair of Ferragamo lace-ups the way a sommelier describes a Brunello. He seemed larger than life, and, in the end, was: he passed of lung cancer a year before I found the knife in the drawer. On the knife's handle Margie has written precisely where and when Bill evaded death. The how and the why she won't forget.

Margie's daughter and son-in-law, Gina and Kevin Correnti, own and operate Trattoria Contadina, a North Beach institution that's been in Kevin's family for three generations. It's at the corner of Mason and Union, only a block off Washington Square yet remote enough that any tourist you pass is likely lost.

Per square foot, Trattoria Contadina is my favorite place in San Francisco, and, quite possibly, on Earth. It's a place where wedding proposals are regularly popped and graduations celebrated, and simply walking in the door raises your odds of photobombing a fond memory. It's an island of consistency in a changing city. Most days, Gina knows most diners. The "new guy" in the kitchen started in 1986.

Signed photographs of local luminaries, minor celebrities, and regular customers fill the walls. A few weeks ago, Kevin pointed to a faded Little League photograph inscribed to Kevin's father in a child's unsteady handwriting. "That's him now," Kevin said, nodding to the slugger at the bar. "He was signed to the Cardinals last year."

Their bestselling dish at present is Il Diavolo, a penne pasta with 'nduja, burrata, shredded basil, and a spicy tomato sauce.

The recipe came to Kevin one night in a dream—this is also how the melody of "Yesterday" came to Paul McCartney, and both masterpieces carry me to similar heights of nostalgia (as my floridness attests). It makes me remember great-aunt Giuseppina's kitchen, or the stories my father tells from his childhood; it is a day pass to a world I descend from but do not belong to.

When you're halfway finished, Gina comes by to ask how your meal is. The question is less a matter of culinary enjoyment than one of mental competence, like knowing the correct year and sitting president. It is a question to which there is but one answer: "It's perfect."

There is one frame without a picture. It's not on the restaurant's walls, but directly across the street, in Gina and Kevin's apartment. One day, while moving furniture, they found jotted measurements Bill had penciled on the wall when he helped Gina move in nearly twenty years ago. Gina bought a tiny frame, and set it over her father's handwriting. If asked, she might say her father had been an artist.

I'd hoped to live in North Beach, but unless you're grandfathered into the neighborhood through rent control, it's largely unaffordable to the literary community that, along with Italians, made the neighborhood famous.

Instead, I moved to lovely, leafy north Oakland, into an old Craftsman divided into four units. It's a perfect area for walking: to the coffee shop, or the bookstore, or the bar where on a Monday five years ago I met the love of my life, a Californian who is bringing me back east next fall.

As we discuss what we will bring and what we will leave, the biggest question has been the books. There are so many: beneath the bed, in the closet, lining the crawl space, towering on shelves,

ANTHONY MARRA

steadying the coffee table. They weigh many times more than the two of us combined.

One of those Little Free Libraries has recently appeared at the end of my block. It looks like a birdhouse for books. Now, on my walks, I leave a book or two inside. My large personal library evaporates, book by book, into this little public one. When the time comes, I'll be light enough to leave.

The problem is that the little library seems to manufacture more marvelous books, and despite my intentions, I can't resist the dog-eared Hilary Mantel, or the Toni Morrison annotated by a diligent student, or the Swedish thriller bookmarked with a takeout menu. I imagine that my own library is reassembled, book by book, inside a stranger's home, and theirs is reassembled in mine, like tapestries we trade thread-by-thread through a keyhole. Every day, as I prepare to leave, I find another reason to stay.

Many of the Italians who built North Beach were "birds of passage," young men who came to America intending to work awhile and then return to Italy. Many were illiterate and dictated their correspondence to professional letter writers. Back in the old country, other letter writers—or the village priest—would read the letters to their recipients and transcribe their replies. Some birds of passage returned home, while others stayed in North Beach and started restaurants. Over a long correspondence, the letter writers on either end would come to identify their counterpart through penmanship, grammatical errors, favored words. Perhaps they would wait as anxiously as the recipient for the next chapter to arrive. Over a long correspondence, two distant letter writers might live as neighbors on either side of a story, speaking only through the words of strangers that passed through their hands.

I am not leaving until the end of the year, but already I know how I will spend my last hours as a citizen of California. I will have dinner at Trattoria Contadina and then, in the morning, I'll head to the airport. But on my way, I will leave this very volume in the Little Free Library at the end of my block. It will be the last book I leave behind, and I hope you read these words, neighbor, because we have exchanged so much but never our names, and it is beautiful to at last meet you, in this sentence, while there is time to say goodbye.

—Anthony Marra

RABIH ALAMEDDINE is the author of *I, the Divine*; *The Hakawati*; *Koolaids*; *The Perv*; *An Unnecessary Woman*; and *The Angel of History*. *An Unnecessary Woman* was a finalist for the National Book Award in 2014 and winner of the prestigious Prix Femina étranger. His most recent novel, *The Angel of History*, won the Lambda Literary Award.

How to Bartend

RABIH ALAMEDDINE

1.

I was the best of bartenders, I was the worst of bartenders. Everyone disagreed, depending on what they were looking for in a bartender. But everyone agreed that I was a mess in those days.

I still find it odd that I bartended. Most of my friends are surprised when I mention it. I never cared much for drinking, rarely spent time in bars, whether gay, straight, or questioning, but for a brief period of time in 1990, tending bar was what I did.

I was thirty, back in school, going for another graduate degree I wouldn't use. You might ask, as any rational person would, why I was trying for a third useless degree. Because I was dying, that's why. That made eminent sense to me at the time. To my mind, it was a most rational decision.

In Lebanon in 1990, the civil war was ending with a mighty crescendo, fifteen years into a regional disaster that tore my country and my family apart. In San Francisco, we were still in the middle of the AIDS epidemic, a disease that killed many of my close friends, and within a few years would decimate an entire generation. Oh, and some four years earlier, in 1986, I had tested positive for HIV.

When I was informed of the news—the nice nurse sat me down in an oddly sized chair that made me feel like I was back in elementary school—I did what any rational person would do upon hearing that he had a short time left on this earth: I quit my nine-to-five corporate job, which was the last time I ever held one of those, and went on a six-month shopping spree. I'm sure I don't have to tell you that the most therapeutic sprees are those where you buy nothing of any use. Since I lived in San Francisco, where the weather was moderate for three hundred and forty-five days of the year, I ended up buying stacks of cashmere sweaters. Which, of course, led me to pack those sweaters and move back to Beirut, where the winter was even milder than in San Francisco. I wanted to be with my family because I was frightened and did not wish to die alone. I'd had to sit at the bedside of a friend as he slowly wasted away, alone because his family had disowned him, a vigil that many gay men and lesbians of my generation had to repeat over and over and over, sitting witness to a man's death because his family refused to do so. I did not want that for me.

Off to Beirut I went, my belongings stuffed in my exquisite, recently purchased luggage. I wanted to be with my family even though they were in the midst of a civil war. I sweated mightily as the bombs fell all about me because I was scared shitless. Or was I just too warm in cashmere?

A year later, I was back in San Francisco, still not dead but soon to be, I was certain. I sat myself down and told myself that I was almost thirty years old and that I should start behaving like an adult. Sure, I was dying, but I had to decide what I wanted to do with the short period of time left to me. In other words, what I had before me was a terribly shortened version of what did I want to do when I grew up.

So I asked myself, Rabih, I said, what would you do if you had one or two years left to live?

And I said, Get a PhD, of course.

So I asked myself, Rabih, I said, you have an engineering degree and a master's in business and finance, what kind of PhD should you go for?

And I said, Clinical psychology, what else.

So I asked myself, Rabih, I said, how are you going to support yourself in school now that you're not working and you're in credit card debt hell because of all the fabulous cashmere sweaters you bought?

And I said, Why, bartend, of course.

See? A most rational decision.

2.

To be completely honest, I did not consider bartending until a friend told me there was an opening for a bartender where he waited tables. I had done nothing comparable in my life, nor had I taken any drink-mixing classes, so I was hired on the spot at that odd establishment. My friend worked in a good old-fashioned diner where every other day the plat du jour was meatloaf (probably the same one). I, on the other hand, was hired to work in the bar upstairs, a faux upscale taproom with an English private club motif: leather fauteuils, pretentiously bound hardcovers in fake bookshelves, and port in the well. In a stroke of genius, the owners had baptized the place the Nineteenth Avenue Diner.

As the newest member of the staff, I was given the day shifts, the slowest. The bar did not have many customers, not at first. I mean, why would patrons of a diner want a spot of sherry or a tumbler of Armagnac after their good old-fashioned burger and fries? Even though I wouldn't make much money, the situation suited me fine, for I'd discovered early on that working was not my forte. It took me less than an hour at the place to realize that I had to change some things in order to make the environment ideal for a person with my temperament. I could not remain standing for ten minutes, let alone an entire shift, so I moved one of the barstools behind the bar, next to the wall on one end, in order to be able to sit comfortably and indulge in my two passions, reading and watching soccer matches.

I don't know why the owners thought an upscale English bar needed four television sets and a satellite system (to show British period dramas?), but I was grateful. I was able to figure out how to find all the soccer games I wanted to watch. For the first month or so, working that almost empty bar was as close to heaven as a job could get.

3.

I'd played soccer all my life. I used to joke when I first moved to San Francisco that I had an easier time coming out as gay to my straight friends than telling my gay friends that I loved soccer. Soon after I arrived, a friend and I started a gay soccer team, the San Francisco Spikes. In the beginning, all the team's energy was directed to playing in what was then called the Gay Olympic Games, as well as other gay tournaments. By 1986, though, the Spikes had registered in a regular league, amateur of course, and by regular I mean that many of the guys on the other teams were homophobic bastards, or to use the Linnaean classification, assholes.

Our team was terrible at first. We would lose by scores of 6-0 or 7-0. We were considered a mockery. A player on an opposing team, a Colombian who went by the nickname Chavo, used to gleefully celebrate each goal he scored against us by using the hand signs for fucking. He would go up to every player on our team, smirking, forefinger penetrating a hole formed by thumb and forefinger on his other hand. We ignored the taunting.

We began to encounter problems when our team improved. I believe it was during a game in the second season, against a team consisting of police officers, that we had our first bust-up. While the referee had his back turned, a cop sucker punched one of our players in the face. A hockey game broke out. For those of us who had been regularly confronting the police at ACT UP demonstrations, that was our first chance to fight back without getting arrested. No one received a red card. We won the game.

Chavo, however, received a red card the next time we played his team. Toward the end of the match, we were leading by at least two goals when he slide-tackled me, taking me out. His cleats dug into my shin, my heels shot skyward. I thought my leg had been amputated. As I lay on the turf, Chavo, ever the gentleman, yelled, "I don't want to get your AIDS, faggot."

Usually, I would not have allowed an insult without some sort of witty comeback. I was a faggot, after all. Even something like "You're not my type, bitch!" would have made me feel better. But I was writhing on the dry grass, in such pain that what I really wanted to scream was "I want my mommy!"

Chavo was kicked out of the match, which set a precedent. He would get red-carded in every game he played against us after that.

We came in third that season, won our division the next. Granted, it was not the highest division, but still. The fights lasted for a season or so before the league clamped down. They even sent a memo to all the teams stating that any player using the word *faggot* on the field would be automatically ejected.

Bless you, Mayflower Soccer League of Marin!

By 1990, when I began tending bar, the Spikes were one of the stronger teams in our division. We became just another regular team, except we looked better, of course, uniforms pressed and shirts always tucked in.

By 1996, half the players on the team had died of AIDS complications. Half the team, eradicated.

4.

I was leaning against the wall, slouched on my barstool, reading a long novel and minding my own business, when two frumpy-looking guys in color-splattered white overalls walked in. House painters, one presumed correctly. They plopped their hefty behinds at the bar, not at a table, which I hated, since patrons at the bar usually expected to be entertained by the bartender.

I knew I was in trouble when they asked, in a heavy Irish brogue, "Is the Guinness on tap?"

I pointed to the handle, which clearly stated Guinness in big white letters.

The answer to their second question was just as obvious. "Is that satellite?"

The third question was the most troubling: "Can we order food here?" No, no, no. These guys expected me to serve them, to actually work. How horrid. I should have kicked them out right there and then. The bar was a classy establishment, but it wouldn't remain so if we allowed Irish guys to drink there. I should have dumped the canister of Guinness. The bar was supposed to be faux English, not Irish.

I had to abandon my stool, present them with a fake smile, and inquire, "What can I get you?" in a disingenuous tone that I hoped would come close to sounding as if I cared. I needed the job.

They ordered their hamburgers, which meant I had to sigh audibly, write the order down, and walk it all the way to the kitchen downstairs. They finished their meal, drank their Guinness, and left me in peace. They didn't know what to make of me, so they didn't engage, not that first day. They just made sure before they left that I knew how to work the satellite system. They told me—warned me, really—that they would return the following day to watch a soccer match. I groaned, they snickered.

Five of them stomped in the following day, loud, violating my space. When I didn't put my novel down, I heard one of them say something to the effect of "I told you." I held my finger up, both to order them to wait while I finished my chapter and to point to the television, where the soccer game was about to start.

Thus began our tug-of-war: they would try to get me to work, or really just do something, anything, and I would try to get them to leave me alone. It was instant chemistry.

That day, one of them ordered something while the others pretended not to know what they wanted, forcing me to put in the order before another of them placed his. Back and forth, down the stairs and up the stairs, et cetera. I allowed that shenanigan just once. I also hated pouring Guinness, which was slower than molasses in winter, and then I had to wait for the damn thing to settle. The time it took for a pint of the dark concoction to come to rest was too long for me to keep standing but not long enough for me to return to my novel. They ordered their beers at different times, and boy, could they gulp them down.

By the third or fourth visit, they began a running critique of my bartending skills or lack thereof, particularly my complete incompetence at pouring Guinness, which was nothing like pouring other beers, as anyone with half a brain would know, they kept saying. Of course I had the best pouring technique: I tilted the pint glass to a mild angle, and with the other hand I flipped the bird at whoever was criticizing me at that moment. Another technique I learned quickly was how to say "Fuck off" the Irish way.

You're doing it wrong.

Fockoff.

When one of them told me I should use an inverted spoon to spread the drip of the beer, I offered him a couple of suggestions on what to do with said spoon. I declared that there were as many right ways to pour Guinness as there were Irishmen in the world. I told them to walk over to an Irish pub, barely a block away, and harass their countrymen with their orders. No, they did not want to. They wanted to stay right where they were, and they wanted their Irish beer. Finally I'd had it. If they wanted their stout poured their way, they could bloody well come behind the bar and do it themselves. I could not be bothered.

Oh, they loved that. All at once, I became the best bartender, and they regulars.

I stopped resenting them for making me work once they started pouring their own beers, a win-win situation if ever there was one. And they were generous with each other. When they went behind the bar, they would always ask if any of the others wanted a top-up, and they'd even wipe up any spillage.

The truth was that I was rude to them because I felt safe from the beginning. I felt at home with them. I had gone to high school in England, and my closest friend at the time was Irish. These men were older than me, but we actually had a lot in common, which was obvious from the first soccer game we watched together. They had a sense of humor that matched mine. They could, and would, make fun of everything. Nothing was sacred, and I couldn't tell you what a relief that was, living in the ever-earnest state of California, which had more sacred cows than all of the Indian subcontinent. They made fun of Americans, the French, the English, you name it. Boy, did they make fun of the

English. They mocked Catholics, Protestants, Jews, and Muslims. No joke was out of bounds. They were ever self-deprecating. They tore into each other ruthlessly. And most of all, they made sure to insult me. I dished it right back, of course. I felt as if I were back with my family.

5.

Memory is the mother's womb we float in as we age, what sustains us in our final days. And I seem to be desperately crawling on my hands and knees to get there. Lately, I can't remember what I had for lunch yesterday or where I put my reading glasses. I finally sold my car in frustration because I had to look for it whenever I wanted to use it, never knowing where I parked it last. But what happened thirty years ago—that I can remember.

What bothers me to no end is that I can't remember specific details about my Irishmen. I recall what happened, how they sat on the barstools, even some of the precise language used in our conversations. Yet for the life of me, I can't remember their faces. I can't tell you their hair or eye color, how short or tall. I'm unable to recall any of their names. I remember the name of another bartender who worked the evening shift because my guys could not stop making fun of it, Riley O'Reilly. They reserved their harshest mockeries for Irish Americans and their green inanities. I remember the names of my manager, of the waiters who worked at the diner. But not my Irish guys.

Incidents—incidents I remember clearly. I remember the Irishmen telling me a joke so good that I ended up sliding off my stool and lying on the perforated rubber mat, laughing my ass off.

I remember this one time, the five were sitting in their usual spot and another customer was sitting on the other side of the bar. She was their age, appeared in good health except for a permanent tracheostomy. When I served her a third martini, she asked me to move closer so she could whisper, "If I faint, please call 911." I was back to reading my book when I heard an immoderate thud. She was nowhere to be seen. All five men rushed over to where she'd been sitting. I leaned over the bar and saw her splayed on the floor. Luckily, one of the guys ran behind the bar, not to pour himself a Guinness, but to call 911. When the paramedics carted my customer off, the guys made fun of me for a week, suggesting I was too short to bartend since I could barely see over the bar.

It kills me that I can't remember what they looked like. All my teammates who died, I remember. I still have team photos that I look at every now and then. I have nothing of my Irish guys. They too might all be dead now. When I walked off my job, it never occurred to me that I would one day wish I had some memento. It never occurred to me to plan against regret.

6.

I should take that back. I don't remember all my teammates who died, not all the time. I had lunch yesterday with a friend who had also been on the Spikes since the beginning. I told him I was writing this essay, and we began to reminisce, about good times and bad. We began to go over all those who left us. We reminded each other of quite a few whom we hadn't thought about in so long: the PhD student whom Thom Gunn wrote a soulful poem about; the best player we ever had, Phil, who played semiprofessionally in Australia and could juggle a ball in four-inch heels. I could barely see their faces in my mind's eye.

I reminded my friend of an Ecuadoran who played with us for two or three seasons before succumbing. I don't know why I think of Wilfredo so much, probably because he was such a character, a combination of terribly sweet and utterly strange. No matter what uniform we wore, he'd have the same top as the rest of us, but he declined to wear any shorts except his favorites, a pair of extremely tight red Lycra ones with no underwear. You could see that he was uncircumcised from the other end of the pitch. And he was a damn fine player too, just peculiar, more so than any of us. Most of the team was there at his deathbed to comfort him, his family having refused to have anything to do with him for years.

I told my friend at lunch that I couldn't remember Wilfredo's face, couldn't reconstruct it. How could we, he said, when we spent all our time staring at those shorts?

So many of my friends died while the world remained aggressively apathetic.

7.

To emphasize how odd the diner was, I should tell you this: Out of a waitstaff of maybe thirty, only three were gay. Before I worked there, we used to joke that "straight waiter" was an oxymoron, but no, that rare breed did exist.

A flamboyant African-American queen joined the staff some four months after I did. Let's just say he tipped the fabulous scale so much that he made me look butch. Of course we hit it off, becoming work-sisters, coining ourselves Butch and Butchette. One day, it was Butchette who brought the Irishmen's lunch order from downstairs. As he was leaving, he pulled himself up toward the bar, standing on the lower rung of one of the stools— he too was short—and puckered his lips. I dragged my barstool over, pulled myself up, and we sister-kissed, both lifting our left legs in the air, synchronized swimming without the water. We separated—he returning downstairs, I moving my barstool to its usual position—without saying a single word.

I tried to get back to my book, but couldn't because the Irishmen kept staring at me.

"What?" I asked.

"Why did you do that?" they said.

"We're friends."

"He's a poof," they said.

Slow as I was, I only realized then that these guys had no idea I was gay. I should have noticed. They had been mocking practically everything about me—my looks, my height, my intellect, my going to school, my bartending, my Arabness, my not being Irish—but they had never brought up my homosexuality. They had no idea, which baffled me. I might not have been the most feminine of men, but I always figured that anyone who had seen me walk would recognize from a mile away that I was queer.

"I am as well," I said.

"No, you're not," they said.

"I am too," I said.

"No, no, you're not," they said.

"Oh yes, I am," I said.

"No, you're not," they said.

For them to believe me, I had to use their language.

"I take it up the ass," I said.

"But you play soccer," they said.

I returned to my book. They finished their lunch in silence. I knew they were shaken, or at least quite surprised, but I understood even then that they would not abandon me. It wasn't only that they could pour their own beer (it wasn't free; I trusted that each paid for what he poured). They liked me. They had always found me odd. Now they had to deal with my being odd and queer.

They did come back, and boy, did they deal with it. It took them twenty-four hours, maybe forty-eight, but they returned with a litany of terrible, puerile jokes. Shouldn't I turn my barstool upside down to sit? How many faggots did it take to change a lightbulb? Did I really nickname my goatee prison pussy? Was I a pain in the ass because I had a pain in the ass? Their mockery was relentless and relentlessly stupid. I loved it. As I already mentioned, we had quite a bit in common. Our emotional development had peaked in middle school. My jabs back were just as stupid if not more so. I told them that Bigfoot had a better chance of turning me on than any one of them, that I liked men, not cheap imitations, nor works in progress. The jokes would ratchet up in intensity when one of the waiters (not the waitresses) came up to deliver food since we had over-under bets as to how quickly we could make them blush.

They did not stop making fun of me until I was no longer there.

To this day, whenever I think of them, I begin to giggle all by myself.

We did not have any serious conversations about my gayness. I don't think any of us were capable of it at the time. I remember once, about a month after they found out, one of them asked me if I was afraid of getting AIDS. I told him I was terrified. I was unable to say anything more than that, wasn't sure I could explain such terror. How could I explain that I had night sweats, not from any disease, but from the fear of it? How could I tell them that my soul had already been crushed, that dread had shadowed itself unto my heart? I could not tell them I was HIV positive. It was eight years before my first book came out, announcing that fact.

8.

The World Cup was on that summer, and the Irish were in my bar almost every day, watching all the games when I worked. One Sunday there was an important second-round game at lunchtime, and the bar was as full as it had ever been, maybe twenty people, maybe thirty. I actually had to work. I made a rule that everyone had to follow: food orders were allowed before or after the game only. I was not about to leave a match to take an order down to the kitchen. My patience had limits, after all. About ten minutes before the start, I made sure everyone was settled. My Irish guys were in their usual seats on my left, already set with their burgers and Guinness. Some American remarked loudly that the announcers were unsophisticated because they called the game *soccer* and not *football*, as it was supposed to be called. My Irish guys let the poor, deluded thing have it. Football meant Irish football, as every enlightened person knew, and he should stop trying so hard to be anything other than the provincial yank that he was. Laughter, uproar, clanking of pint glasses.

And in walked Chavo.

I wasn't sure which of us was more surprised to see the other. His expression changed from stupid at rest, to shocked, to venomous. He hesitated a second or two before reaching the bar, but then he made his decision. He would proceed as his usual nasty self, bless his rancid heart.

"What the fuck are you doing here?" he yelled, loudly enough that the bar quieted.

I did what I always did when faced with a stupid question. What would I be doing standing by myself behind a bar, holding a wiping rag in my hand, surrounded by customers on the other side? Product modeling? My hands Vanna White-ing, *On this upper shelf we have the vodkas and gins?*

I just replied with a sigh, "I work here."

"Heineken," he ordered.

Why did assholes always drink Heineken? I placed a bottle in front of him, noting that it would not be his first drink of the day. I began to wonder whether he played soccer sober or not. I waited for him to pay, but he went off on a mini-tirade.

"They shouldn't let someone like you work here," he said. "This isn't one of your neighborhoods."

I expected one of my Irish guys to say something. From the corner of my eye, I noticed them drinking their pints.

"What if you give us your disease?" he said.

"Get the fuck out of here," I said. "I'm not serving you."

I took away the beer bottle, turned my back to him, and with a dramatic flourish poured the undrunk Heineken down the sink. He went nuts, high-tirade time. He was going to kill me. I was a lowlife faggot. He was going to jump the bar and break my bones. I was going to regret being born. I was about to order him to leave before I called the police when he quieted, and then I heard a scramble. I turned around and he was already at the door, stumbling out.

Soon after a threat dissipated, the terror always peeked out from behind the patina of bravura and camp. As much as I was loath to admit it, the motherfucker terrified me, on the soccer field or off. I had to control the swell of shaking, steady my breathing.

"What were you doing?" I yelled at my Irishmen when I was finally able to turn around without worrying that anyone would see the panic in my heart. The delicious comfort of rage flooded my veins in hot, resuscitating waves. "How could you allow him to come into our bar and say those things?"

All five were clutching the pint handles the same way, glasses in front of them in the same position, completely dry. They stared at me. I noticed just how menacing they looked, and it took me a minute to understand what had happened.

"We should explain the Irish Hello," one said, holding the empty pint glass and punching the air as if it were a face. "Very popular greeting in Ireland."

"We were going to kill the cunt."

"We were so looking forward to painting his body black and blue."

"The son of a bitch ran out as soon as he looked our way."

"You may be a poof, but you're *our* poof."

"No one but us can call you *faggot*. That fucking faggot."

I told them I had many witty insults to throw at them but I was going to give them a break for twenty-four hours. I would even pour them their Guinness myself, an offer they refused, anything but that.

9.

I stopped working at the bar not long after that. Never saw my Irishmen again. The diner and its taproom would shortly turn into a Chinese furniture store.

I didn't get another degree. Somewhere along the line I would once again perform a one-eighty and reinvent myself again and again.

I did not die. So many friends did. I lost count of how many deaths I witnessed.

These days the San Francisco Spikes have about one hundred and fifty members. They field four teams in different divisions.

I haven't been able to play soccer in quite a while. These days I run or swim, solo activities.

I did not die and I did not recover.

D. A. POWELL is the author of five collections of poetry, including *Chronic,* winner of the Kingsley Tufts Poetry Award, and *Repast: Tea, Lunch, and Cocktails. Useless Landscape, or A Guide for Boys* received the National Book Critics Circle Award in Poetry. He lives in San Francisco.

The End of
The Pride Parade

D. A. POWELL

I went to the parade and watched people wave at Wells Fargo.
I watched them wave at Harvey Milk, now more than
thirty years dead, and lift up their phones. Look at me
with a drag queen, they'll scream at their kids one day. Love
has been sponsored into law but a lot of you didn't vote
for it. I did not come for the free t-shirt. I came for the free
condoms that'll sit in my hopechest like a bill that keeps
getting tabled in congress. Where is the fuck brigade? I went
to the dick parade. It was the same as this but I didn't get
a lei from the US Bank. There was no Chipotle float
¿Homo Estas? with a giant foil-wrapped cylinder representing
the burrito of equality. Folks are cheering in the streets
for Walmart whose workers have shown up pushing unironic
shopping carts. After them comes Dignity Health and Yahoo,
Orlando Strong. Then Macy's and the Berkeley Free Clinic.
Someone ran off with our dildo and turned it into a marketing
tool. Bring back the street heaux, bb. Don't step in the vomit.

KAREN TEI YAMASHITA is the author of *Letters to Memory, Through the Arc of the Rain Forest, Brazil-Maru, Tropic of Orange, Circle K Cycles, I Hotel,* and *Anime Wong. I Hotel* was selected as a finalist for the National Book Award and received the California Book Award, the American Book Award, the Asian/Pacific American Librarians Association Award, and the Association for Asian American Studies Book Award. She is currently Professor Emeritus of Literature and Creative Writing at the University of California, Santa Cruz.

Omaki-san

KAREN TEI YAMASHITA

M ukashi mukashi, the war came with planes that dropped bombs and destroyed everything. Not that the planes were anonymous nor the men who piloted them within, but from that distance in the sky who could know where exactly the bombs fell? Would it have been different had the eyes of the child who pointed upward and those of the bombardier met? In this assumed indifference, many people died, but there were those who crawled away from the rubble and found a way to survive.

Postcard from Bob Hannoki
to Charley Hannoki

April 14, 1946
Tokyo

Charley Lil' Bro!

Arrived in Tokyo. Supposed to be cherry blossom time, and here's a postcard pic of the old days. You can use your imagination. Entire neighborhoods blasted away, but we're here pulling together reconstruction. Weird to be here in uniform with this face. Guess that's the job.

How's UCLA treating you? Hope you're keeping up your schoolwork, buddy.

Bob

Aerogram from Bob Hannoki
to Charley Hannoki

February 3, 1947
Tokyo

Charley Bro,

Thot I'd write to you before I let Mom know. Been dating a gal here and planning to get married. Met her in a bar here, but it's not like what that sounds. She was doing errands for the owner and pouring tea, just trying to get by. It started that I'd pass on to her some cigarettes that she could sell to scrape up something to eat. Then I started to bring k-rations or leftovers from my lunch, and we'd eat together. Thing is she lost her entire family in the war, grandmother, mother, and little sister. Her father and brother were called up, died somewhere out there in the Pacific. She thinks Guam or Burma, but all the letters and documents were lost. She thinks maybe she has some relatives in the countryside, but she doesn't know. When she visited the village with her mother, she was too young to remember. We went over to see what's left of her home, scraped around in the char, and this was just before they bulldozed the site clean. Sad story. Now I'm all she has. I don't want this to sound like she's a charity case, but she is. Maybe she's my fate. Irony of getting out of camp and getting drafted to come back to a homeland I never knew and finding it pretty much destroyed. Believe me, I have mixed feelings, but I've never felt this kind of tenderness and love for anyone. Well, when you hear it from Mom, means it's official. Just wanted to be sure you knew the backstory. Got no one else to tell this to.

Miss you, bro. Keep up your studies and write me when you have a minute.

Bob

Aerogram from Bob Hannoki
to Charley Hannoki

June 1, 1947
Tokyo

Charley,

By now you've heard from Mom that Omaki and I tied the knot in a simple ceremony in May. According to custom here, we did it Shinto style, though Mom would have preferred a church wedding. Maybe we can come to L.A. and do it again, though that doesn't seem likely for a long time.

How's college? At least you get to start in as a freshman and can finish, won't have to get your studies disrupted by a war, and you can plan a future. It looks like I'll be here awhile since the pay is good and comes with housing, and now I've got a family started. I used to think maybe I'd get back home and get another degree, but got to save that dream for another time. Keep me posted on your studies, not that I'm looking over your shoulder, just living the college life vicariously.

Did I say start a family? What I didn't tell you or Mom is that Omaki is pregnant. I would have married her anyway, but this sealed the deal. When we went to get registered to marry, we had to try to dig up her records, but everything is pretty much gone. But what I found out was that she had lied to me about her age. She's actually only sixteen, so imagine my shock. Turns out it's all legal, but to register with the government, she'd have to get parental permission. So then I had to get death certificates, and so it's been a hassle. And I admit I've been pretty angry about this because we could have waited and you know me, straight arrow kind of thinking. So I feel like I've been had, but then Omaki apologized and cried, and I melted. I'm fine now, just blowing off steam with no one to talk to. Anyway, you wouldn't get into a situation like this, but let my experience be a warning.

Sorry to lay this on you. Don't mean for you to get distracted by my problems. Just between you and me.

Bob

Wedding invitation from Dr. and Mrs. Reginald Higuchi to Captain and Mrs. Robert Hannoki

Dr. and Mrs. Reginald Higuchi
request the honor of your presence
at the wedding of their daughter
Catherine Ichiyo
to
Charles Kiyoshi Hannoki

Saturday, the twelfth of August
Nineteen hundred and fifty-eight
at four o'clock in the evening

Centenary Methodist Church
Thirty-fifth and Normandie Avenues
Los Angeles, California

reception to follow

Note accompanying invitation from Charley Hannoki to Bob Hannoki

Bob,

Hope this finds you and Omaki well. I guess it was about time.

Yours,
Charley

Card from Bob Hannoki
to Charley and Cathy Hannoki

July 15, 1958
Tokyo

Dear Charley and Cathy,

Sorry we can't be there. Glad I could see you last year at least, even if it was at Mom's funeral. Sorry that Mom's not alive to see you married.

Sending you a photo of our little girl Midori. She's already ten. Hard to believe. Omaki sends her good wishes too.

Cathy, take care of my little brother. I know he's a handful, but he's a good guy.

Yours,
Bob

Christmas card from Charley and Cathy Hannoki
to Bob and Omaki Hannoki

Christmas 1959
Los Angeles

Dear Bob, Omaki, and Midori,

Merry Christmas and Happy New Year!

Here's a photo of our little Timothy, just born.

Love from Charley, Cathy, and Timmy

Christmas card from Charley and Cathy Hannoki
to Bob and Omaki Hannoki

Christmas 1962
Los Angeles

Dear Bob, Omaki, and Midori,
  Wishing you Love at Christmas and Peace in the New Year
  Sending you a photo of your namesake, little Bobby.
  Photograph of Timmy (age three) holding newborn Bobby
          With love from Charley, Cathy, Timmy, and Bobby

Letter from Omaki Hannoki
to Charley Hannoki

July 4, 1963
Tokyo

Dear Charley,
  I have a hard time to write this letter to you. I should tele-phone you, but I cannot. I got the news that Bob died. They said it was an accident. It happened in Korea. I don't understand. The war there is over many years. I know that was Bob's work, but I cannot forgive. I will come to America. I will bring Bob's ashes to bury with his mother and father. I think this is what he would want. I am sorry to write this to you.

Omaki

Letter from Hannoki Omaki
to Sato Otsuma

オつまマちゃん
  お元気ですか。
  ボブが亡くなってから、遺品を整理したり家を片付けたりで大変でした。弟の チャーリーが一週間来てくれて、アメリカのほうの書類

などを手伝ってくれました。これでやっとこっちを離れて、サンフランシスコで会えるわね。貴女と一緒に暮らして新しい人生を始められることに、本当にほっとしています。貴女のお店にきっとお役に立てる。前に夢見ていたように、ついにアメリカで暮らすのね。これはボブが約束してくれたこと。私がさんざん頼んだのをボブがちゃんと聞き入れて、とっくに任務を辞めていてくれたらよかったのに、あの人は死んじゃった。貴女はやり手のご主人が見つかって、運がよかったわね。

　美登利は寮のある学校に入れました。卒業まではこっちにいます。あの子の歳のころには私は完全に自立していたのよ。あの子は甘やかしちゃって苦労を知らない。アメリカで学校に入れるほど頭が良くないと思うの。いずれはアメリカに行かざるをえないけれど。だって、ボブの年金だけでは学費がいつまで持つかわからないから。

　またすぐ、東京からの旅程を知らせますね。

　こっちは寒いのよ。貴女と一緒にサンフランシスコの春を迎えられるのを楽しみにしています。

かしこ
おまき
１９６４年３月１０日、東京

(translation)

Otsuma-chan,

　My dear friend, I hope this letter finds you well.

　Since Bob died, I have had a difficult time sorting out his things and closing down this house. His brother Charley came for a week and helped me with the American paperwork. I am ready to finally leave and to join you in San Francisco. I am so relieved to be able to live with you and start a new life. I know I can be useful to your business. As you and I dreamed, finally I will come to live in America, something Bob promised me. He should have resigned his commission earlier, and I kept asking and insisting, and now he is gone. You were so fortunate to find a man with business prospects.

I have placed Midori in a boarding school here to finish her education. At her age, I was already completely on my own. She has been spoiled and is innocent of hardship. I don't think she's smart enough to come to America and go to school. She will have to come later anyway, since I don't know how long I can spend Bob's pension on her schooling.

I will send you very soon my travel itinerary from Tokyo.

It is still very cold here. I await a springtime with you in San Francisco.

Your old chum,
Omaki
March 10, 1964
Tokyo

Letter from Omaki Hannoki
to Charley and Cathy Hannoki

March 10, 1965
Tokyo

Dear Charley and Cathy,

I will come to America in a few weeks. My friend Mrs. Otsuma Sato lives in San Francisco. She is married to Mr. Sato who owns Daikokuya Import store near Nihonmachi. She can help me with a job there. I think this is the best decision for me since Bob died. Midori will stay in Tokyo to finish school. When I arrive, I will write to you again.

Yours,
Omaki

Letter from Omaki Hannoki
to Charley and Cathy Hannoki

September 9, 1965
San Francisco

Dear Charley and Cathy,

I am in San Francisco for six months now. I should come to Los Angeles to see you now. I will bring Bob's ashes to bury with his parents. I can stay at your house. Thank you for this imposition. I will arrive by Greyhound bus.

Yours,
Omaki

Letter from Cathy Hannoki
to Dr. Reggie and Natsuko Higuchi

September 30, 1965
Los Angeles

Dear Mom and Dad,

How are you both? Have you settled in by now? It's difficult to imagine that you'll be in Nagasaki for an entire year. Though you've just left, I miss you already. I know the work there will consume Dad, and I know Mom will find a lot to explore. Keep us up on everything, what you see and do.

The news here is that Omaki has come to live with us. She kind of just moved in, but Charley is, of course, very nice and solicitous of her. It's his way of mourning Bob, even though he won't talk about it. I try to be supportive, but the boys keep me very busy. Omaki tries to be helpful playing with the boys. Sometimes she talks to them in Japanese, and they laugh. Maybe they'll learn the language.

Charley's been terribly busy. He's partnered with another dentist, and they are making a go of orthodontics. I think he's a bit stressed, and it's difficult to have another person to take care of. I feel sorry for Omaki, but in her needy way, she's rather pushy. I'm sorry to complain.

Timmy just started kindergarten. On the first day, he was shy, but as soon as he saw another child crying, he showed me a look of disdain, looked back at me once, and broke away. I admit I'm surprised at his independence at such an early age.

Here's a recent photo of the boys. Tim (age five) Bobby (age three).

We're fine. Send us news about your adventures.

Love,
Cathy

Letter from Hannoki Omaki to Sato Otsuma

おつまちゃん

やっと涼しくなりました。インディアン・サマーっていうのかしら、このお天気、よくわからないわね。でも東京とちがってこっちは暑いといっても湿気がなくて乾燥しているから、しのぎやすいけれど。暑かったせいで、サンフランシスコのひんやりとした霧を恋しく思っていました。慣れていたから。スチュワートと一緒に桟橋に行ったりゴールデンゲート橋を歩いたりして、夕陽が沈むころ霧が流れこんでくるのを見ていたのを思い出します。こういうとなんだかバカみたいにロマンチックに聞こえるかもしれないけれど、彼のことをとてもなつかしく思っているのよ。あんなに生き返ったような気持ちになったのは、本当にひさしぶりだったから。ボブはいつも家にいなかったし、もちろん私にもやることがいろいろあったけれど、家にいるときでもあの人は私が何を必要としているかに、スチュワートほど気を遣ってくれなかったから。スチュワートの噂を何か聞いたら教えてね。こっちではすごく退屈しているの。どこにも行くところがない郊外

56

で、家から出歩くこともできない。時期が来るのを待って方針を決め
なくちゃいけないとはわかってるんだけど。毎日、がまんしなさい、っ
て自分に言い聞かせています。ご存知のとおり私はこうと決めたら決
意は固いけれど、計画は慎重にしなくてはね。アメリカという国が、や
っとわかってきた気がしています。

　ここではチャーリー一家と一緒にいます。奥さんは、まるで私の
ことはちゃん とわかっているとでもいうように、用心している様子。
私を信用してないみたい だけど、チャーリーはとても親切です。二
人とも私を哀れに思ってるんでしょう。少しでも役に立ちたいと思っ
て、男の子二人の世話をしています。いつもうるさくかけまわって大
げんかばかりしている、やんちゃな子たち。テレビを見ていい ときだ
け静かなの。キャシーは子供にテレビを見せないけれど、彼女が出
かけて しまうと漫画番組をつけてやるでしょう、すると私はのんび
りできるというわけ。そして隙を見て自分の部屋に逃げこめば、やっ
と落ち着けるのよ。それでいま、こうして部屋で手紙を書いている。

　貴女、あのお年寄りの旦那さんをどう操っているの。佐藤さんは
いずれはお亡くなりになって、あなたにお店と財産を遺してくれるで
しょう。そうなったら私たち、旅行でも何でも好きにできるわね。でも
あの姪っ子、ルーシーには気をつけなくては。泣き言ばかりいって。
本当に、あの子はスチュワートの人生をみじめにしなくちゃ気がすま
ないんでしょう。

　あ、やんちゃどもが私の部屋のドアのところで騒いでるわ。晩ごは
んの時間。また時間を見つけて書くわね。いまは取り急ぎ。

おまきより
１９６５年１１月５日、ロスアンゼルスにて

(translation)

Otsuma-chan,

Finally the weather here has cooled down. I don't understand
this climate they call Indian summer. But unlike Tokyo, when it is
hot here, it is dry and not humid, so bearable. Because of the hot
weather, I have been longing for San Francisco and the coolness

and the fog there. I had become accustomed to that. I remember walking with Stuart on the pier or over the Golden Gate and watching the fog roll in with the setting sun beyond. I must sound like a silly romantic, but I do miss him very much. It had been such a long time since I felt alive again. Bob was always away, and of course I had my other interests, but when he was around, he was never as attentive to my needs as Stuart. If you've any news about Stuart, please write to me. I'm really so bored here, stuck in this house in what they call the suburbs with nowhere to go. I know I must bide my time and find my way. Every day I tell myself to be patient. As you know, I am very determined, but I must plan carefully. I think I am beginning to understand this America.

Meanwhile, I am here with Charley and his family. His wife is rather cautious as if she knows something about me. I don't think she trusts me, but Charley is very kind. I guess they pity me. I have tried to be useful, taking care of the two boys, both brats who are constantly running around, fighting, making a commotion. They are only quiet when they can watch television. Cathy won't let them watch television, but when she leaves, I turn it on to some cartoons so I can have some peace. And when I can, I flee to my room to get some quiet. That is where I am now, writing to you.

How are you managing with that old husband of yours? Old Sato should one day keel over and leave you his business and fortune. Then you and I can travel and do as we like. But you must be careful of that niece of his, Lucy. Such a whiner. Really, she must make Stuart's life miserable.

Oh, those brats are making a ruckus at my door. It must be dinnertime. I will find another moment to write to you again. In the meantime, sending my affections.

Omaki

November 5, 1965

Los Angeles

Letter from Sato Otsuma
to Hannoki Omaki

おまきちゃん

　ご存知のとおりサンクスギビングで、あのぞっとする七面鳥とか他にもアメリカ人の大好きな食べ物を耐え忍ばなくてはならない時期ね。でももっと困った問題は、親戚の集まりを我慢しなくてはならないこと。佐藤家はいたるところに子供たちがいて、一族郎党、集まりたくてたまらないの。もちろん私はこういうお料理はできないので、佐藤と私は毎年ウォルナット・クリークの、彼の甥のところにご招待されます。部屋がたくさんあるすてきなお家で、時々都会から逃げ出せるようにあんな家を買いましょうよと、佐藤を説得することもできるかもしれない。でもこういうことを書こうと思ったのではないのよ。

　サンクスギビングの時ね。もちろんスチュワートとルーシーも来ました。みんなディナーの食卓について、ご自慢のあの巨大な黄金色の七面鳥が切り分けられて、スイートポテトや詰め物やあのげんなりするクランベリーソースやグレイビーの器が回されたりなどなどがあったわけ。スチュワートとルーシーは互いに話をすることを避けていたけれど、ふたりのあいだのこのピリピリした感じに気がついていたのは私だけだったわ。スチュワートは相当みじめに見えたのよ、ほんとに。ふたりは一見幸せそうなふりをしていたけれど、ルーシーはいつものごとくおしゃべりで話が飛ぶし早口で、私はあの人の話はさっぱりわからないので正確なところを伝えられないんだけれど、ルーシーの話し声がどんどんどんどん大きくなって突然ヒステリーみたいな金切り声になり、テーブルの一方の端からあの人スイートポテトのマッシュしたのをスプーンでたっぷりスチュワートのお皿に投げこむのでお皿からそれた分が彼の胸にこぼれて、あげくの果てには器いっぱいのグレイビーを彼のお皿に空けちゃったの。それでグレイビーがお皿からあふれてテーブルにこぼれて彼の膝にこぼれて、彼は立ち上がって怒鳴り、彼女も大声を上げながら部屋から飛び出していったのよ。ほんとにねえ、おまきちゃん、とんでもない場面だった！　想像できる？

貴女がいないと、ここはとても退屈です。またすぐお手紙頂戴ね。
かしこ
おつま
１９６５年１１月２５日、　サンフランシスコ

(translation)

Omaki-chan,

As you must know, it's been Thanksgiving here, and I have to endure that horrid turkey and the rest of the food that Americans are so in love with. But the bigger problem is to endure the family gatherings. The Satos seem to have procreated everywhere, and they are so in need of inventing reunions. Of course I don't make this food, so Sato and I are invited every year to his nephew's big house in Walnut Creek. It is a lovely house with lots of rooms, and I have been thinking that I might persuade Sato to buy us a place like it somewhere outside the city to get away from time to time. But this is not what I wanted to write about to you.

So there we were at this Thanksgiving, and of course Stuart and Lucy were there. We all sat down to dinner, and there is the carving of that gigantic golden bird that they are so proud of and the sweet potatoes and the stuffing and that awful cranberry sauce and the passing of the gravy and so on and so on. Stuart and Lucy were not talking to each other, but only I noticed this tension between the couple. Stuart looked quite miserable really. They both pretended to be happy, but Lucy has a way of chattering about anything and very quickly, and I cannot understand anything she is saying, so I cannot tell you exactly what was said, but Lucy's chatter became louder and louder and suddenly screeching and hysterical, and I saw from one end of the table that she served a scoop of those mushy sweet potatoes to Stuart in a large plop that spit from his plate and onto his chest, and then to top it off, she poured the entire dish of gravy into his plate. It spilled over the plate and the table and onto his lap, and he stood up suddenly yelling, and she ran screaming from the room. My dear Omaki-chan, what a scene! Can you imagine?

How dull it is here without you. Please write to me soon again.

Yours always,
Otsuma
November 26, 1965
San Francisco

Aerogram from Cathy Hannoki
to Dr. Reggie and Natsuko Higuchi

December 1, 1965
Los Angeles

Dear Mom and Dad,

How are the both of you? Thanks for your last long letter with all the details about Dad's work with atomic bomb survivors. I can only imagine the intensity of your work and what you must be feeling. And I'm glad to hear that Mom is also doing some traveling outside of Nagasaki. We received your recent postcard from Kyoto. The snow-covered Kiyomizu Temple is most beautiful.

Well, we just had Thanksgiving here, and Kevin came home to join us. So it was Kevin and us and the boys and Omaki. We missed you. I made the turkey, but it was not as good as last year when Mom roasted it. But I will say that my stuffing was pretty good. I will send you some photos when I get them processed.

61

Kevin is looking toward his residency and wants to relocate back to L.A., which I hope is possible. So you'll be proud to know your son is seriously following your footsteps toward a medical degree. He is ready to leave the East Coast and those cold winters. He'll be here for a few weeks to look at some opportunities here, will leave again to wrap up work in Baltimore, then return for Christmas. It's so good to have him back with us. The boys adore their Uncle Kevin.

Omaki continues to live with us. She is probably bored, but she goes over to the cultural center and retrieves books and reads the Japanese newspapers to keep up on the news in Japan. And every chance she gets, she makes me take her shopping, usually to May Co. or to I. Magnin. Bob must have left her a nice bank account. Occasionally she makes us a Japanese dinner, but the boys don't like fish. I have to make spaghetti on the side. I asked her about her daughter Midori, if she's heard from her, but she doesn't seem much concerned. I asked her if she doesn't miss Midori, and she didn't say. I've asked her about her life with Bob, about those early years when they met, how Japan has changed. Maybe it's still too painful to talk about, or she is shy. I don't know how really to relate to her. I don't think it's just a matter of the language barrier, but perhaps you can enlighten me about this since you are living in Japan. The good news is that she and Kevin really seemed to get along and that suddenly she seemed to open up with him.

The boys miss you and ask when grandpa and grandma are coming home. Well, enjoy every moment in Japan. We'll miss you this Christmas, but I promise to take lots of pictures.

Love,
Cathy

Aerogram from Cathy Hannoki
to Mrs. Natsuko Higuchi

January 8, 1966
Los Angeles

Dear Mom,

Happy New Year. We missed you this year, but of course you are enjoying the real thing in Japan. I did my best to make the ozoni. Omaki tried to help, and she must have thought me incompetent. She told me that we should have the spread made outside by professionals. She actually said "professionals," but all Japanese businesses close for the holidays. I pulled out the Nisei church cookbook, and Omaki looked at the recipes and shook her head. Every region in Japan apparently has their style of cooking, and whatever we're doing is not what they do in Tokyo. She was especially dismissive of the recipes that are probably from Hawaii, like the guava kanten, which I love. What style of New Year's food did you enjoy in Nagasaki?

Actually I am writing to ask you for advice. Kevin came home for Christmas and stayed through the New Year, and he and Omaki seem to have really hit it off. That is to say, it's more than that. I think that they are involved romantically. This has been really awkward for all of us. Omaki is older, in her thirties, but of course Kevin is not that much younger. Maybe I'm just being a prude, but Charley also feels strange about this, since Omaki was married to his brother. I don't want to worry you with this. I feel like I'm tattling, and Kevin is a grown-up man. But he is my brother. Maybe it's really nothing and will go away. I guess I just want your reassurance and wisdom.

Love,
Cathy

Letter from Cathy Hannoki
to Mrs. Natsuko Higuchi

February 3, 1966
Los Angeles

Dear Mom,

Thanks for your letter and reassurances. Kevin returned to Baltimore as he should have, but he promises to be back here, actually in a few days. He was really angry at me for suggesting anything to him when I had the chance to talk to him, but he seems to have his head in the clouds. Before he returns, though, I need to tell you some gossip I heard that I figure, considering the source, is probably true.

None of us, except for Charley who went to Japan, had ever met Bob's Japanese wife Omaki. So I had no idea of what to expect. To be honest, she is really a striking woman, and when we go out, you can see that men turn their heads to look at her. She also came with quite a wardrobe of clothing, which seems to be growing. Bob, the one time I met him before we were married, was a pretty down-to-earth guy, but living with Omaki, now already almost five months, it's been interesting to imagine their lifestyle in Tokyo. I try to understand this considering Bob's work for the military occupation and his descriptions to Charley of Japan after the war. Maybe you can enlighten me about this. After all, they've just built that bullet train.

Do you remember Susan Sato? She's my old roommate from college from San Francisco. She's related to the Sato family that owns the Daikokuya Import store where Omaki went to work last year when she first arrived. Apparently, Omaki and Mrs. Sato (the second wife) are old friends from Japan. I met Susan for lunch in Little Tokyo, and she told me that her cousin Lucy is married to a Stuart Kusari, and Stuart has been working for their Uncle

George Sato at the import store. Long story short, while working at the store, Stuart got involved with Omaki.

Kevin arrives in a few days, and I'm sure he's rearranging his schedule with promises to Omaki, but this is time Kevin really can't afford, considering his studies and finances. As I said, Kevin got really angry when I suggested that maybe he was infatuated. Of course, I didn't say that exactly. But now, with this news, I can't believe Kevin is so dumb.

Anyway, glad you are far away from this nonsense.

Love,
Cathy

Letter from Hannoki Omaki
to Sato Otsuma

おつまちゃん

　前に手紙をさしあげてから、キャシーの弟のケビンに会いました。ケビンはアメリカの反対側ボルティモアで医学を勉強しているのですが、サンクスギビングとクリスマスに家に帰ってきたのです。やっと話し相手が、お出かけしたり人生を少し楽しめる相手ができました。ディズニーランドとプラネタリウムに一緒に行ったのよ。一時もじっとしてられない甥のティミーとボビーを連れていかなくてはならなかったので、こんな子守りは時にはほんとに疲れる辛いことなんだけど、ケビンは私にとても親切にしてくれました。あの子たちがうるさかったのを埋め合わせるために、彼は私だけをディナーと映画に連れて行ってくれて、私はやっといくつか観光もできました。

　わかると思うけど私のサンクスギビングは、貴女のとは大変にちがっていましたが、貴女の手紙を読んだら笑って笑って涙が出てきちゃった。佐藤家の人たち も、これでルーシーがどれだけ非常識な人かわかったでしょうね。すてきなスチュワートのことを私は忘れてはいないけれど、将来お医者さんになる人のほうが 安楽な未来を保証してくれそうだという点については上よね。愛だけで結婚でき るいいけれど。貴女も私も親が決めた結婚をさせられることから

65

は逃げられたし、それを不幸といわれても報われる部分もあるけれど、とにかく私たちは自分で相　手を見つけなくてはならない。この点、貴女はすでに私より一歩先を行っている　わね。

　ケビンは昨日帰っていったばかりですが、その前に姉のキャシーと喧嘩しました。これがまた私の信用と計画にとっては邪魔なの。彼はできるかぎり早くまた来るよと約束してくれました。こっち、ロスアンゼルスで仕事を探すって。

　また手紙で大笑いさせてね。

かしこ
おまき
１９６６年２月２０日、ロスアンゼルス

(translation)

Otsuma-chan,

　Since I last wrote to you, I've met Cathy's younger brother Kevin. Kevin is studying medicine in Baltimore, on the other side of the country, but he came home for Thanksgiving and for Christmas. Finally I've had someone to speak with, to go out and enjoy life a bit. He's taken me everywhere in Los Angeles. We went to Disneyland and the Planetarium, although we had to bring along his overactive nephews, Timmy and Bobby, but even though it was quite tiresome and trying at times, Kevin was so kind to me in every way. To make up for their commotion, he's taken me alone to dinner and to the movies, and finally I have seen some of the sites.

　As you see, my Thanksgiving was very different from yours, although in reading your letter, I laughed so hard that tears came to my eyes. Now the Satos can see how preposterous Lucy can be. I have not forgotten my handsome Stuart, but certainly a man who will be a doctor has better prospects for a comfortable future. If only one could marry for love. You and I escaped the consequences of being married off in family arrangements, although that misfortune may be its own reward, but we must find our own proper arrangements. You are already a step ahead of me.

Kevin just left yesterday, but not without a fight with his sister Cathy, yet again another impediment to my good plans. He promised me that he will be back again as soon as he is able, that he is looking for a position here in Los Angeles.

Please send me another letter with more hilarious news.

Yours,
Omaki
February 20, 1966
Los Angeles

Aerogram from Cathy Hannoki to Mrs. Natsuko Higuchi

February 20, 1966
Los Angeles

Dear Mom:

Kevin just left yesterday, back to Baltimore. Before he left, we got into a terrible argument. Well, I told him the story I heard about Omaki in San Francisco and the probable reason why she left the city. He was outraged and said that I was spreading lies, that Omaki has had a very difficult life, that she is still mourning her husband, that she misses her daughter, that she feels like a stranger, is embarrassed by her English, and is very aware of her imposition on our family but doesn't know what to do. He said that she told him she had hoped to make some money by working for the Satos, but that Mr. Sato was particularly difficult and she felt that she could not make her friend Omatsu's life more difficult by staying. What Omaki told Kevin, confidentially, was that Mr. Sato was hitting on her, and she really didn't want Omatsu

67

to know about her husband's infidelity. This was all amazing to me, and I didn't know what to say. Then he said he would come back for Omaki and hoped I would be more understanding of her situation.

I don't want to bother Charley with this situation. He is so busy building the business, and it is finally taking off. I go in every day for a few hours to help in the office with accounting and scheduling, and to be fair, Omaki takes care of the boys when I leave the house. But I can't keep my mind off this. Be honest, and tell me if I'm overreacting.

Charley and the boys send you their love. Love to Dad too.

Love,
Cathy

Letter from Natsuko Higuchi
to Cathy Hannoki

March 2, 1966
Nagasaki

Dear Cathy,

So grateful to get the photos of you and the boys. But I admit I'm feeling uneasy about your letters about Kevin and Omaki. I shared your letter with Dad, and you know him, always philosophical about these things. And he's really very busy working with patients who are so in need of his help and expertise. But I know you are there in the thick of it, having to interact every day with Omaki and then with your brother who can be very stubborn. And Omaki seems frankly to have invaded your household. I know you and Charley want to be charitable, but there are limits. If Kevin has become so close to Omaki, perhaps he can guide her to another future (job?) in the US. Not marry her, though. I wish I could come and take care of the boys and give you some time off.

While Dad has had to remain in Nagasaki, I've been able to travel with friends to other parts of Japan. Kyoto was so lovely, entirely preserved from the devastation of the war, but then most of Japan has been or is being rebuilt, and the physical evidence of the war is all but disappearing. I have been taking Japanese lessons and flower arranging and tea ceremony, and any other activity that's suggested. I have also been asked to teach English to a small group of women who come once a week to the house. They are all so polite and kind to me, bringing gifts all the time. I feel very fortunate, but the conversation, even when I try to complicate it, is always very limited. There is a great reticence to speak or perhaps there are signals that I cannot comprehend. I feel very isolated here. Perhaps this is what Omaki too is experiencing. Not to excuse her actions, but perhaps to give you some perspective.

Missing you and the boys in particular. Hugs all around.

Love,
Mom

Letter from Sato Otsuma
to Hannoki Omaki

おまきちゃん

お知らせがあります。お宅の美登利ちゃんがサンフランシスコの私の家に来ています。昨日着いたばかりよ。ひとりで飛行機に乗ってアメリカにやってきました。そんなことありえないと思われそうだけれど、あの子はきっとあなたとおなじくらい反抗心と勇気があって、あなたはあの子を見くびっていたのかもしれないわね。東京の学校の寮から逃げ出してきたんだって。ロスアンゼルスに行かせましょうか？ とてもいい子にしてるわよ。さしあたっては、私が面倒を見られます。

　別のお知らせもあるの。あの何度かお店に来て、古い漆塗りの簞笥や十八世紀の屏風をいくつか買ってくれたお金持ちの白人、ジム・マーティンを覚えてる？彼はすごいお金を遣ってくれて、品物はぜんぶロスアンゼルスの自宅に送ったでしょう。そう、あの人はサンフランシスコに一軒、そしてベバリーヒルズにも大きな家を持っているのよ。テレビのプロデューサーらしいわ。その彼がこのあいだ、貴女のことを知りたくて、訪ねてきました。貴女がどこにいるのか、どうやったら連絡が取れるのかを知りたいんですって。しつこいくらいで、自分が手紙を書いたら貴女に転送してくれるか、といっています。それでその手紙を同封します。

　美登利ちゃんをどうすればいいか、忘れずに知らせて頂戴。

かしこ
おつま
１９６６年３月１７日、サンフランシスコ

(translation)

Omaki-chan:

　I have some news for you. Your daughter Midori is here at my house in San Francisco. She just arrived yesterday, having taken a plane by herself and come to America. I know this sounds impossible, but she is perhaps as rebellious and courageous as you, and you have not given her enough credit. She has run away from that boarding school in Tokyo. Shall I send her to Los Angeles? She is quite well, and I will take good care of her in the meanwhile.

　There is some other news. Do you remember that rich white guy, Jim Martin, who came into the store several times to buy some old lacquer chests and several 18th-century screens? He spent a great deal of money, and we shipped everything to his house in Los Angeles. That's right, he has a house in San Francisco and a large house in Beverly Hills. I think he's a television producer. He has been here lately asking about you. He wants to know where you are and how to be in contact with you. He's been very persistent and asked if he wrote you a letter if I would forward it to you. Well, here is the letter.

Don't forget to let me know what I should do about your Midori-chan.

Yours,
Otsuma
March 17, 1966
San Francisco

Note from Jim Martin
to Omaki Hannoki

March 15, 1966
San Francisco

Dear Omaki-san,

I was so disappointed to come into Daikokuya and find that you were no longer there. There is no pleasure shopping there without you. I have given this note to your friend Omatsu-san in hopes that you will read it and find some time and heart to correspond with me. When I met you, I knew I had found the perfect woman, the very Japanese woman I have been looking for all these years. I have been thinking of you constantly since we first met, and I cannot get you out of my mind. Wherever you are, I will come to find you. I promise that my intentions are the most respectable. I will move and shake the world for you. I beg you to answer me with some sign but more importantly your current address.

With great sincerity and true love,
Jim

71

Aerogram from Cathy Hannoki to Mrs. Natsuko Higuchi

April 1, 1966
Los Angeles

Dear Mom:

How are you and Dad? Thanks for hearing me out and for your thoughts about Japan and the Japanese. Speaking of which, my house just got more Japanese in it. Omaki's daughter Midori arrived a few days ago. Apparently she ran away from the boarding school in Tokyo, found a way to get on a plane, and came on her own to San Francisco. She was staying with the Satos, then they sent her to Los Angeles. Midori just turned eighteen, but this must have been a very brave thing to do. Omaki is pretty upset about it, and I have heard her fuming and yelling at Midori. Midori, for her part, is very quiet and shy. Her English, however, is quite good. She went to American schools on the military base in Tokyo. I think she was in a Japanese boarding school that must have been very strict and even abusive from the little I've learned. I've suggested that she can go to the local high school and meet other students like herself. We went together today to meet a school counselor and get her classes arranged. Well, we'll see how this works out.

I haven't heard from Kevin who usually writes us a few lines every week, if just a postcard to the boys. He does seem to be writing to Omaki however. When I hand Omaki his letters, she stuffs them away in her pocket or purse without comment.

Timmy is very happy in school. He's already reading. Dick and Jane and Dr. Seuss.

Bobby loves to ride around on his tricycle. While Timmy is in school, we go to the park. Your Japanese picture books just arrived. Thanks!

Sending love to you and Dad,

Cathy, Timmy, Bobby, and Charley too

Letter from Sato Otsuma to Hannoki Omaki

おまきちゃん

　美登利はぶじロスアンゼルスに着いたことと思います。美登利はとても引っ込み思案に見えるけれど、じつはあの子を見ていると貴女を思い出すのよ。何を考えているのか絶対に分からないけれど、あの子はいつもよく見ていろいろ学んでいるにちがいありません。

　新しいお知らせよ。スチュワートとルーシーが離婚する、そして別れる以上、スチュワートは大黒屋を離れなくてはならないということを、ついさっき聞きました。佐藤のお父さんはこの件についてはとてもきっぱり決めていて、ルーシーの側の言い分しか聞こうとしません。スチュワートは、ロスアンゼルスに移って新しい仕事を探すといっています。彼は日本の骨董品を売るのはそもそもあまり上手じゃなくて、いつも誰の作かとか何世紀のものかとかをまちがえていました。私は教育がないけれど、その私だって日本の歴史は勉強してきたわ。こうした骨董品は、それにまつわるいい話をしてあげられるのでなければ、けっして売れないもの。あの人は嘘ひとつつけないから。でもとてもチャーミングでハンサムだから、きっと何か見つかるわよ。もちろん彼が引っ越しについて私に話してくれたのは、私がそれを貴女に話すと思ってのことでしょう。だから予め警告しておくわね。

　この件がこれからどうなるか、そして貴女が最近どうしているのか、教えてね。

かしこ
おつま
１９６６年４月１４日、サンフランシスコ

(translation)

Omaki-chan,

I trust Midori arrived safely in Los Angeles. Even though Midori seems very shy, actually, she reminds me of you. You cannot know what she is thinking, but I believe she is always watching and learning.

I have new news for you. I have just heard that Stuart and Lucy will get a divorce, and with that separation, Stuart will have to leave Daikokuya. Old Sato-san is adamant about this, only willing to hear Lucy's side of everything. Stuart told me he will be moving to Los Angeles to look for a new job. He was never very good at selling Japanese antiques anyway, always confusing the artisans and the centuries. I am not educated, but even I have been studying Japanese history. If you cannot tell a good story about these old objects, you can never make a good sale. He could not even lie. But he is very charming and handsome, so something should come his way. Of course he told me about his plans to move so that I would tell you. So you are forewarned.

Let me know what happens and how you are faring these days.

Your friend,
Otsuma
April 14, 1966
San Francisco

Letter from Cathy Hannoki
to Mrs. Natsuko Higuchi

May 5, 1966
Los Angeles

Dear Mom,

It's Boys' Day today, but you know this. We are flying two large koi in the backyard for Timmy and Bobby. It's also Cinco de Mayo. There was a dance program at school, and Timmy danced the hat dance with his classmates in the schoolyard.

Midori is going to school and seems to be doing just fine. She's a very sweet young girl and very helpful and kind to the boys.

Bobby can't wait for her to come home to play with him. I think she genuinely loves to play with the boys, even when they are rough and uncontrollable. I have seen her roll around on the lawn together with the boys. It was Midori's idea to fly the koi. We went together to Little Tokyo to buy them. In a short time, we've all become very attached to Midori. Despite her crazy mother, Midori seems to be her father's daughter, like Bob, down-to-earth, open and very earnest.

The new development here is that lately there is a hakujin guy who comes around and takes Omaki out on dates. Apparently Omaki met him in San Francisco. He has at least two cars, a big black Cadillac and a sporty red Mustang. Depending on the date, he'll arrive in one or the other and escort Omaki away. Midori has joined them a few times. They've taken day trips to Santa Barbara or to Palm Springs. Omaki's also mentioned going to concerts and the opera, and she said he's promised to take her to the Emmys. I guess he works in TV. Omaki calls him Jimbo.

Last weekend, Kevin arrived suddenly, I guess hoping to surprise Omaki. But Omaki wasn't here but in San Diego or maybe Tijuana. Kevin moped around the house all Friday and Saturday and just before his flight out of LAX on Sunday, Omaki arrived in that red Mustang with Jimbo, the convertible top down, laughing gaily. I was pulling the car out of the garage to take Kevin to the airport, and he was lugging his bag across the front porch. Somehow everyone got introduced, fakely cordial. Then Kevin got in the car, and we drove in silence to the airport.

Well, enough said. Love to you and Dad. I miss you so.

Love,
Cathy

Letter from Hannoki Omaki
to Sato Otsuma

おつまちゃん

　ベバリーヒルズでの私の新しい住所をお知らせするために書いています。ジム・マーティンと私が結婚したと知ったら、貴女は驚くでしょうね。簡単な急ぎの式でしたが、いずれパーティーを開くし、そのときは誰よりも貴女に来てほしいわ。ジム坊はパームスプリングスにも家を一軒もっているので、パーティーをどっちでするか、決めなくてはなりません。でもいうまでもなく、サンフランシスコにジム坊がもっている東洋趣味のビクトリア式の大きな邸宅にも、貴女をご招待できます。

　美登利はハイスクールを卒業して、それからもチャーリーとキャシーと一緒に暮らしたいといっていますが、これは本当に助かるわ。二、三年のうちには美登利がきっと大学に入れると、キャシーは考えているみたい。

　もうひとつのお知らせです。あなたが教えてくれたとおり、スチュワートはロスアンゼルスに引っ越してきました。彼はいい仕事が見つからなくてお金が尽きてしまい、気まずくてそれが私にいえなかったのね。ある晩、ジム坊と私がハリウッドで夕食をとっていたら、テーブルにウェイターとしてやってきたのが、なんと私の最愛の、最高にハンサムなスチュワートだったのよ。私は顔を上げると息を呑んでしまい千回もとろとろに溶けてしまったけれど、なんとか間をおかずにジム坊に紹介できるまでには回復したの。「大黒屋時代のお友達でね、私にとっては兄みたいな人」って。それからはトントン拍子に、ジム坊がスチュワートを助手として雇うことに。助手といって、スチュワートがどんな仕事をするのか全然わからないけれど、それよりもいいのは彼はトレーラーハウスとかいう物を借りてうちの土地に住んでいるのね、だからいつも手が届くところにいるというわけ。

　やがてはこんなふうになるのよって、貴女か私に予言できたかしらね。

いつも貴女のお友達である

おまき１９６６年６月１８日、ベバリーヒルズ

(translation)

Otsuma-chan,

I am writing to you to let you know of my new address in Beverly Hills. I guess you'll be surprised to know that Jim Martin and I got married. It was a simple and quick ceremony, but we will have a party, and you will be the first invited. Jimbo has another house in Palm Springs so we must decide where to have the party. But soon, as you realize, I can also invite you to Jimbo's oriental Victorian house in San Francisco.

Midori wants to finish high school and to continue to live with Charley and Cathy, and that is a big relief. Cathy is sure Midori can get into college in a few years.

Another piece of news is that Stuart arrived, as you let me know, in Los Angeles. Unable to find a good job, he ran out of money and was too embarrassed to tell me. One evening, Jimbo and I were having dinner in Hollywood, and who should come to wait on the table but my dearest handsomest Stuart. I looked up and gasped and melted a thousand times, but recuperated my senses in time to introduce to Jimbo "my friend from Daikokuya, practically a brother to me." Well, one thing led to another, and Jimbo has hired Stuart as an assistant. What Stuart must do as an assistant I have no idea, but the better thing is that Stuart is renting what they call the carriage house on our property, so he is never very far away.

Could you or I have predicted how things would turn out?

Your friend always,
Omaki
June 18, 1966
Beverly Hills

MAI DER VANG is the author of *Afterland* (Graywolf Press, 2017), which recounts the Hmong exodus from Laos and the fate of thousands of refugees seeking asylum. The book received the Walt Whitman Award from the Academy of American Poets, was longlisted for the 2017 National Book Award in Poetry, and was a finalist for the 2018 Kate Tufts Discovery Award. Vang is a member of the Hmong American Writers' Circle, where she co-edited *How Do I Begin: A Hmong American Literary Anthology*. Born and raised in Fresno, California, she earned degrees from the University of California, Berkeley, and Columbia University. In Fall 2019, Vang will join the Creative Writing MFA faculty at Fresno State as an Assistant Professor of English in Creative Writing.

Prayer to the Redwood

MAI DER VANG

Senescent and dwelling
      In your tower with sorrel

    For shoes, I come to you fleshed
With intention,

A muted engine
        Dismantled at your coastal throne

    In doubt and daring
Intuit from you:

> *Tell me if you've*
> *Heard of the Apis dorsata and I*
> *Will affirm*
> *What I know of its innocence.*

    Take this confession to your
Wildlife, mahogany limbs

Grasping the upper
      Avenues of your genius memory

        As readily there a
Nursery for hemlock and new firs.

    How would you have guarded your pine?
These sudden flecks, you would have

Known its taste as factory-born far from organic consent,
      You would have deemed its

                              False footprint.
                    Here in your globe's

Fluent echo, you exhale the words:
            Stockpile, degrade, human subjects.

I make sentient
My palm over your bark of suede,

        Dense as it were to defy

A passing inferno,

                Stockpile, degrade, human subjects,
No secret must ever be singed of your knowing.

WILLIAM T. VOLLMANN
is the author of ten novels,
including *Europe Central*,
which won the National Book
Award. He has also written
four collections of stories,
including *The Atlas*, which
won the PEN Center USA
West Award for Fiction; a
memoir; and eight works of
nonfiction, including *Rising
Up and Rising Down: Some
Thoughts on Violence, Freedom and Urgent Means* and
Imperial, both of which were
finalists for the National Book
Critics Circle Award. His latest books are *No Good Alternative* and *No Immediate
Danger.* He lives in Northern
California.

The Fires

WILLIAM T. VOLLMANN

1

Not long ago I wrote a book called *Carbon Ideologies*, which directed its explanations and excuses to some hypothetical readership in our hot dark future. Why did we keep on warming our atmosphere to the point of ruin? Maybe someone in the future would want to know. Unfortunately for my generation (I had hoped to be safely dead), the future came early.

For more than a quarter century, I have lived in Sacramento, California. Night after night in August 2018 I woke up tasting smoke—it was worse than the August before. One evening I laid myself down on a river barge out in the Delta, inhaling the fresh river breeze (although the sunset, I admit, was a trifle lurid), and at midnight was pulled out of sleep by a pain in my chest. The winds had shifted; whether I was inhaling smoke from Redding or the Sierras I cannot tell you, but there was nothing to do but keep on breathing that stinging foulness, feeling that I was harming myself; so I lay there for what seemed to be a long time, trapped and discouraged. Finally the winds changed direction again, and by sunrise the air grew almost clean.

In Sacramento most dawns came nastily gray that month. Lacking an air purifier, I ran my air conditioner day and night. When I went out for coffee the air was mostly tolerable; my eyes hardly ever watered, and the smell remained a mere dirty suggestion.

On Thursday, August 9, 2018, the morning sky actually appeared blue—a quaint survival from California's pre-apocalyptic summers. (Two weeks before, the *New York Times* had announced that the Golden State had suffered wildfires every single month since 2012.[1]) The prospect of traveling into the source of that unseen smoke was not enticing; on the other hand, having written *Carbon Ideologies*, I thought it my duty to see what I could see.

2

For the sake of people fortunate enough to be unafflicted by the dreary pages of *Carbon Ideologies*, let me summarize: Climate change is a scientific theory. A scientific theory cannot be proved, only disproved. What it offers is predictive reliability. The theory of gravitation predicts that anytime we let go of an object in midair, it will fall. Should that fail to happen, even once, the theory would need revision. For its part, the climate change model predicts, among other things, that our oceans and our average surface temperatures will keep rising, as indeed they have done. Tide gauge measurements around the world, some of them dating back to 1901 and farther, record sea level increases of about 1.7 millimeters per year until the 1990s, when the rate

---

1. Scott Bransford, Jennifer Medina, and Jose A. Del Real, "As Carr Fire Kills 2 in California, Firefighters Reflect on a Job Now 'Twice as Violent,'" *The New York Times*, July 27, 2018.

of change increased to 3.2 millimeters a year and kept going up. Satellite measurements show that in 2012, the minimum extent of Arctic sea ice fell 49 percent below the 1917 through 2000 average.[2] Etcetera, etcetera.

Climate change deniers will point to a cold day and say: "See, this disproves global warming." It does not, because the meteorological conditions on a single day fall under the rubric of *weather*, which varies much like the daily jig-jogs of the stock market. *Climate*, on the other hand, is weather averaged over a long period, such as thirty years. Of course one could cook the books, and cherry-pick a particular period in which temperatures decline, but if the climate change theory is accurate, then over a string of such periods, average temperature readings will increase.

Deniers like to claim that our temperature measurements have been historically inaccurate. But they have no accurate measurements of their own with which to correct the record. Carbon combustion shills hope to reduce the climate change debate into a game of he-said, she-said. They refer to left-wing conspiracies to suppress evidence that there is no global warming. In fact the consensus that global warming *has been proved* shows up in documents from scientific bodies and national governments all over the world. The U.S. may well be the only developed country in which I would see any need to write these few paragraphs in defense of the global warming theory. If you have any doubts, educate yourself about the science, which is not difficult. If you lack basic math and science skills, ask yourself: Should I believe

2. Thomas F. Stocker et al. (Working Group I Technical Support Unit), Climate Change 2013: *The Physical Science Basis: Working Group I Contribution to the Fifth Assessment Report of the Intergovernmental Panel on Climate Change* (New York: Cambridge University Press / Intergovernmental Panel on Climate Change 2013), pp. 46 and 136.

climatologists who get paid whatever their numbers are, or carbon lobbyists whose financial interest must be to deny that our planet is heating up?

At any rate, the global warming theory predicts that wet areas will get wetter, and dry areas drier. Hence the wildfires of California. If the theory is accurate, we can expect ever larger, faster, more dangerous wildfires for the rest of our lives. To be sure, torrential winters may extinguish those fires, at the cost of stripping away topsoil, and drowning a few humans. Then summer will return, ever earlier and for an ever longer period. We will choke on smoke until most of our trees are gone.

I hate the global warming theory. I long for it to be wrong. So far, unfortunately, whenever I let go of my pencil in midair, the pencil keeps falling to the floor.

3

The horrendous Carr Fire began on July 23.[3] On August 9, I set out for Redding, California, in company of the photographer Mr. Greg Roden. Crossing the Sacramento River on Interstate Highway 5, I found the fields already grayed out, with narrow stripes of smoky whiteness where the vague grayed out trees met the fields. My tongue tingled with smoke, and my chest ached a little but, as usual, it was perfectly tolerable. When we fueled up at a convenience store in Woodland, I found the air-conditioned interior a treat. A few minutes later the sky had gone blue again and breathing was easier. In a big-box hardware chain in that town we bought the best paper respirators they had (a sales

3. Cal Fire Incident Update [online, accessed by Greg Roden], updated 8/11/2018, 7:00 p.m. My statistics on the Hat and Hirz fires also come from this source.

clerk said all the fancy ones had been sent to Redding). When we came out it was 7:10 in the evening, and the big white sun wore a great white halo in the bluish-gray sky. We reentered I-5, where an electronic sign warned of the closure of Highway 299 West in Redding. Past a metal silo we encountered a smell of woodsmoke, delicious like barbecue, not yet stinging my throat or hurting my chest. The sun hung orange and vague on our left.

Four or five miles south of Williams, that round sun grew redder and more ethereal, with strange dark markings on its surface like the mountains of the moon. It paled, its redness presently vanishing into the smoke from the bottom up. Just then a truckload of tomatoes was paralleling us, the tomatoes vermilion and washed out like the sun. We hummed through Williams at 8:00 p.m. I felt much as I had in 2011, that first time going north toward Fukushima, Japan, right after the tsunami and nuclear accident, because everything kept getting more silent and more alien. I remembered not liking it as I drew near the radioactive Tepco Nuclear Plant No. 1; and this time I found myself trying not to take deep breaths for a slightly different but equally infantile reason (as if inhaling less were even possible!), while grain silos loomed like mists out of the mauve dusk. For a mile the odor of manure overwhelmed the smoky smell, and I could pretend that life was "normal."

Just as we entered Glenn County the smoke began to irritate my throat, although the sky looked no worse. The Sacramento National Wildlife Refuge exit sign had lost contrast in the smoke, and I wondered how the water birds were. Then came a lovely fragrance of fresh alfalfa; but soon the glowing signs and headlights had haloes around them in the thickening smoke and my eyes began to water. The traffic stayed light. Rolling out of Red Bluff at ten at night after a quick dinner in a mediocre Mexican restaurant I found the night looking ordinary but my eyes smarting, the night air somehow not satisfying. Then I began to get a headache; the road was empty and my nose stung. Greg, a former smoker, remained unaffected.

I put on the respirator in Redding, but my tongue burned and an almost nauseous feeling grew in my chest. I felt outright discomfort by the time we turned onto Lake Boulevard, heading toward the Carr Fire on Highway 299 West. We rolled down into a valley or dip, with vague lights visible ahead. There was a fire truck in a motel parking lot, a sign: THANK YOU FIREFIGHTERS, then an ambulance. In downtown Redding the smoke thickened. Passing the Thunderbird Lodge where a lady friend and I had once stayed happily, we read THANK YOU ALL FIREFIGHTERS AND FIRST RESPONDERS. By now I was feeling impaired. My chest pain worsened, and I evaluated my condition as moderate but significant respiratory distress. Greg had only a mild sore throat. The sign advised: HWY [299] CLOSED 6 MI AHEAD. It was seven miles to Whiskeytown. A man in a yellow suit waved us through the roadblock. Now everything grew gray in our headlights and I felt what I unimaginatively called *a nauseous distress*, while a single cricket sang. No one else was driving that road. I experienced a kind of tunnel vision. We kept curving round in the grayness, closer and closer to the fire. My head ached. After a police car on a side road came the bent sign for the municipality of Shasta, accompanied by a fouler smell of smoke. The sign said five miles to Whiskeytown or was it Weaverville; I could not think; another glowing sign said forty-six miles per hour, and another announced that in half a mile the road would be closed. At the closure, where a pilot car waited, we went to speak with the police officer who said that we could go about twenty-five miles farther to the "hard closure" but not off the road. Greg wanted to continue but I was feeling faint. The policeman wore no mask. When I remarked on this, he said he was from here and used to fires. Greg proposed that my symptoms were psychosomatic, and maybe they were, although it might also have been that after years of printmaking and photochemical processes I had become chemically sensitive; I was the sort who upon going into the hardware store's aisle of sealed turpentine tins almost retched. I said that I could not go on, so we drove back into Redding.

Outside an establishment called Alehouse, the alley was slightly gray fogged in the dark, and I experienced mild burning of the eyes. The barmaid said whenever she went home the smoke made her sick, so she lay down, or else tried to go back to work. She said that the Carr Fire had burned many houses in the northwest part of town. In her opinion, climate change was not so responsible as "neglect," which I believe meant failing to thin out the forest undergrowth. (Apparently the president had just announced that more logging and culling would save us. Maybe one of his toadies owned a furniture factory.) "It's always hot here, and always on fire," the barmaid added. When I asked for advice on my trouble, she recommended Mercy Hospital, where they could give me a better respirator. Sighing, she said: "They talk disaster preparedness, but no one is prepared."

When we went out into the parking lot I needed my mask again and when I pulled it on, its inner surface immediately stung my skin. Greg remained almost unaffected. I experienced the sense of being in an inimical zone, as though the air had been misted with some powerful insecticide.

So we drove up to Mercy Hospital. By then it was midnight, and the security guard informed me if I entered I must pay for emergency care, so I asked for his suggestion. He told me to get an N95 mask, a blue one, much thicker than mine; any evacuation center would hand them out for free. At our hotel by Shasta Dam the kindly Gujarati hotelkeeper gave me a free white paper N95, which appeared almost the same as the kind I already wore. I tried it on, standing in the parking lot, slowly, wearily breathing. Maybe it was better.

The hotelkeeper had turned on the air conditioners in our rooms. I went and lay down. Slowly I began to recover. In greedy gasps I kept breathing and breathing the good cold air. It was one in the morning. Lying down in my clothes, I fell into a deep sleep almost instantly. Shortly before five the winds must have altered, for I woke up with smoke in my chest. Now my eyes were stinging, although I hardly cared about that. I reached for the new mask, which cut out most of the smoke but made it harder to breathe. Next I tried to dial up the air conditioner but it was already at maximum strength. In misery I lay taking shallow breaths through my mask.

That morning, a gray mist was coloring the hotel parking lot with muted smoky light, smoke-filtered, one might say, or in Greg's words, "like a big soft box." I asked him what color it was, and he replied: "I think it's whiter than gray." Where the trees joined the grass, that was what Greg called "bright shadow." "And look at our shadows. They're very undefined." While he packed up his gear, I sat outside my room with my respirator on, studying the road, which was a surprisingly bright whitish-gray stripe behind the greenish-gray trees. I decided that the respirator actually excelled the kind we had bought in Woodland. It was a Friday morning, and there were darting cars on that high narrow ribbon of road, but somehow a strange wrongness hung in this hollow of smoke where the hotel was. Everything was almost dreamy in that smoky softness.

So we drove over the hill and then toward the horizon, bemused by the utterly gray, apparently melting trees, then onto I-5, where the trees were green on our side and gray on the other side, Greg thought because the closer ones were backlit by the sun. The overpass to the Oasis Road wore a fence that had almost vanished in the smoke. Reentering the Redding city limits, we passed a convoy of army lorries, maybe Corps of Engineers, then descended into that nasty whiteness, with gray-green trees and tan-gray houses for stage props. Next we crossed the Sacramento River, which was wide and blue-gray with strange streaks like reflections of long fat smokinesses, with the blue-gray trees all still. Here came a truck from the Albuquerque fire department, then a long line of blue Pacific Gas and Electric trucks. A hand-lettered sign on a school fence said THANK YOU FIREFIGHTERS. On the sidewalk, a lean young bearded man stood fighting the smoke by dragging on a cigarette while looking down at his cell phone. We were then on Tehama Street. The message on the fancy steakhouse read THANK YOU FIRST RESPONDERS. On South and Market, a stocky white-haired fellow in short sleeves ambled through the smoke as if he had all the time in the world. I looked down South to a single tapering blue-gray tree a block away with nothing but grayish-whiteness on either side of it.

Cindy, the waitress at Corbett's Restaurant, said: "Well, I have chronic bronchitis, so I try to either stay in or just go straight into my vehicle. I don't wear a mask." She lived in Anderson, a bit southward and by the river, so it was not bad in her house. "Well, today it seems worse," she agreed. But hardly anybody outside wore a mask.

I sat there across from Greg in a booth in that wide restaurant with the gray morning outside, where visibility was surprisingly good; in a photo it might merely have been foggy. It was a marvel how as soon as I came inside I could think and talk better. Even so I did not feel completely right, so I tried to breathe shallowly. A man at the next table was saying: "It went over the hill and burnt them houses right up. It's really funny."

Another couple came in, maskless, and the family at the next table fussed about the decimal point on their bill until the baby pooped in his diaper. Finally, one white-haired man entered wearing sunglasses and a mask.

Cindy agreed that the fires around Redding were getting worse and worse. "Well, the fires that we've had in the past have been in further areas from the town. But we've just had a lot of people lose their homes. I lived in Florida for nineteen years and everybody talked about climate change and how it's gonna affect the coastline. Whether climate change is real, I'm not a hundred percent certain. It's not as hot here in Redding as before, but a lot drier. Since I live in Anderson, this one pretty much didn't touch me. I've been watching it on the news. My first thought was oh dear God. I really thought it would head toward Weaverville but when it started to come here I thought oh my God."

I was starting to feel the smoke even inside the restaurant, so I asked her where I could buy a better respirator, and she advised a place called Everything Medical. Greg called them for me, and they recommended a construction supply store, so we decided to go there.

In the smoke outside in the restaurant's parking lot there sat a handsome young fellow named Josh, with the cuffs of his jeans rolled up pale against their dark blue and his baseball cap pulled backward. Originally from the Sacramento suburb of Rancho Cordova, he had now been homeless in Redding for a year and a half because "I got in a van going up to a Rainbow gathering and got stuck in Anderson and after like the fourth flat they told me get the fuck out of here."

When I asked him about the fires he said: "I think it's deliberate. I think there's a lot of people that like fucking hate homeless people. Some homeless did it out of hate or else someone did it knowing it would wrap around and get the homeless."

Then I asked for his Carr Fire story. He said: "I was actually like doin' this exactly. I woke up down the street an' this one chick picked me up in a jeep 'cause it was super smoky and I guess she was tryin' to save me and like that. She was hot lookin'. I was on Eureka Way when the fuckin' National Guard showed up. Then she just kinda like pulled over, and was like hailin' me, a hot blonde in a fuckin' jeep; this don't fuckin' happen to me. She was a different character. I don't think I like her too much anymore even though she's beautiful. Night before, I was in a Carl's Jr. parking lot across the bridge, layin' on top of my shit, because you have to lay on top of it to keep it. Then the smoke came. We were driving all over and ended up in Anderson, in the river park over there and it was still just as smoky. She thought her Mom got burned out. I was freakin' out because I didn't know if my Mom . . ."

"How do you manage in the smoke?"

"I have a couple 3M masks but I always forget before I go to sleep. I fell asleep. I was thinkin' about putting on my mask, but I forgot. Woke up with a lump in my throat. Had to cough it out. Honestly, I'm just kinda like ridin' it out 'cause there's so many beautiful women here. Bein' homeless, it's like a half an' half. I really meet people who say, my house has just burned down and, like, *wait*, so they actually come back with a dollar or two."

"Do you believe in climate change?"

"There's like these fuckin' weather changes that are like government caused. Like they'll put out rain clouds and like that. You'll just notice cumulus clouds that just show up out of nowhere."

"What's your plan for today?"

"Right now I gotta kill off this beer."

Thanking and paying him for his trouble, we proceeded to Liddell Construction Supply, Inc., where kindly Ms. Toni Magee, who had actually called the manufacturer on my behalf, outfitted me with a half-face rubber and plastic respirator with a carbon filter on each side of the nosepiece. Greg adjusted the straps for me, and after that I was able to wander about through our future as well as any Redding local. I asked Ms. Magee whether she believed in climate change, and she replied: "Well, I'm of two minds about it. After all, volcanoes put out twice as much carbon dioxide as we do." Thus educated, I put my mask back on, and we went outside.

4

We rolled down the windows, driving toward journalistic glory on a thoroughfare called Churn Creek. It was another nasty hot day; after lunch, when we checked into our next hotel, the clerk pegged the temperature at 101 degrees. In the lane to my immediate right, a young woman was driving a station wagon with the windows open, probably because her air conditioner didn't work; and, grimacing, she held a bandana over her nose and mouth with one hand while steering with the other. I pitied her; she was a weak remnant of the present like me. With the new respirator I felt almost healthy again.

Spying firefighting vehicles in the whitish haze by the town's auditorium, Greg proposed that we seek background information from someone with the appropriate knowledge and authority, so we walked up to the fire chief, Chris Varnum, who like Greg got by quite well without a mask.

First I wanted to know whether the Carr Fire was contained. "I wouldn't say it's contained," he replied. "And it never stops. Now we have the Hirz Fire and the Hat Fire. It was four hundred and fifty acres last night, totally unrelated. That's the thing. Don't let your guard down. Every day we're getting new fires and that's the one that's gonna come around and get you."

About the Hirz Fire, which had broken out not far to the north, he said: "That whole area in a normal year should not have been touched because it's near the river."

"Would you say that these fires are caused or influenced by climate change?"

"Well, whether it's a one million year thing or not, it's definitely ass-backwards, things we've never seen."

He sat in his vehicle, tired and sad and polite; one of his crew, Jeremy Stoke, had been recently killed; the memorial service was today. A female colleague handed each of us a decal with the dead man's name on it. She told me to be sure to drink plenty of water.

They gave us directions to a nearby neighborhood that the fire had reached. We thanked them. Sitting in the parking lot while Greg looked for a forgotten piece of his camera, I enjoyed a brief cool wind, which did not taste smoky thanks to my respirator, although I felt that unpleasant something in my chest. If I keep going on and on about my symptoms it is merely because my body, like my camera and laptop, was one more recording machine whose organic data may help you from our present to imagine yourself into the future.

And that is why I also tell you that when Chief Varnum's vehicle groaned slowly out of the parking lot, after we waved to him, I studied that red and silver truck's muting and softening in the smoke as it swept around the bend. I took note of the way the headlights shone more than usually silver-white, with larger vaguer disks than in the present where I was from; from previous summer visits to

Redding I remembered their hurtfully bright micalike glare, which the fires now considerately smoothened and softened.

Turning left onto Riverside Drive, then right, we descended into a valley of smoke and crossed the Sacramento River, which appeared glassy and grayish-green. Left onto Quartz Hill, left onto Harlan Drive, where our horizon became a wall of smoke-stained trees, and we saw: WE LOVE FIRST RESPONDERS THANK YOU. A sign by a house read: THE LOVE IN THE AIR IS THICKER THAN THE SMOKE.

Greg parked in a cul-de-sac, and we went our separate ways to better inventory the future, which for me began at the very edge of the sidewalk, where I stood listening to my own slow breathing through the mask. I saw a gentle hill, on which some trees remained in leaf, and as I waited to perceive and understand I began to hear birdsong; here came a big fat jay lording it over the ashes. This hill was not uniformly black but varied within the blackness, much as a Rothko "dark painting" starts to show its secret undercolors to one who waits; there were also browns and tans, and conspicuous patches of white.

I strolled around the neighborhood. Down a grand and winding driveway, past a red declaration of unsafety, I reached a new temporary fence that guarded a lonely chimney on a field of rubble, with two nubs of house wall still standing not far away, and an untouched pole lamp, and some kind of scaffolding around a charred black tower.

In a scorched place, affixed to a scorched truck, a sign read: BURNED UP BUT NOT BURNED OUT JESUS IS LORD JOHN 3:16.

An old couple went past me, pulling an empty wagon and walking their dog; I greeted them and they did not answer, probably because I was photographing the burnt remains of some neighbor's property. I wondered if they had been distributing bottled water. I listened to the rustle of the yellow police tape, which read: DO NOT ENTER DO NOT ENTER UNSAFE.

On the other side of the street was another driveway beauti-
fully decorated by the smoke-softened shadows of maple leaves
that the fire's breath had wilted on the tree. The driveway took
me to a wide low mound of broken plaster or Sheetrock, with
the metal skeletons of chairs standing or fallen in it, and a waste
bin already filled by some order-lover with some of those white
flakes, behind which stood a scorched metal tomb that might
have been a refrigerator. Pathetic squares of brickwork guarded
ceramic pots with the burnt stalks of houseplants still in them,
and there were pathetic squares of brickwork near some moatlike
construction disinterred by the flames.

Then I saw an almost untouched house, with its back fence
scorched and partially nibbled, flaunting its luck beside the next-
door neighbor's charred foundation.

During my researches into the Fukushima nuclear disaster I had paid a number of visits to the abandoned town of Tomioka, which this street now brought back to me, for it was formerly so ordinary and now so hideously extraordinary—but only to those of us who still lived in the present. Thanks to climate change, the Carr Fire would soon enough be a typical West Coast summer vista, from Canada right down to Mexico.

It was now Friday afternoon and a man in shorts and a bright green T-shirt parked at the edge of the fortunate house and took a photo with his cell phone, even as one of his neighbors worked with a chain saw, seeking to clear away the future, and a few other cars very slowly came and went, with those smoky grayed out trees looming over the edge of the cul-de-sac.

5

Chief Varnum had mentioned the Hirz Fire and the Hat Fire, so we decided to cut our baby teeth on at least one of those before covering the Carr Fire. For some days now there had been an even more impressive conflagration in Mendocino, the largest on record in California, they said, but the way I looked at it, it would only be the largest until next year or the year after. "What's the difference anyway?" I mumbled to Greg through the rubberized speech enhancers of my mask. "What did you say?" he replied. Thus one of our typical exchanges. In our three days we drove about eight hundred miles, which I considered adequate, and reader, if you feel disappointed in us, why not outshine us by visiting the fire nearest you? Of course it was easier for me than for Greg. All I had to do was emote. To raise his photographs up to Pulitzer quality, he needed walls of flame, swarms of helicopters and, ideally, people screaming with their clothes on fire. Well, in twenty or thirty years nobody would give a damn about all that.

At 4:30 we were on I-5 North, rolling past the unseen gray smokiness of Castle Crags, where I once used to hike, innocently enjoying the views. The hills ahead were an ugly tan with gray-green trees on them. My lungs continued to be tip-top thanks to the new respirator; I didn't mind my stinging eyes at all. Our first glimpse of Shasta Lake resembled nothing more than a pit of hellish smoke. Presently we saw more of that water body, blue-gray to the right, gray to the left, with an unreal gray haze of mountains behind it. Speeding into a dip where everything looked and felt slightly better, then up around a curve with blue-gray ridges ahead, where my chest ached a trifle, we headed toward the Gilman Road exit, since the Cal Fire website had advised us to avoid it if at all possible. A turkey vulture rode the smoky thermals. Here came a drop to the left: blue-gray ridge-tops, serrated with trees and two-dimensional. We turned onto Exit 698: Gilman Road. This forest zone was much less smoky than anywhere we had been in Redding, so that when a fire truck groaned by it seemed out of place. We sped over bend after bend, everything quiet with blue smoke below and behind the trees, and I wondered whether, if the Hirz Fire came roaring around the bend, we would be, in Chief Varnum's words, outflanked. Here came a ROAD CLOSED sign, courtesy of Shasta County, and behind the orange and white traffic cone sat a white van with its doors open, its yellow top light whirling by a spool of cable. Its occupant, a man in yellow vest and coveralls, said the fire was five to eight miles away.

"Could we get outflanked if we go down that curvy road?" I asked.

"You could," he said.

He would not let us through on his own authority. We were to be vetted by law enforcement, which presently appeared, in the person of a slender, fit young person named Harper. "No, it's way the hell down deep," she said. "I've been driving all over hell and gone trying to find it, but there was too much smoke."

"Can I take your photo?"

"No."

I liked that. She was someone who knew her mind.

Because our assignment had come through at the last minute, all we had in the way of a press letter was something "virtual" on Greg's cell phone—which lacked reception out here; so Harper refused to let us through. She said the Hat Fire was more convenient anyway for us journalistic slugs: easily visible, right off the edge of Highway 299 East. According to the Cal Fire website, it had started the day before, on August 9. As of today it had carbonized 1,900 acres and was 45 percent contained. So we drove back to Redding, on the way admiring a blue-gray island rising out of the silver-blue smoke of Shasta Lake, amended the letter to include the Hat Fire, got the desk clerk at our hotel to print it out, and finally, since it lacked our editor's signature, I, always eager to help and please law enforcement, added one of my own. Thus accoutered, we gassed up, bought cold liquids, and headed toward Hat Creek.

Shortly before seven, speeding east on 299, we found ourselves in a surprise patch of that good old-time golden light with trees the way they used to be and beautiful yellow grass, so I tried breathing unassisted and even got to enjoy the fragrance of evergreens, but presently the trees ahead began to go gray, the sky silver-white; so I put my respirator back on, feeling sickish, and we flashed through the tiny town of Ingot. It was a nice long drive. In the higher elevations there were quarter hour stretches of fresh air. Coming down from Hatchet Mountain's summit to about four thousand feet we gained a futuristic vista on our right: sharp green tips of pines on the roadside, then meadow and forest dulled down foully far below.

Just before dusk, we reached Officer Smith at the checkpoint on Sand Pit Road. He accepted our press letter. Future-adapted, he too wore no mask. He said that the fire was on the other side of that blue-gray forest ridge straight ahead. Like all the police and firefighters in those parts, he was a calm, fit, brave, pleasant sort who told us to be careful. A firecopter was about to take off across the road from the round red sun.

Following behind a red and yellow fire truck, we saw a gray-charred ridge some distance to our left, and then, closer to hand, black streaks in the pale grass. There was a strong woodsmoke smell, although I could not see anything actually smoldering. We watched for the place where Officer Smith had warned us that the guardrail was burned away, found it, and passed two firefighters in yellow coveralls. I saw my first smoke-wisp at the Pit River campground, which was now thoroughly blackened, so that it harmonized with the huge red-orange sun. Helicopters droned over the sad foulness.

It was ghostly gray down off the righthand side of the curving road. We stopped so that I could describe it, and Greg erected his tripod. My eyes were stinging. Our future began at the pavement's edge. It went down into blackness and grayness and blue-greenness with a blue-gray wide mountain, perhaps Lassen, almost beautiful in the southwest, blocking the dirty yellow-gray sky. I stood there feeling very sad.

Two red fire trucks from the Sugar Pine correctional camp whined by, followed by two white vans and a police car. My eyes

were still stinging, but at least no smoke blew in my face. As it turned out, for the rest of our time in this area the air would never be as bad as it had been on that first night, so I had full leisure to describe for you that wide vale of ashes, with a few trees untouched in it and even a peeping bird.

It was almost sunset. As I stood watching, something like a black snake uncoiled across the sun, becoming a great black bat or dragon—what was it? what could it have been, but smoke?— and within a few seconds it blew away, leaving the sun yellow-red on top and vermilion on the bottom; such colors kept crawling and shifting across its surface, reminding me of the storms our telescopes pick out on Jupiter.

Around the next bend, we found those two blocky red trucks of the Cal Fire crew from Sugar Pine: prison inmates. They formed up in their orange suits, with their small caps and backpacks. One man scraped a shovel against the ground. I called out my best good luck to them, and they laughed and waved back. Then they filed up the dirt road from the dry golden meadow in which they had parked, toward another snaky line of vehicles and then green-gray bushes that drew into the dimness of distance, where bluish-white stalks and funnels of smoke bloomed here and there, widely spaced, not dramatic: another day in paradise. And that orange column of firefighters vanished into the landscape, and the red sun went down.

6

The next morning (August 11), the sky was actually bluish in downtown Redding, and when I walked around at 8:00 a.m. I tasted smoke on my tongue but my throat did not hurt. We set off for the Carr Fire, which had now munched up 186,416 acres, 1077 residences, 22 commercial establishments, and 500 outbuildings. Against it fought 335 fire engines and 4,665 human beings in 76 crews.

In Greg's truck I commenced without my mask. Looking past the red light of California Street, I could see a good four blocks into green trees whose undershadows only were gray. Pretty good for the future, I said to myself.

Now we were back on Highway 299 West, passing the sign that warned of limited access, rushing toward smoke-hazed gray trees, and then I had to put on the mask, seven miles from Whiskeytown Lake. We were still in greater Redding. More handwritten signs thanked the police, the National Guard, and "all kind people." In the strip mall to our left, many yellow-clad workers formed up into two open-backed personnel carriers. Three yellow fire trucks and one red one turned in ahead of us as we entered the lanes of orange cones. A woman in a yellow suit waved us through, and we entered a landscape of mostly living trees on black and white burned ground. Then we rolled down into a hollow of smoke. Greg said: "I had no idea it was this bad when we were here the other night. Well, that's because we couldn't see anything," and we rushed like eager beaver journalists into a future world decorated with the black skeleton-fingers of trees. Greg pulled on his disposable mask. I asked how he felt, and he said it was no big deal; he only had a sore throat. After winding past burned houses, a fruit stand most definitely not open for business, an old brick ruin in the town of Shasta, black trees sticking out of whiteness, we pulled over by the marker for a PIONEER BABY'S GRAVE.

There on the edge of the road, tasting smoke on my tongue but almost entirely escaping lung-unpleasantness, thanks to that magic mask with its disposable carbon filter, I looked down a nude dirt-hill through a line of partially scorched trees, then across undulating funereal swales of gray, brown, tan, and mostly black, the soil fire-stripped, the most colorful thing being the reddish-yellow of dying pine needles, although here and there a few gray-green trees had escaped. The farther away I looked, the grayer grew the trees and the air; in a way it was almost beautiful, although not as pleasant as the planet we were leaving behind. With this fire half-contained and the winds on our side, the sky had a blue tint even here, and I could easily distinguish the helicopter that hummed overhead.

Past Rock Creek Road, the road ascended up a hill into smoke, and I took slow breaths in my mask. A transmission tower loomed surprisingly clearly out of the gray. The road was fairly busy, almost entirely with fire vehicles, and we passed the Whiskeytown turnoff. It was almost a pretty summertime drive for a second or two. Now we came to the roadblock where one must follow the PILOT CAR NEXT 30 MILES, and then, after the policeman approved our documents, we descended into the near-blue sky with Whiskeytown Lake blue and preposterously pretty on the left. When I was young I used to go there with friends to camp and swim. Oh, well. On the right stood many yellowing pine trees in bare burned ground.

That last officer had been another future-adapted type who wore no mask. When I complimented him on his tolerance, he remarked: "Well, it was pretty good earlier this morning but now it's starting to creep back." What *it* was he did not have to say.

We came to a spot the fire had neglected, and heard the hissing of poplars in the breeze. Crows and jays announced themselves on this hill of mostly green trees (thanks to climate change several pines were reddened by bark beetles). Five red fire trucks, evenly spaced, came around the bend. All in all, it was a dull enough place, too much like the world from which we had come, so I proposed that we swing back around to go deeper into the Carr Fire. We pulled up to a bearded man in a truck. I asked how he was and he smiled and said if he felt any better he'd be high or dead. Greg asked where the action might be. He said that if we went up Trinity Mountain we would see some cool shit, lots of helicopters taking off, but, remember, we hadn't heard it from him. So we turned off on the Trinity Road, heading up toward Jackass Springs.

Passing a well-vehicled laydown yard whose most interesting occupant might have been the blue Incident Command Support Unit truck, we came to a big thank-you sign by the town of French Gulch which, smoke-wreathed against a hill, had been mostly spared. At the other end of town we saw THANK YOU FIRE PERSONS AND THANKS 1ST RESPONDERS.

Not far up out of French Gulch there came a place where two scorched cars paralleled each other, one on each side of the road. Beneath the front bumper of the closest one, something had melted into a silvery puddle-shaped ingot. I gave it to Greg for a souvenir. He thought it might be from a mailbox.

I walked down a path of ashes to Clear Creek, which still flowed in apparent conformance with its name, although its bed might have been browner-green than usual. (When I mentioned this to Greg, he said that in Redding he had seen a swimming pool with a dark green tint.) In this eerily preserved strip of moderately blighted greenery, with dead grayness on either side, I listened to the sound of the water with my mask on. The far bank commenced with bare gravel, then rose into a hill of dark ashes, burnt trees, and smoke. I heard a woodpecker not far away; its pecking was strangely slow.

For several miles we now wound up the mountain road, right up to the first smoke-wisp, where a worker in a truck told us (admitting he could not command us) to go back because it was dangerous and we were hampering operations. Over the horizon hung something like a great white cumulus cloud. Greg wanted to get sight of it, so we rounded a few more bends, but there was no vista. I did not like the wind, which might be on the verge of shifting. We stopped up there in that high forest of very dry oaks with the wind blowing through. Looking over the pavement's edge, I saw more white smoke creeping up a few feet away. I walked around the next bend. Smoke was seeping up from a black burned stump and there was an evil red eye in the center. I heard a hissing, not of wind. Smoke blew steadily across the road; if the wind changed we might be burned. In spite of the hissing everything seemed very silent.

Returning down along the ridgeline of the burned canyon, looking across burned patches into the opposing blue-gray ridge of trees and smoke, we noticed more stealthy irruptions, none of them as dramatic as the smoke we'd seen at the Hat Fire. On the far side of the highway, beyond a barbed wire fence and a freshly bulldozed stripe of firebreak, I gazed across the creek where the fire's many small fingers came up thin and then funneled out, blue-gray and rising.

Pulling back into French Gulch as the Red Cross van rolled through and a helicopter whickered unseen in the smoke, we parked to see what we could see. The fire had been stopped right at the edge of the town. Even up in the burned hill on the western side a large white house stood untouched. The firefighters had done a magnificent job. Along the main street there were two facing shaded stretches of sidewalk, and on the railing of the long, shaded porch of the two-storey French Gulch Hotel, one sign said WE WILL REBUILD and the other, written in a rainbow of colors, perhaps by children, read: THANK YOU FIRE CAMP PRISONERS, with a heart.

We stopped to talk to Mr. John Vella, who said: "It started right down the street, on 299. It shoulda been called the fuckin' French Gulch fire. When I first heard about it I drove down the road to where it started. I saw the whole hill goin' up in flames, a quarter mile from 299. I left, spent a couple nights, but it got too smoky so I finally got the hell out. Sheriff said, you got five minutes; we gotta go. I went down to my brother's house in Elk Grove. Spent two weeks there. I got updates from everybody around town. Everybody took care of each other. Took care of my cat. I wasn't here in '04 when the fire took twenty-nine homes, but this time they came in strong, had twenty-eight fire trucks. Protected the town. Yeah, but the fire came back two times, tried to burn the town down."

I wondered when it would come back again. He was patient with me, so I asked him what he believed about global warming.

"Yeah, it's gettin' drier and drier. Trump doesn't wanna say it, but it's fuckin' climate change. It's just dry. And all our . . . There's over five hundred fire trucks up here. Utility trucks, too. I've seen 'em come in today from Fremont, Oakland, Los Angeles, Alameda County. I saw one from Iowa earlier this morning. PG & E got crews up the butt up here."

He was about my age (I was born in 1959). I inquired whether French Gulch would be uninhabitable in his lifetime. He said: "In my lifetime, yeah, probably another twenty years it should be all right. Probably gonna be all right. At least we got power. Thank God."

Then Greg and I drove out of the future, although I kept my mask on for much of the way back to Sacramento. The next day there was hardly a tint of gray in the sky.

ELAINE CASTILLO was born
and raised in the San Francisco Bay Area, where she
graduated from the University of California, Berkeley,
with a degree in Compara-
tive Literature. *America Is
Not the Heart* is her debut
novel, and was named one
of the best books of 2018 by
NPR, *Real Simple*, *Lit Hub*,
the *Boston Globe*, *San Francisco Chronicle*, *New York
Post*, *Kirkus Reviews*, the
New York Public Library
and more. It has been nominated for the *Elle* Award, the
Center for Fiction Prize,
the Aspen Words Prize,
the Northern California Independent Booksellers Book
Award, the California Book
Award, and Italy's Fernanda
Pivano Prize.

Facts From the Story []'ll Never Tell You

ELAINE CASTILLO

1. [] don't talk anymore.
2. When [] visited [] in jail the first time, back in 2014, [] hadn't been back to the Bay in three years.
3. The last conversation [] had was over Skype, two days before [] was supposed to surrender to police custody.
4. [] said [] was thinking of enlisting, after [] got out, after [] years of probation were up.
5. [] said, *I know how you feel about the military. I know. I'm sorry. It's just . . .*
6. [] said, *No, I—listen, come on. You know people from our community—dudes—I get why they enlist, I'm not gonna. Like J., like—*
7. The screen was blurry.
8. If [] looked closer [] would have seen [] shaking, but [] couldn't, so [] didn't.
9. *I mean, you know me, I'll—whatever—I'm gonna be a pain in your ass like always but I'm not gonna, I'm not gonna, disown you, like—I know what the options are, if you feel like you—I don't—. Don't be dumb.*

10. [] nodded, blank with shock, like someone who'd been slapped but was still waiting for [] brain to bring the message of pain.

11. *Thank—thank you—*[] said.

12. Then dropped [] face into [] hands and started sobbing.

13. *Shit—shit, honey—*

14. On the Skype window, just trembling hair: coarse, black, same as [].

15. Hidden in [] palm: [] eyebrow: thick, with a cowlick in the left one, same as [].

16. [] said, *Did you think I was gonna disown you if you told me? Because of what, my politics? Did you just think I was gonna—*

17. [] kept sobbing for a long while.

18. When [] lifted [] face, [] looked surprised, almost disconnected from []; some dwende had taken over [] body in some holy sympathy, given [] a breather from the scale of [] feeling.

19. But now it looked like the dwende had left, so it was [] turn to feel it.

20. [] said, *Were you afraid of telling me? Because you thought—*

21. [] didn't say anything. Nodded, jerkily.

22. *I love you.*

23. The next time [] saw [], [] were in the same room; still behind a glass screen.

24. [] was in the Bay for two weeks.

25. [] mom and [] saw [] twice a week, the maximum number of visits.

26. [] always went late at night, when the streets around the jail were so wide and empty [] could be pretty sure that any car [] glimpsed was either coming from where [] were about to go, or going where []'d just been.

27. For the first four years of [] life, [] mom raised []—along with seemingly every undocumented Filipino in [] family, around seven to nine people at a time, most sleeping on the floor—in a two-bedroom apartment not far from the jail.

28. [] elementary school and [] local church were both walking distance from the jail.

29. In middle school, [] dad bought an Accord from the Honda dealership next to the jail.

30. This winter [] almost bought a Honda Accord from the Honda dealership next to the jail.

31. Nearly all the visitors in the jail whenever [] went were women, predominantly Mexican, Filipina, or Vietnamese.

32. Once [] forgot the closed-toe shoe rule and had to rush back home for sneakers, racing to make it back before visiting hours ended.

33. [] thought [] recognized one girl from elementary school, but she didn't see [], and [] didn't say anything.

34. [] sent books to [] multiple times.

35. The jail rejected the books every time.

36. Even got a writer friend to get [] publisher to send books direct.

37. The jail rejected the books every time.

38. On the first visit, [] wore a freshly shaved head, a brown uniform, and a grave, wry expression.

39. [] told [] about another inmate, nickname Triste, who was an artist and wanted to paint [] portrait.

40. *He's never even seen me.*

41. [] shrugged, eyes rolling in the manner of someone who's already told everyone the worst version of who [] are: *I think he's heard enough.*

42. [] don't talk anymore.

43. The last of those jail visits, before [] had to go back to London, was on the Fourth of July.
44. Before [] went to the jail, first [] had dinner at a local Filipino barbecue joint in Milpitas.
45. On the big television playing Filipino cable in the restaurant, the screen showed Senator Juan Ponce Enrile surrendering to authorities at Camp Crame—the Philippine National Police's headquarters—on charges of corruption and plunder.
46. [] mom and [] didn't talk much.
47. The day before []'d had a screaming fight, a tradition for [].
48. Same old things: family, the past, why [] are the way [] are; things that happened that []'ll never admit happened, the happening of which made whole people.
49. Unmade whole people.
50. Afterward, [] went to the jail to spend Independence Day with [] brother.
51. [] don't remember much of what [] talked about.
52. [] think [] talked about how [] was getting used to being woken up at three in the morning for dinner.
53. [] think [] talked about how [] was still trying to mail books to [].
54. [] had some books in the jail, so [] was reading the *Hunger Games* trilogy, which [] hadn't read yet.
55. [] promised [] that [] would read every book in the trilogy so [] could send [] letters about [] thoughts.
56. In the months that followed, [] read every single book in the *Hunger Games* trilogy, and sent [] letters about [] thoughts.
57. [] couldn't send any letters back.

58. On the way out of the jail for that last visit, halfway between the last security gate and the parking lot, in the middle of a vast asphalt walking path bordered by electric fences, [] mom stumbled over nothing, then stopped to weep in [] arms.

59. [] didn't cry; not there.

60. Afterward, [] mom and [] did something [] hadn't done in years.

61. [] went to watch the Fourth of July fireworks in town.

62. [] parked the car in the Golfland parking lot next to the old liquor store where [] father, grandfather, and eldest brother used to buy lotto tickets every week, along with Benson & Hedges menthol cigarettes.

63. [] walked the mile it took to Cardoza Park, along with seemingly every other soul in Milpitas.

64. [] had never seen that many people on the street in [] entire life.

65. It's still the longest distance [] ever walked with [] mother.

66. July in Milpitas is hot enough for tank tops well into the night, but [] wore a jacket and [] wore a sweater, and were still shivering.

67. Anyone who wasn't part of the sidewalk procession to Cardoza Park was sitting in [] driveways, garage doors open, mahjong tables and garden loungers arranged, beers clinking, fireworks vantage points already set up.

68. Everyone on the street was speaking Tagalog and Spanish and Vietnamese and Cantonese and Hindi and Urdu and English.

69. It took [] a long time to walk that mile to the park; not just because of the crowd.

70. [] were clutching each other so closely that [] could only take tiny steps at a time.

71. [] arm tight around [] waist, [] arm tight around [] shoulders, [] other hands clutching, [] head nestled into [], [] hair against [] cheek and mouth.

72. Like lovers, or the shipwrecked on a makeshift raft: holding on for dear life.

73. What [] went in for is not a new thing in this family.

74. [] didn't go to jail for it, though.

75. [] have to protect [] own, someone said to [] once.

76. [] protected [] own for a long time, too.

77. [] partner and [] came up with a safeword to use if something [] do brings up a memory.

78. [] left the Bay Area for almost a decade.

79. [] not the only girl who left, but.

80. [] not the only one who came back, but.

81. [] is not the only brother [] don't talk to anymore.

82. [] mom doesn't talk to one of [] sisters anymore, either.

83. One of [] older brothers doesn't talk to the other one.

84. One of [] aunts doesn't talk to another aunt.

85. One of [] cousins doesn't talk to two of [] sisters.

86. When [] lived outside of the Bay, [] used to go on real estate websites and look up houses for sale in Milpitas, Daly City, Hayward, Union City, San Jose.

87. It never took [] long to find the kind of house [] wanted to see.

88. Last Supper portrait in the kitchen, big fork and spoon on the wall.

89. Gaudy tapestries, portraits of Jesus, statues of Mary.

90. Plastic-covered furniture, dark wood chairs.

91. Money plants, bamboo plants.

92. Healthy orchids, plastic; dying orchids, real.

93. Bay Area Filipinos leaving, selling their houses; sometimes for over a million dollars.

94. *Good for you*, [] thought back then.
95. [] didn't look up the houses all the time.
96. Not all the time, but not infrequently.
97. [] got out on [] birthday.
98. [] wasn't there.
99. [] don't talk anymore.

HÉCTOR TOBAR is the Los Angeles-based author of four books, including the novel *The Barbarian Nurseries*, and the nonfiction book *Deep Down Dark*, an account of the 2010 Chilean mine disaster and rescue. His work has appeared in the *New York Times*, the *New Yorker*, and *Best American Short Stories*. He is an associate professor at the University of California, Irvine.

A Portrait of the Artist as a Latchkey Child

HÉCTOR TOBAR

Humberto was in a trance, though it took his mother a while to notice. She was whirling about the apartment in a cloud of hairspray, sculpting her brunette strands into a jaunty wave. When she finished, she found her son sitting over his breakfast and saw his eyes were fixed on something outside the large window of their second-story living room. She followed his gaze through the glass and saw the same ficus trees as always, with their old, robust, and billowing canopies, and the same cube-shaped apartments of smog-soiled turquoise and salmon. The boy was not looking at those things. He was daydreaming. And his expression was so serious and monklike, he looked as if he were twenty-six years old instead of six. Her son was a strange still life sitting there at the table, holding a spoon that rested, motionless, inside a bowl of floating green, pink, and blue cereal loops. The corners of his lips rose suddenly in amusement. A part of his boy self was alive, out there, in an imaginary world beyond the window. His head bounced with a suppressed laugh.

"¿Por qué te ríes?" she asked, but of course he didn't answer. So she returned to herself, to her harried and underappreciated

91

self. She spoke a motherly instruction in a stern, clipped sentence of accented English. "Eat your cereal before it gets cold."

Her command broke Humberto's trance. He turned to her and said, "But it's supposed to be cold."

She walked to the window and pulled a thick curtain of grayish green fabric across it. "I'll be back at the same time," she said, and she gave Humberto a kiss on the forehead, picked up her purse, and headed for the door.

By now, Humberto's mother had grown used to leaving Humberto on his own, and so she skipped the admonitions she'd given him the first few times: "Don't turn on the stove or play with fire or matches. Don't open the door if anyone knocks. Don't play with the electrical plugs." Humberto routinely broke two of these three rules, though his mother did not know this. She locked the door behind her and began her journey into the stuccoed, stylized metropolis called Los Angeles. A city of short skirts (like hers on this day) and floral print sundresses and pastel lipsticks and pretzeled neon, of men on the prowl, each day filled with economic and libidinous possibilities. Nothing like her native country. She wanted to be lost in Los Angeles. She wanted a muscled hero to drive her on avenues that led to rocky beaches and rocky deserts.

Humberto listened as her high-heeled steps click-clacked down the stairs. With his mother gone, he began his day as he always did. He walked to the curtain and inched it open and squeezed his face against the glass to see if he could catch a final glimpse of her. This was the moment of the day he most felt like crying, and the first week she had left him to go to work he bawled and snot-coughed and wailed because the closed door and the quiet were horrible things. As she disappeared around the corner he heard a snap coming from his bedroom. A comforting click. The lemon-yellow digital clock on the dresser by his bed dripped the minutes, one numbered leaf at a time. Humberto stepped into his room and saw the time: 8:35 a.m. He kept his eyes on the numbers, trying not to blink (though he did, twice) until the clock flipped to the next minute. With each day Humberto spent alone in this apartment the snap became louder and Humberto became more obsessed with the clock and its movement. Sometimes he lifted up the box of the clock and studied it without unplugging it, trying to guess at how it worked by the vibrations he felt through his fingertips. There was a cylinder inside that turned at the speed of the Earth itself, a single rotation each day, a journey of three inches in twenty-four hours.

After listening to the clock snap hundreds and then thousands of minutes, the imperceptible rotation of the mechanism inside and of the Earth on its axis became one and the same thing in Humberto's mind. His apartment and the street below his window were all turning on the surface of this planet, and he imagined the Earth rotating under his tennis shoes, racing toward a horizon. Hills and plains and the oceans, turning. The clock snapped another minute. When the minute leaves reached 5:45 p.m. his mother's heels would click-clack back up the stairs, and Humberto would hear the musical notes made by her keys, and the door would open again. Their apartment stood on stilts above a parking garage that itself rested atop the great ball of the Earth. At school he had learned about the solar system. And he understood that he lived on a celestial object speeding through unending blackness, in the stillness of something his teacher called "a vacuum." The hours of wordlessness that followed his mother's departure felt like the kind of quiet in which a planet could float, and when he thought of himself and his lonely body in the cosmos, he was as close as a boy his age could be to understanding the Infinite.

Humberto returned to the living room. I should probably turn on the television. Mommy told me to watch as much as I want.

93

After several weeks alone, Humberto had memorized many of the words and pictures from the shows he liked to watch and the commercials in between. The cowboys, the car sellers, and the jingles. The television sang and guffawed and chortled and laughed its tin laugh, and after a few weeks its amusements had come to feel as flat and unalive as the muffled speech of the neighbors coming through the walls of the apartment. The electronic components inside the wood and steel box that contained the device were more interesting to Humberto, and he often sat on the carpet and peered through the small ventilation holes in the device's rear panel. He saw a fantastic, miniature cityscape of glass towers, of twisting copper paths, of plastic cylinders and disc-shaped men standing on wire legs. Twice before he had taken a screwdriver and removed the television's rear panel, and he wondered if today would be the day he finally disassembled the entire apparatus, to study and play with it.

Humberto imagined the television in pieces scattered across the living room and knew that this would make his mother cry. So he did the obedient thing and returned to the front of the television and stood before it; he saw his own reflected image filling the screen, a boy alive and three-dimensional inside the curved space of the glass. He turned the television on and watched as the boy disappeared and a single point of light expanded from nothing to fill the screen, and the electric miasma inside the glass became a two-dimensional cartoon bear. Before the creature's voice began speaking, there was a moment of silence, and Humberto heard the clock in his bedroom drip another minute.

Cartoon animals ran and jumped and fell off cliffs, and looking at them Humberto remembered himself running and jumping and falling in the schoolyard during the school year, and in the park where his father once took him before his father stopped seeing his mother. His father, his cologne, Humberto running around his father's legs, outside, in the sunshine of a California winter weekend. When he emerged from this daydream he saw flames on the television screen. He saw a newsman whose black hair was on fire, and Humberto realized that images of a burning hillside were being projected behind this man. The flames gave way to a map that showed a cartoon fire rushing toward a cartoon beach labeled MALIBU.

"It's a fire," Humberto said out loud. "A fire!"

He went to his mother's room and climbed on her bed to open the window, to see if he could spot any flames. Then he jumped and bounced on her bed, his feet sinking into the huge belly of the mattress. He trampolined up and down for two minutes, and then he lay on his stomach and stared at the clock on his mother's nightstand. This clock had a black face and a turning white hand that moved in a smooth, steady motion across the circle of the seconds, never stopping, always turning, turning, turning, and he watched this turning, turning, turning until it hypnotized him and he slipped into a daydream in which this room became dark, and it was the night his mother was here, on this bed, with the Man with the Long Sideburns.

Humberto had been asleep, and he had been awakened by a rhythmic clattering coming from his mother's room. He rose to his feet, and peering through her open doorway he saw that the Man with the Long Sideburns was on top of his mother, who was on her back. They were exercising, it seemed, and the exertion involved was causing them to grunt and moan and make other noises he had never heard adults make before. Humberto had thought it best not to interrupt them, and he had gone back to bed. The next morning the Man with the Long Sideburns was gone, and after his mother had left for work Humberto had seen the blankets covered in blackish-red patches and snaking pearly streaks that were mysterious to him.

The blankets were clean now, white and unblemished, and at this moment and for many years to come, deep into his California middle age, Humberto would wonder if his memory of those red and white stains was real, or just a dream. The blankets smelled of bleach, but that scent wasn't nearly as strong as the perfume that came from the jar of his mother's cold cream. The flowery aroma inside the jar brought his mother's presence most vividly to him, and he was about to open it and release a burst of the smell into the room when he heard a knock on the front door.

The knock repeated. Someone's there! Three beats on the wooden seal of the door. Humberto froze in place. I can't let them hear me. Dangerous. They'll know I'm alone here. Humberto held very still. Finally the door-knocker turned and went back down the stairs, and by the heaviness of the steps, Humberto could tell he was a man.

When the man's steps had faded, Humberto walked toward the door with slow, light strides. He noticed a folded piece of paper had been slipped under the door, and he kneeled down to look at it, and then snatched it up.

It was a brochure, printed on thin, delicate paper, its cover illustrated with a drawing of a stone tower with parapets. That's a nice castle. The message on the brochure was written in a style that was too dense and too grown-up to pull him in, but on the back of the page he saw three words that were bigger than all the rest, as if they had been placed there for a boy his age to read.

GOD SEES YOU

Humberto turned and scanned the room behind him; then he looked up, in the general direction of the sky, which was where everyone said God lived. He saw the rough, uneven surface of the acoustic ceiling, a choppy alabaster sea that hovered over him day and night. Whenever Humberto stared at this plaster ocean he saw different patterns—resembling birds, rivers, the moon—but now he saw faces, flashing glances at him one right after another. A series of dark eyes, chiseled noses, and the stern straight mouths of masked deities.

The paper was wrong; there was not just one god looking at him, there were twenty. Maybe there were extra gods to make certain he remained obedient. The plaster gods wanted him to stay away from the fire and the electrical sockets; they wanted him to eat the lunch his mother had prepared, which was cooking in an electric pot. He turned off the switch on the pot, and got a bowl and served himself the stew of potatoes and meat. Humberto ate this same stew most days he was alone, and as he chewed he looked up at the ceiling gods and wondered if they had been telling his mother how he behaved. Probably not, because there were many things Humberto had done while he was alone that would have made his mother angry and sad had she known about them: like the time he'd toasted and re-toasted his bread over and over again until a cloud of smoke filled the kitchen; or the time he'd put a fork into one of the electrical sockets, sending a shock through his hands and wrists that caused him to fly backward and that produced a tiny explosion of sparks, leaving scorch marks on the wall. The gods did not tattle on him then, and he sensed they would remain mute on the ceiling no matter what he did, even if he opened the door and walked down the stairs and onto the street. Or if he opened the second-story window and jumped out, using his mother's freshly bleached sheets as a parachute.

I'll float down to the street below. Like Superman. Like a bird. The spell of his daydream was broken when Humberto realized

97

that, even if he landed safely on the concrete, he'd be locked out of the house. He returned to his bowl of stew. When he finished he retrieved a spiral notebook he kept by his bed and began to draw. He began to create a highway map of Los Angeles County from memory, including freeways that were under construction; and he sketched the sun dipping into the Pacific Ocean, as he had seen it on the beach in Santa Monica with his mother. While he drew and wrote he forgot about the snap of the clock. Finally he stopped and looked back at all he had drawn, today and the days before. Once before he had ripped out two sheets from the notebook and set them on fire, and now he decided he should send all his pages up in flames, but then changed his mind and grasped the notebook against his chest. He started to shiver, even though it was a hot summer day, and he thought about how much he wanted his mother back. When he heard the next snap of the minute-leaves on his clock, he would scream. He opened his mouth and flexed his throat, but stopped himself, because this would bring the neighbors to the door. Instead he ran in a circle in the living room, and the walls and the framed photos they held rushed past him in a blur, as if he were on a merry-go-round. Finally, he stopped, and when he felt the urge to scream again he pulled the curtain violently open.

A blinding torrent of sun flooded the living room and kitchen, and in this light the rooms and their contents seemed to shrink in size and grow older and lose their color. All the gods on the ceiling disappeared, and Humberto could see a thick layer of dust on top of the television. He walked toward the daylight until his nose touched the pane of glass.

The windowpane was summer warm, and Humberto closed his eyes and allowed himself to linger there, until he heard a voice.

"Yeah, over here. This is good."

Two boys were standing on the driveway directly below him. They were older, fourth-graders at his school. One of them was bouncing a ball. They disappeared beneath his feet into the open garage and began throwing their ball against the wall beneath his living room, each impact causing a tremor in his apartment.

"Curveball got him looking!" one of the boys yelled.

The second boy shouted back: "You can't make a tennis ball curve, dummy!"

They threw the ball against the wall, tossing it rhythmically, causing the floor, the ceiling, and the walls of his apartment to pulse, as if the building were a huge animal made of wood and plaster, and he was inside the animal, listening to its heartbeat.

Humberto returned to his room and sat on his bed. The leaves on the lemon-colored clock snapped: 3:26 p.m. He touched the timepiece with his fingertips, and felt it humming. Beneath his feet the two boys kept playing and bouncing their ball, and the walls of the apartment throbbed. He thought about the turning Earth and felt the street and the building moving toward a distant horizon. A summer afternoon. In his mind's eye he saw waves of heat rising from the asphalt outside. Birds sipping at wastewater in the gutter. The skin of the playing boys turning mahogany in the sun.

The plaster gods had returned to the ceiling. He could set fire to his notebooks and watch the smoke rise up and cover their masked faces. Or walk out the door and look for the man who knocked. Ask him to take me to Mommy. Take this bed sheet and fly out the window. Fly over those two boys. Now Humberto became the boy who sailed out the window, and many other, different boys all at once. The boy reflected in the television glass. An intrepid trailblazer marching over a snowy mountain pass lined with boulders. An astronaut on the surface of Mars, running scarlet sand through his gloved hand. Humberto no longer heard the snap of the clock, and his visions became more real than the room, and in their realness they were exhilarating. He lived inside them and felt their light and saw their textures. Martian sun, an icy pathway through pines, the orange dirt of the baseball diamond at Lemon Grove Park, here in Hollywood, and the leather skin of a baseball in his palm. Humberto wandered about the metropolis of steel and concrete he saw when he went shopping with his mother, Los Angeles, a city where electricity pulsed in the buildings and in traffic signals shifting from red to green to yellow to red. In this imaginary Los Angeles he spoke words to other boys, and he floated over hillsides that were on fire, and the spectacle of the flames was orange and menacing and beautiful. He became a mischievous giant blowing the brushfire smoke into the atmosphere, drawing lines of floating ash and soot around the globe to amuse himself.

When his mother returned at 5:45 p.m., Humberto did not hear the clank of her keys or the sound of the door opening. She found him sitting on the carpeted floor of the living room, staring out the picture window at the sullied blue of the California sky.

LAUREN MARKHAM is a writer focusing on issues related to youth, migration, the environment, and her home state of California. Her work has appeared in outlets such as *Guernica, Harper's, Orion,* the *New Republic,* the *New York Times,* and *VQR,* where she is a contributing editor. Markham is the author of *The Far Away Brothers: Two Young Migrants and the Making of an American Life,* which was awarded the Northern California Book Award, the California Book Award Silver Medal, and the Ridenhour Prize.

The California Pageant

LAUREN MARKHAM

If you look at a topographical map of California you see a hollow basin in the state's center that spreads fifty miles east-west between the Sierra Nevada mountains and the Coast Range, and some five hundred and fifty miles north-south between the towering crags of Mount Shasta and the creeping section of I-5 called the Grapevine that twines its way through electric poppy fields before dumping into Los Angeles. This massive level basin is California's Central Valley, whose shape resembles the state in miniature, a state nestled within the state. It's flat and vast, like the skin of an upside-down drum. But in the northern quarter of this great expanse, near Chico, is a tiny cluster of topography: the Sutter Buttes, or what's been called by NASA the smallest mountain range in the world.

In a state that loves its vistas, the Buttes come as a welcome relief from the Central Valley's fertile, flat monotony that, on closer look, isn't so monotonous at all, only flat: the twisting rows of raisin grapes, the sturdy olive orchards, the low leafy lettuce patches, the waving safflower fields that burn so bright golden in late spring that my aunt always felt driving through them to visit her godmother that she was galloping on wheels upon her own personal yellow brick road. This part of California feeds millions in the United

States, and abroad; only one percent of the nation's total farmland, it contributes more than eight percent of its crops. There are the nut orchards (eighty percent of the world's almonds come from California), the tomato fields where my mother worked so many summers that she still can't stand the smell of a vine-ripened tomato. When it's their season there are also the oranges and the lemons and the broccoli and the pomegranates, the perennial emerald alfalfa that sucks the water and feeds the cows and that, increasingly, is shipped overseas to China, to Japan, to Saudi Arabia, so their drought-stricken cows too, can be fed. California is the most productive agricultural state in the country, and by far. In the winter the rice paddies flood and populate with hundreds of species of birds along the Pacific Flyway, lithe creatures that feed and rest and are shot down by the duck clubs, before the water is diverted through canals and into further farming pastures and then back into the river, where eventually, now just a piddle, it empties into the ocean. The Buttes rise out of these vast, fertile flatlands like a dazzling cluster of fangs. They are magnificent and strange, these volcanic formations appearing suddenly within the great, golden bowl of California and then folding back into the level expanse, as though a trick of the craving eye, a mirage.

The Buttes, which are now the single largest uninterrupted habitat in all of the eighteen thousand square miles of the Central Valley, were formed some 1.4 million years ago by tectonic activity and volcanic eruptions, and they have created a sense of wonder for millennia, too. Mountains have a magnetic quality, particularly when you can behold them in full; people want to see them, to climb and to know them, even to possess them. This being California, and the United States, these formations are historic indigenous land. What are now officially named the Sutter Buttes were formerly known as Middle Mountain, or Spirit Mountain, or the Histum Yani. This was a sacred place to many

Native people of this area before the settlers came, and long after, and still today.

Now, with the exception of a small state park that's nearly impossible to access due to the fact that it's surrounded by private property whose disgruntled owners don't favor visitors or the park's very existence, the Buttes are a collection of privately owned parcels. The Buttes consist largely of undeveloped rangeland and almond orchards (which people in the area, my entire family included, call *amand* orchards, for after all, they insist, what do you call the fish that's pink?). To visit the Buttes you have to find your way into the park or pay for a guided hike or you have to be lucky enough to own some of it. Most of the year the park is closed. This mass of land fascinates me because it is magnificent, because it is sacred, and because members of my extended family own parts of it—and it thus twines me directly to questions of ownership and of theft, two of California's most persistent stories, and to aspects of my identity and my state from which I've long preferred to shy away.

When I was growing up in California in the eighties and nineties, students at my school—an all-girls, private, K-8 institution where we wore uncomfortable, ill-fitting uniforms—studied California history in the third grade.

My class learned about the Missions, the transcontinental railroad, Angel Island and immigration, the Gold Rush and the Forty-Niners. The local indigenous communities—such as the Coast Miwok and the Ohlone—were presented to us as wise and noble and simple; these were people who ground acorns, who lived off the land, who carved arrowheads out of obsidian, that gleaming volcanic stone that we found spellbinding. History, as our teachers presented it to us, wasn't all that complicated. The making of California was presented as fully glorious and good: westward expansion, pioneer possibility, our great and golden state. The history we learned was a blend of memory and romance, our flawed history books and the dim, tattered photos within them, and our own imaginations. The Native people were here, the story went, and then after a while they mostly weren't anymore.

As part of my school's California history curriculum, the third grade class put on an original play. Each student portrayed a key character, each of us reenacting part of the great Golden State's unfurling. There was John Muir, Wells Fargo, Bill Graham, Jerry Brown. My best friend, Dani, played a wealthy San Francisco aristocrat and activist, Sally Lilienthal, who was part of an extended Jewish family credited with helping transform San Francisco into a booming metropolis; much to my jealousy, Dani got to wear a hoop skirt and a gown. Susanna Meyers played an infamous Mexican stagecoach robber. Susanna donned boots and a mustache and, when the Haas Lilienthals and Wells Fargo traveled an open road in their finery, Susanna leapt before the improvised stagecoach, and, as directed by our drama teacher, Mrs. Whitsel, and much to her delight, whooped dramatically and ridiculously, "*andale, andale, arriba, arriba!*" while brandishing two shiny cap guns, like Speedy Gonzales.

I've considered this play again and again, and how its genius was that it would forever intrinsically connect these characters from history with a real, lived experience, such that I was so much less likely to forget them. Which, of course, is a problem. For its more pernicious genius was how it laid bare the fundamental danger with the study of history, itself. All it takes is one zealous and giddy conductor—Mrs. Whitsel, say—to enact an elaborate, ecstatic lie.

The play opened with Ariel Levine playing Junipero Serra, the Franciscan Monk responsible for starting some of the first Spanish missions throughout California—missions that would forcibly convert, displace, and enslave hundreds of thousands of Native people in the name of God. Junipero Serra walked onstage in his humble, mud-brown robe tied with a fraying cord, spoke kindly to a handful of students in Native garb, and delivered his speech. "I am Junipero Serra, and this is California."

"Inherent in the myth we've been taught," writes Roxanne Dunbar-Ortiz in *An Indigenous Peoples' History of the United States*, "is an embrace of settler colonialism and genocide." History is just a collection of the things we teach and the stories we tell one other, piecing them all together as fact. Immigrant stories. Pioneer stories. Stories of striking it new in a bleak, fresh world. "Origin narratives form the vital core of a people's unifying identity and of the values that guide them," writes Dunbar-Ortiz.

We know the things we know because they've been taught to us, sometimes directly, sometimes obliquely, legend-by-osmosis. The things we don't know are things we've never heard about— whatever has been left out of the conversation, struck from the record, or simply never even considered. We sometimes have to unlearn these early teachings, or at least learn that some additional facts inhabit the legends we've been passed down like heirlooms, each as solid as a land mass and casting long shadows, just like the Buttes themselves.

The Buttes, as far as I ever heard growing up, were a beautiful, untrammeled place that belonged to members of my family. My great-grandfather Thomas Brady, who by all family legends was an important figure in the state's history at the turn of the century, accumulated parcels of the Buttes from other private landowners to graze his sheep. "The invasion of North America is told almost entirely from the eyes of the invader," writes scholar John Mohawk in his essay "Indian Nations, The United States, and Citizenship." What am I but a descendant of the invaders?

Here's how a 1935 article in the *San Francisco Examiner* tells the story of the settling of the Sutter Buttes: "A young United States Army captain fought his way through hostile Indian bands to pitch a camp on the curious volcanic buttes that form an interesting geological landmark on the otherwise flat Sacramento valley." The Maidu communities native to this area were killed or forcibly removed from their lands by Spanish conquistadors, by trappers, by the U.S. Army, by missionaries, and then—after the cry of gold was heard round the world—by settlers hell-bent on claiming the land for their own. "The young captain was John C. Fremont," the article continued, "and the events that followed his encampment at the buttes may have saved California for the United States." The Buttes were precious and storied, and coveted, and were a key part of the grand, murderous march toward what we now know as California.

Maidu Natives didn't live on the Buttes themselves; there was no year-round water source in the Histum Yani. But nearby communities relied on the mountains to hunt, to gather and pound acorns, to hold ceremonies of prayer. Until they were displaced, many Maidu communities—who were and are numerous and diverse—lived in the flatlands within sight of the Buttes. Eventually, once the settlers came, they were forced into slave labor in work camps, mill operations, and Catholic missions, or, in what were often the best of circumstances, onto reservations and rancherias at a considerable distance from where the communities originated, and thus from the resources on which they had come to rely. "The Indians were attacked and killed, enslaved and abused, their land seized and their children forced into alien schools solely because they possessed land other people wanted," writes John Mohawk. Settlers headed toward the Buttes were hungry for land, and would take it at any cost.

Dunbar-Ortiz points out that many of the settlers moving to the "New World" from Europe had, themselves, been disenfranchised of their land, which had been taken over by their countries' rulers, thus pushing them from the farmlands into the overcrowded cities and, eventually, across the sea in search of something of their own. The settlers in the early colonies, and long after, carved up the territory according to their sacred covenant of ownership: that myth of a wide-open space, theirs for the taking, full of possibility and profit. As an *Images of America* series booklet on the Buttes puts it, "to own land offered one a chance to make something worthwhile of his life." What had the westward slog been for, if not to own something, to stake one's claim and try to prosper?

In the eyes of the settlers, the Buttes were *theirs*—their discovery, their mysterious and alluring mountains that shot up out of an incomprehensible nowhere, their fertile rangelands, their refuge from the monotonous flat and the winter floods, their bounty and their beauty. Images of the Buttes appear in photograph after photograph taken by the settlers in the 1850s and onward—farmers in their tractors, merchants in their cars, families having a picnic in their Sunday best, the Buttes always looming marvelous and mighty overhead. In her book *Sutter Buttes: Land of the Histum Yani*, Louise Butts Hendrix refers to the mountains as "literally sentinels of the valley"—as a force keeping watch over whatever marauding bands might be out there, waiting. The description of their beauty is cast in the language of conquest.

In 1949, one hundred years after settlers struck gold at *Sutter's Mill*, the mountains were officially—by which I mean, in the eyes of the U.S. government—named the "Sutter Buttes," after John Sutter, the early California kingpin and swindler who was lauded for his ability to "break" Indians enslaved in his mines and logging camps. Even the name carries a legacy of violence.

*   *   *

A key California-related vocabulary word we learned in the third grade was *entrepreneur*, which, we were taught, meant something a bit more pioneer-fabulous than a mere "business-man." Levi Strauss was one example, and he also featured in the California pageant. According to what we were told, Strauss, a Bavarian immigrant, came to California to strike it rich in the Gold Rush but, upon arrival, realized just how brutal the mining life was, and how unlikely a prospector was to actually find much gold. But he noted how quickly a miner's pants wore down in what were considered California's unfettered wilds. According to our teachers, Strauss fashioned a pair of pants for himself from an old ship sail; they were sturdy and stood up to the elements. He used rivets to fasten them at the places where pants often turned to tatters. Each day more pioneers clawed their way over the Sierra Nevadas and more trading ships scudded through the Golden Gate. Strauss made another pair, and another; they sold like hotcakes. Denim was born. Nevermind that Strauss actually got the idea for riveted blue jeans from a friend who worked as a tailor up in Reno. A legend is a legend. And an entrepreneur was someone who spied untapped opportunity, seized it in his grip, and made a fortune.

By this definition, my great-grandfather Thomas Brady was a certain entrepreneur. Members of my family refer to him as a self-made man: a trailblazer emerging out of the great sea of everybody else. He started out collecting trash in Yuba City, a rumbling pioneer boomtown in the Central Valley, eventually making enough money off other people's refuse to purchase a small plot of land, and then more land. He sold land to turn a profit and then turned around and bought some more. He quit the trash business and began herding sheep, leasing land in Oroville on the eastern side of the valley near the foothills, and then purchasing a large swath of the Buttes. Spring and summer he'd spend in Oroville with the sheep, then herd them through the valley's great sink to the Buttes which, though brown and coiled with rattlers in the summer, were good and green in the winter— perfect land on which his animals could graze, and it belonged to him and him alone. After they were fattened, he'd load them into Chicago-bound railcars for slaughter. The meat was sold on the East Coast. With the money from the sheep he bought more land, and more sheep, and then more land. Thomas Brady was at one point one of the largest sheep herders in all of California, with about twenty thousand head of sheep.

Eventually he was rich. In 1917 he bought a stately Victorian farmhouse along West Butte Road from one of the original Buttes ranching families. He lived there with his wife and five kids. My grandmother was the youngest. He added a second porch above the first one so that the family could sit outside and watch the cars and coaches go by, often Buttes-bound, along the same road that indigenous people had traveled for millennia before the road was taken over. People loved to take drives by the Buttes to inhale their beauty, to take a rambling walk or sit in the shade of an oak or feel the breeze cool their faces.

In spite of her grandfather's wealth, my mom mostly grew up poor, number six of seven kids in an old farmhouse that was colonized each winter by crickets. They farmed almonds (amands) and my grandfather worked off and on in the Highway Patrol. My mother was made fun of for wearing secondhand clothes. But even though they were cash poor, my grandmother had inherited some of Thomas Brady's land—bits that hadn't been sold off or ended up in other family members' hands. There were the two parcels in the Buttes, and a swath of seasonal floodlands in the Butte Sink. Owning this land didn't bring my family much money, but it did convey a status, and a particular possibility—this land could make us rich again, one day, if we did things right.

To pay for her seven kids' college, my grandmother and her sister sold the floodlands to the state, after which they were turned into Gray Lodge, a protected wildlife refuge. Her decision was ridiculed by their neighbors and friends. How could they sell good, private property, and turn it over to the state? Owning property in California, being, of course, something like a religion. But my grandmother had tuition to pay.

The thing that made it possible for my mother to go to college, and thus made my life as I know it possible, was stolen land. This is at once a woefully basic and perhaps even bland consideration, but also one people don't often enough speak aloud: that my ability to be successful in life—to get an education, jobs, and opportunities of my choosing—occurs on the backs of people who, because of the trajectory set in place by my ancestors, didn't have such opportunities or luxuries, or who had ceased to exist at all, by which I mean, were exterminated.

But my grandmother's generation never sold those final two parcels of the Buttes. She and her siblings took their kids there for Easter picnics, for the occasional strolls through the hills just like in the olden days. That land was too meaningful to the family. Its felt value was, as is often the case, out of step with its value on the market. Once the land was passed on to my uncles' generation—the girls got some cash, but the Buttes were for the boys—they felt much the same way: the land was sacred, in part because it was the last gasp of a family empire. "Once in the hands of settlers, the land itself was no longer sacred, as it had been for the Indigenous. Rather, it was private property, a commodity to be acquired and sold—every man a possible king, or at least wealthy," writes Dunbar-Ortiz. To sell the Buttes would be leaving that all behind.

* * *

112

The Buttes weren't only the pristine wilderness turned pastoral paradise of the settlers' imaginations; they were also an opportunity for urban boom. In Thomas Brady's day, when mining life got too hard and the gold began to dry up or reveal itself as too elusive to bother with, pioneers began leaving the mining camps in the hills and heading down toward the flats to start life again as farmers, and as merchants. They purchased land and they built homes. After indigenous residents were killed or relocated, settler camps and outposts became towns and then cities. Cities created yet more opportunity for capital, for ownership, for getting rich quick. Many of these cities cropped up in the fertile valley around the base of the Buttes. The gentle shadow of the Buttes: what a perfect place to build a town, to launch an empire.

A slick pioneer entrepreneur named Pete Gardemeyer saw dollar signs at the south base of the Buttes, and the possibility of an emerald city. A former door-to-door salesman of gates and sewing machines who married a wealthy Buttes widow, Gardemeyer began dreaming his boomtown into being. Starting in 1887, he bought up land and carved it into lots. Hotels would be built there, a railroad hub, agricultural plots, universities, houses and estates for all of California's newly rich and newly-arrived hopefuls. The entirety of South Butte would be terraced and a "luxurious hotel" built there for people of means to relax, to revel, to hunt the abundant game—antelope, elk, deer, rabbits—in the hills. The Buttes would be the city's backdrop and its backyard playground.

Like my great-grandfather did, Gardemeyer bought some land and staked out more. "We intend to bring out a colony of industrious people of some means and give them a chance to see their way clear to an income before asking payment for the land," an investor announced to a local paper. He offered these mortgages for a hundred dollars an acre, and invited investors

113

from San Francisco to bond and purchase land in his city, which he insisted would become the state capital, the urban center of the new westward expansion, destiny manifested.

His team laid out the lots and collected the cash as eager investors and settlers arrived; they had come to California for its promise, and here was yet one more migration, tugging at their willingness to believe. Coal was discovered nearby; that enticed people all the more. There wasn't enough timber to build fast enough, so Gardemeyer and his partner purchased one million bricks. They started a newspaper, which, as a sweeping, folksy history Sutter City published in the 1966 edition of the Sutter County Historical Society points out, functioned as the de facto PR wing of their settlement operation: "Never was the country more beautiful with its carpet of flowers," read a story in the paper, "especially the poppies, its stately oaks with their new green dress while the play of color on the Buttes is majestic." The landscape, combined with the fizzing prospect of wealth, captured the imagination of settler Californians again and again and again. They named the town—what else?—Sutter. Come one, come all, to the city of Sutter, beneath the Sutter Buttes, start a life and prosper.

I didn't know much about the Buttes growing up, only that they were there, majestic, that they belonged to my mother's family—the side of my family that, though I saw them often enough, was always shrouded in some mystery which, I understand now, was in part a product of tight-lipped, pioneer stoicism. I didn't know much about my ancestors, or my mom's upbringing, or even about my grandmother, who died long before I was born; we didn't talk about all that. This was perplexing to me when I compared it to the Greek side of my family, where everything was articulated and loud, deeply felt, likely shouted across the room or the dinner table, often with thunderous feeling and even fury, but always with some kind of love. Growing up, my mom knew that she was loved but cannot recall ever once being told by her parents, "I love you."

My mom's generation always knew their grandfather had been a big deal, and that he had been murdered when his kids were young. My grandmother was only ten at the time, and she never spoke of it. Somehow my mother's generation gathered that he died at a poker match: a gambling dispute. But my mom's cousin Johnny did some digging and found out that that wasn't how it went at all.

After winters herding sheep in his land in the Buttes, my great-grandfather would move them across the valley to Oroville to spend a few months fattening on leased land. But in 1925 he arrived at his usual spot to find a South Asian turkey farmer named Ali Kahan (which some papers spelled "Hakan") on the property with his flocks. My great-grandfather was irate and began throwing all of Kahan's belongings out of the small ranch house and onto the dirt outside. Kahan protested; he'd taken over the lease on the first of the month and had every right to be there. Brady threatened and taunted and told him to get the hell out, but Kahan stood his ground. Brady then picked up an axe and raced toward him, but Kahan had a gun and shot at him three times. Brady fell to the ground. Kahan knew he was in trouble—he'd likely killed a white man—so he ran. "Following the shooting the Hindu took a Chalmers auto and in his haste to get away ran through a band of sheep killing about thirty of them," a newspaper story read. He was apprehended several days later in the Midwest and brought back to California for trial. My great-grandmother lugged her two young daughters—ages ten and twelve—fifty miles each day to the trial, dressed prettily in black. EYE WITNESSES SAY HINDU WHO COMMITTED ACT WAS ATTACKED, read one headline. In spite of being a brown man on trial before an all-white jury for killing a wealthy white man in 1925 California, Kahan was acquitted.

Though two eyewitnesses told the investigators that Brady had come at Kahan and was ready to kill him, my mom's cousin Johnny doesn't buy that he would have actually done it. "I really don't believe that a man of his stature, with that kind of money and with young kids, would really try to kill a man."

There was a lot I probably preferred not to know about that side of the family's ancestry, and even that, as an adult, I shied away from. I was proud of being a fifth generation Californian, and enjoying this pride required a degree of ignorance and avoidance. Eventually I learned—how long can you turn away?—that my great great grandfather, my grandfather's grandfather, was an army general who was in charge of an Indian Camp in the 1860s—meaning that he was in charge of corralling thousands of indigenous people as if they were cattle, robbing them of their land, their homes, their families, their dignity, in many cases, their lives. Who wants to know that about her own family lineage?

"You know," Johnny added, "it's very probable that we're related to Tom Brady the quarterback."

They buried my great grandfather in the family plot at Sutter City, the former boomtown, just at the foot of the Buttes.

The problem with the two parcels of land that my uncles and their cousins own is that access to both requires passage through other privately-owned property, on privately-owned and maintained roads. The other problem is, now that several generations have passed, too many family members own it. There are nine of them. In theory, the two parcels are worth quite a bit of money. But in reality, it's hard to say. There's no water there, or electricity, and hooking up to the grid or a sewage system would be devastatingly expensive. To build anything on the Buttes would cost a fortune. And who would want to live there? In the summer it's hot as hell. "Nothing up there but rocks and rattlesnakes," Johnny's mom used to say. Do they sell it? (Who would buy it?) And what is it really worth?

Once, over Thanksgiving when we were kids, my cousins and I overheard the uncles whispering about how perfect a place the land would be for growing pot. But that was too risky. One of the owner's kids used to lead unpermitted hunting trips up to the Buttes to shoot boar and birds. He was arrested for secretly baiting the birds with seed, ensuring his customers would get a kill and thus would pay to come again. When some of the owners have been broke or short on cash, they've felt stymied by having all that land—theoretical wealth—but being unable to sell it because the others don't want to.

For now, they lease it for cattle, earning eighteen thousand dollars a year. Property taxes are around four thousand. That leaves fourteen thousand dollars' profit, but then there's the occasional upkeep, like the fence they just installed to ensure no one goes through. Best case, it's fourteen thousand dollars divided by nine people, which, though nothing to sniff at, isn't much if you consider how much land there is and how much trouble it takes to keep it up, manage the books, file taxes, and the endless conversations they have about the land and its future.

Naturally, the uncles could put it in a land trust, return it to Native communities, or to the state for a park, but—as when my grandmother sold the floodlands that became Gray Lodge, or when the state bought a parcel of the Buttes and turned it into a public park—that would rub up against the pioneer sanctity of private property. Will it stay in the family forever, the shares carved into smaller and smaller bits as the generations mutate and bloom?

Johnny now considers himself something of a steward of the place. To him, developing the property would be a crime. Because of its human and natural history, he feels, it needs to be protected; Johnny sees himself a willing and valiant custodian.

"The energy up there, it's different," he told me recently, when I was asking him what it was about the Buttes he so loved. He's not a full-blown spiritualist, but he's open to the unseen world in a way that I found somewhat surprising, given the more conservative nature of much of my family, and endearing. "It's just different. It changes you. You can feel it."

For a while he thought the land should really be given over to the state for a park. But the more he talked to other landowners and people who'd spent time up there, the more he changed his mind. The state, he felt, wouldn't leave it as is; it would bring in roads, porta-potties, too many visitors. They couldn't have their land go the way of the Peace Valley park, open to just anyone who could trample it, graffiti it up, start a fire that would burn the whole place down. In his estimation, common among landowners up there, the private citizens who own the property and keep it for themselves are the most suitable stewards.

As nice as it is up there, Johnny feels it best that the land is only available to a few—people who know how to care for it. He doesn't like the idea of people traipsing through his land uninvited, even though it sits there empty and beckoning. Part of being a responsible landowner, Johnny believes, is keeping people who don't belong there out. "Would you be okay with someone just walking into your house?" He knows it sounds selfish, he told me. But it is the way it is.

Johnny has spent years collecting family history, digging into archives about Brady, about the Buttes, about early California. He has assembled a rich archive of his own. Once, Johnny arranged for a naturalist and historian to take our family on a hike up to the

Buttes. It was spring, a bluebird day. "You packing?" one of my uncles asked the other, meaning, *you got your gun?* They both did, for no particular reason, just because that's the kind of thing one brings along. We huffed and puffed our way to an overlook on a peak called Destiny, where a low cave was carved into the hillside from which we had a perfect view of the craggy, verdant valley below. The naturalist pointed out that this very spot, according to property maps, belonged to the Brady family: to us.

Johnny was stunned. This was the first place he'd ever visited in the Buttes' interior, on a hike led by the Middle Mountain Foundation that he'd paid for. He'd bought a trip to a place that he himself owned. From then on, Middle Mountain didn't take treks that way anymore; Johnny put a stop to that.

To own land in California is not necessarily to be wealthy, but to be *somebody*, to be connected to place, and to offer the promise of future wealth, sparkling, just around the corner. The Buttes are emblematic of a settler mentality, one that combines a reverence for land and place, a hardscrabble work ethic, and an insatiable desire to possess and to grow, to both protect things as they are and boom things into oblivion.

I will admit to feeling relieved that, due to happenstance of gender, I'm not set to inherit the Buttes; however untrue, it lets me feel that, as bound as I am to the land's past, I am, in part, let off the hook for its future.

In the late 1880s the Sutter City project continued to roar away at the base of the Buttes. "Sutter City: The Pride of Sutter County," read a full-page spread about the boom town in an 1889 issue of the *Sacramento Daily Record-Union*. They built a school, a hotel, a stunning, elaborate new Victorian residence for the Gardemeyers with turrets and gables and dormer windows and ornate balustrades.

119

But doubts began to spread about Gardemeyer's solvency. He was paying off new business deals with old ones, cheating people out of money, double selling the land titles, all while insisting on an outward myth of prosperity. The university project stalled, as did the railroad. Then the lawsuits piled up one after the other: obtaining money under false pretenses, petty larceny, selling the same lot to two different people. The thieved land was thieved again. The Justice of the Peace issued an arrest warrant, and Gardemeyer fled town (only returning every now and again, as rumor has it, to visit his wife under the cover of night and disguised as a woman) and sold his interest in the city for ten dollars—not a cent more. Then he ran. Later, Gardemeyer's gardener, a German immigrant whom Gardemeyer had cheated badly, purchased a gun and murdered Gardemeyer's wife for revenge.

I learned about the swindle of Sutter City from the newsletters at the Community Memorial Museum of Sutter County, which doubles as an archive: a modest operation off the four-lane thoroughfare in Yuba City packed with books and papers, maps and deeds, pioneer ephemera crammed into all its nooks and crannies, stacks and shelves and drawers. I was certain I'd find something out about my great-grandfather, but there was nothing. His name wasn't on the old maps of Yuba County and the Buttes that hung around the museum and were stuffed into record books. He wasn't in the papers, or the photographs, or the pictures, or the books. How could that be?

Lots of people are of course erased from history but rarely are they wealthy white landowners. Perhaps Thomas Brady was not the area bigwig that our family fancies—that I thought he was, or maybe even, if I'm being honest, that I hoped.

The thing that's best documented about my great-grandfather isn't his life—his riches, the contributions he made, his kids, how he was remaking the state in his image along with the rest of the pioneers—but rather his death: how he went after a brown man with an axe, and how he bled out on the land he was fighting for.

"Are mythic narratives real?" writes Mohawk. "They are as real as the power the people have invested in them." Thomas Brady was swept into the myth of manifest destiny—that insatiable greed—and we, his descendants, in turn, made a myth out of him.

I recently went to the Buttes with my uncle, my aunt, and my mom. The holidays had just passed and it had rained substantially, blessedly, coating the hillsides in that rare and fleeting incandescent, emerald sheen. We opened the neighbors' gate with the code they shared with us, lurching slowly over the dirt roads through their property, past the big open space where they hold their annual Easter picnic, and toward our own land. My mom and aunt hiked the low road, a jeep trail that led from where we parked the car along the seasonal stream and up toward the base of the ridge past where my grandfather's ashes were scattered in a humble clearing. Uncle Mike and I went the other way, walking the north-south property line up to the ridge, then hooking west toward the ocean, through the snake grass and ankle-twisting notches of the pasture. It was lovely up on that ridge: the blue sky, the quiet calm of the valley, not many sounds apart from our own breathing, some insects, the occasional groan of cattle newly let out to pasture. Uncle Mike loved it up there, I could tell. He smiled as he tramped up the hill as he pointed out his duck club, Gray Lodge, the canal through which the Feather River was diverted to the rice fields, Mount Lassen in the distance, and where, if the day were a bit clearer, we'd be able to see Mount Shasta. He even told me some old family stories, as ever a generous and jolly host—for after all, I was his guest and this was his home.

"You can learn whatever you want from books and from the archives," Johnny had told me, "but there's no replacement for just taking a walk up in those hills." Especially when they're still green, he added. One truth about most parts of this state is that they don't stay green for long.

Johnny kept all his research—about Thomas Brady's life and death, about past owners of the Buttes, about the trial and the sheep and the old property maps and the current property lines—in a safe-deposit box in a tiny little foothill town called Paradise, a few miles from where he lived. This past October, he looked outside and spotted flames. He went to pack his car to evacuate—common enough in California these days—but he was low on gas, so, to be safe, his girlfriend took him in her car, which was already packed to the gills. He could only fit himself and his dog, but good thing he did, because his house, and a good part of his town and the entire town of Paradise, burned to near nothing. All that work and time: gone.

But then he got news that the safe-deposit boxes at the Paradise bank had miraculously survived. He hasn't been able to go back yet, since the town is still pure char. One day, he hopes, the bank will be back up and running and able to let people peer through their boxes to see what, if anything, remains.

I should have said earlier that my role in the California pageant was John Grubensky, a firefighter who lost his life in the 1991 Oakland fires. The play was performed in 1992, so his death was a fresh wound. The hillsides where my cousins lived were still scarred with rubble and char. My godmother's house—made of steel and iron and glass—was a flat mess encasing Grizzly Peak, as though a cascade of water had met a deep and sudden freeze. Unlike my classmates whose role was to represent the stories of people from olden times, my part in the play was to tell a piece of the contemporary story, the one of devastating wildfires, a reality that at the time was just emerging and one that now, as I write this in my mid-thirties, is a curse we can't kick. We're drying up and we're burning. We descendants of settlers haven't been such fine stewards of this stolen land, after all.

Though the hills and the valley formed a slick sea of green that December day that Mike and I walked the property line, those fields would dry up by April, May at the latest and, depending on the way things went in the spring and summer, the hillsides would likely be little more than kindling until the following December. All it would take was a poorly managed campfire or a flicked cigarette and the whole place could go.

Up there on that ridge I thought of the California pageant again, that modest attempt to re-enact the historical narrative that comforted us all, and thus to bolster it, to batten it down. We girls—not one indigenous student among us—received a standing ovation as we gathered at the front of the stage in our costumes, linked arms, and took a grand, ecstatic bow. We were being raised to understand that the world was ours for the taking, because that had long been true, even after the gold dried up, even after the cities burned or failed to be built at all, even after our origin stories were revealed for what they were and we outgrew our costumes and our grandparents and then our parents began to die—heroically or no—even after our memories failed and the stories flew away.

If the Brady family's wealth and prominence has been diluted over generations, along with Thomas Brady's land, there's still that mythic possibility right around the corner of being or becoming something. It seems to me that after millennia of meaning associated with the Buttes, the new story that my family has enacted there is about having land at all. It makes us feel that we really belong. There are many reasons my uncles haven't sold, but perhaps one of them is that it's nice to tromp around those gilded hills with their dazzling quiet and hypnotizing views, thinking, *this is mine, this is mine, this is mine.*

At the Shore

FRANK BIDART

All over the earth,
elegies for the earth.

The shore is in mourning. It mourns what it must soon

see, the sea
rising—

implacable, drowning chunks of the intelligible, familiar world.

Creatures of the earth filled with the instinct to wound
the earth. We fear that by an act of immense, unconscious

will, we have succeeded at last in killing NATURE.

Since childhood, you hated the illusion that this
green and pleasant land

inherently is green
or pleasant

or for human beings home. Whoever dreamed that had

not, you thought, experienced
the earth. *We needed to rewrite in revenge the world that wrote us.*

＊

My parents drove from the Sierras (Bishop), to the almost-
city of their parents, carved from desert (Bakersfield).

To get anywhere you had to cross the Mojave Desert.

It was World War Two. In the Sierras my father was a big shot.
He said *It's better to be a big fish in a little pond.* The government

didn't draft—even

refused to enlist—rich
farmers. So to my mother's dismay, night after night in bars

drunk, wronged, he fought soldiers who had called him a coward.

They drove their gorgeous Lincoln Zephyr across the steaming
                                        Mojave at night.
Half-

carsick, I was in the back seat, inside,
protected.

Unprotected. Phantasmagoric enormous

tumbleweeds in the empty
landscape rolled aimlessly outside the speeding car.

MANUEL MUÑOZ is the author of a novel, *What You See in the Dark*, and two short-story collections, *Zigzagger* and *The Faith Healer of Olive Avenue*, which was shortlisted for the Frank O'Connor International Short Story Award. He is the recipient of a National Endowment for the Arts fellowship, a Whiting Award, and three O. Henry Awards. His most recent work has appeared in *American Short Fiction*, *Glimmer Train*, *The Southwest Review*, *ZYZZYVA*, and *The Best American Short Stories 2019*. He has been on the faculty of the University of Arizona's creative writing program since 2008.

Susto

MANUEL MUÑOZ

No one in town even knew the old man's name, but they pretended they did after he was found dead by the foreman one day at the end of winter. The foreman, as he told it later that morning to the others at the Royal Dutch Bakery during their usual coffee, had stopped the tractor midrow when he couldn't make out the strange silhouette deep in the vines. The grape farmer had sent him out at dawn to begin the spring prep on the vineyards and he had spotted something in the distance. The foreman had shut off the tractor, spooked by the dark form lying in the row. A dead coyote maybe, or a rabid stray dog that had collapsed on its way to hiding out before dying, as sick animals sometimes do. Whatever it was, it was too big to be something like that. The dark form didn't move. The quiet of dawn only made it worse.

The foreman didn't tell the men at the bakery that he had stayed on the tractor and waited for the sun to break into its truest light before he dismounted to see what the shadow was. As he got closer, he made out that it was a person, a man by the look of the clothes: a white T-shirt yellowed in the armpits, pants that may have been part of a good suit too many years ago, and leather shoes worn and woeful at the soles. That's all the foreman saw of him—the clothes had been all he had to confirm that the body was indeed a man's, because the body had its head buried in the dirt. Like a goddamn ostrich, the foreman told the others gathered around the Formica tabletop listening to his story.

He hadn't meant to spit the words out as he did, just as the young waitress came around with the coffee pot. The other men had fallen silent from both his story and the belief that the waitress shouldn't be overhearing terrible things. She served their coffee and looked at none of them, but she caught the foreman's eye just as she finished her pour, and she seemed to search his face for the root of his contempt.

Did she know the man, he wanted to ask her, since she was a Mexican girl whose family let her work on Sundays, and the man whose head had been lifted from the dirt was as brown as she was? He might have guessed from the brown of the man's hands if he had been brave enough to look, but it had taken the weekend deputy, pulling the man's head from the ground like a dandelion weed and brushing the caked dirt from the eyelids, to confirm that the dead man was an older Mexican.

But the foreman didn't ask the Mexican girl anything and she had walked back behind the counter as if she hadn't heard a word. The other men took over the story. They knew the weekend deputies and who would have been on the Sunday shift and that the man was probably some drunk who wound up so far out in the fields and that it was probably Dennis, the youngest of the Kenmore brothers, who had shown up from the sheriff's office. The foreman let them talk. He said nothing about just how long he had sat on the tractor before he had felt safe enough to go back to the farmhouse and summon help. He kept quiet about needing the sun to come up to chase away his darker suspicions that this was the devil's work and to help him see it all in the colder logic of a robbery gone wrong. He didn't say that he had waited for Dennis Kenmore at the side of the road, the tractor idle in the middle of the field and the shape of the man with his head buried in the dirt so still in the distance that he swore at one point it moved.

One of the men remembered, a couple of years back, a teen-aged boy who had been found in one of the town alleyways, a dropout from the high school who dealt measly amounts of weed but had nonetheless been knifed for whatever he'd been carrying. The boy had been as thin as his empty wallet, the man said, on account of all the weed he smoked, but he was proof that even a few dollars was more than enough reason for someone to do such a thing.

The Zacarías kid, confirmed another. The oldest one in that bunch, too. His mother raised him better than that.

It's one thing to be looking for trouble at that age, said someone else. But an old man? Probably buried his head himself out of shame for whatever he'd been up to.

Who said he was old? The quietest man finally spoke. Who said he had anything to be ashamed about?

Well, he wasn't a teenager. And what's an old man doing out in the middle of a field if he ain't working?

The other men turned to the foreman. Did he work for you?

I'd never seen him in my life, the foreman answered. But he didn't tell them that he hadn't been able to bear looking at the man for very long, Dennis Kenmore holding him up by the scruff and roughly brushing the dirt from his eyes. The eyes had to have been shut and yet he wasn't sure.

He would've recognized him if he had been a worker. He would've told us the name.

Like I said, I'd never seen him in my life, the foreman repeated.

Last night was Saturday and it's the beginning of the month so people have money in their pockets. Poor guy probably got drunk at John Henry's and went off with some new people and they robbed him and dumped him in the fields. That's what happened.

An ostrich? someone asked.

The foreman didn't answer. He didn't want to say the words again. The waitress behind the counter slid a tray of bread into one of the cases as if she hadn't heard them talking.

If he's a good Christian, someone will miss him in church, the quietest man said, though it was Sunday and not a single one of them had been to service in years.

For the rest of the morning, the foreman's discovery left him at a strange crossroads of somberness and dread. The other men had exited the bakery by noon, but the foreman had sat alone, reluctant to return home. Some churchgoers had stopped by after services and he had watched them select bread from the cases for their evening meals. They were older people overdressed for the cold in the Valley, still wrapped in scarves as they waited, their gloved hands holding on to dollar bills. Once they turned their backs to him, the foreman couldn't tell if they had come from the Catholic service on the far side of town or from the Presbyterian church with the manicured lawns and high green shrubs. They were dutiful no matter who they were, waiting patiently for the waitress to serve them, saying hardly anything beyond their pointing fingers and maybe a thank-you he could barely hear. His coffee cup had gone cold but he hadn't bothered to raise his hand for a refill. The foreman listened to the older churchgoers shuffle their feet along the floor, tap on the glass cases for the better bread, rustle their paper bags tight against the cold before they went back outside. What little he could catch of their faces when they passed by betrayed nothing of what they might have heard in church that day. He found himself surprised that he thought this, watching them, his mind on how another Sunday morning had moved silently by. Had they heard that it was not wise to love this world, nor anything in it? What would that mean, he wondered, if they knew a man had been found dead in the fields?

What else was there but the fields and the orchards?

By one in the afternoon, the bakery had emptied. The waitress stepped away from the register and wiped down the counters. She slid trays of unsold bread out of the cases and took them one by one to the back of the bakery, not looking at the foreman. The longer the silence went on between them, the more he knew he wasn't to ask for another refill of the coffee. Though he knew the bakery wouldn't close until three, the foreman waited until she went to the back of the shop, then rose and stepped into the day, the bells on the front door jingling behind him. He imagined she was relieved by the sound of his leaving and he felt freed in a way as well. He didn't want to think about that man, or look at a face that knew what he was thinking. The foreman took in the empty street, looked this way and that, but no one was about. Everyone had retreated to their own homes and he had no choice, he knew, but to return to his, a small house he rented just on the edge of town, close enough to the county road to see the cars coming and going from bigger places in the Valley. He walked up the street to a corner market, its windows already starting to glow against the meager light of the winter day, and he bought a bottle of whiskey from the bored-looking clerk who, for a moment, had looked at him as if he had a sudden and burning question, only to give him his change without a word.

The foreman got back to his small house by three in the afternoon. He took his whiskey to the front porch and unscrewed the cap on the bottle. The daylight had gone milky and the Sierras in the distance had already steeled themselves purple. He would drink, the foreman thought, until he could no longer give himself over to the chill of the winter trees sinking into the dark. He would watch the endless parallel rows of the fields blend their green edges beyond discernment, no moon rising. He would track the first few wisps of the winter fog forming almost as soon as the sun slipped down. By then the day would be over and he could forget about the terrible way in which it had begun.

The whiskey was warming him. The bare branches of the fruit trees, which had let in the afternoon's craggy light, closed in. The fog deepened, coming in low at about the height of the vineyards. Far off in the distance, the red taillights of the cars heading to bigger towns reminded him of the woman who had been in his life at one time, just long enough to begin talk of marriage, but not long enough for doubt to break its hold of his heart. Frustrated with him, she had gone to Los Angeles and the foreman had never heard from her again. Years ago, so many years ago, and why remember now, he thought. His eyes followed the red taillights getting smaller and smaller in the distance. He expected them to disappear, but they steadied after a moment, two pinpoints of red light in the winter dusk. He traced the lights moving along the road, then followed them as they froze, seemed to change direction, coming now toward the farmhouse. The foreman blinked his eyes to be sure, losing the lights in the fog momentarily before making them out again. The red lights traveled too slowly to be a car, he thought, and they floated along what he was sure was one of the outer vineyards. The foreman stood up to get a full view. He squinted against the dark and the fog, against the whiskey, aware of the anonymity of his small house, of the enormity of the dark world.

The distance was not so far now. He could make out the edge of the vineyard where the red pinpoints finally emerged from the leaves and fixed on him like a set of eyes. No, they *were* a set of eyes, his sight adjusting to the darkness of the field, and now he could make out the vague outline of a man's body, the glow of a white shirt, still and unmoving. He could make out the slumped posture of an older man. The foreman sensed a stern grip deep in his chest, seizing him to complete attention. It was not alarm or terror, but something like pity. He knew who it was.

What do you want? the foreman finally called out, but nothing came.

What do you want from me? he tried.

The figure did not move. Nor did it make a sound. The foreman kept waiting for something to break, to hear soft footfalls in the dirt, or the vines snapping to let pass whatever needed to return to the darkness of the field. He tensed for something sudden, but nothing broke, and he felt his body give way to a lightness, like stepping off the last bit of solid ground and into a deep, calm pool of water. He was still on the porch—he could sense the wooden slats beneath his boots and the wintry air pinching at his skin— but he trusted the buoyancy of the voice he knew he was about to hear, and he closed his eyes, hoping to understand what it had to say. The voice was on the brink. He could feel it about to come out of his own mouth, an involuntary, flattened whisper, a last word in a dream. The foreman felt himself floating, first to the edge of the porch, and then somehow retreating into the darkness of his house. Out there, at the edge of the vineyard, the foreman caught the flicker of the old man before he returned to the fog. The night collapsed around him and when he opened his eyes, he heard the call of the rooster greeting dawn at one of the farmhouses across the fields. He was in his bed, his clothes still on, and at his side, the letter that had been returned to him from somewhere in Los Angeles. He did not remember opening it. *I miss talking to you, though I know it is hard for both of us*. The light in the hallway had been left on, brightening the house. *I keep hoping you still want to hear from me*.

He rose and put the letter in the back of the top dresser drawer. He had work to do—there was always work to do in the fields—and he walked out to his truck, his head still buzzy from the night's drinking. Not all of the men from the usual Sunday gathering would be there. Some still worked, but the retired ones and the ones without wives drank coffee there daily. He had gotten into bed somehow without eating dinner and he convinced himself that he was going to the bakery because he was hungry. His stomach growled in agreement, but the bakery served no breakfast. That would be at the P&A diner around the corner, but he knew no one there. If he peered through the diner's plate-glass window, he would recognize no one, and no one would turn to look at him, as did the three of the Sunday men now, spotting his truck with surprise.

You look like hell, said one of them, and waved the waitress over. Bring him a sweet roll, something with a little sugar in it.

Sit, said another one, and when the foreman did so, they all waited until the waitress poured him a cup of coffee and placed the pastry in front of him.

Lots of things can drive a man to drink, said the third man. Ain't no shame in it.

Who says I've been drinking?

They scoffed at him. Come on now, said the eldest one, the one who had been retired the longest and knew how to temper a conversation. Maybe not this morning, but you sure look like you were up to something last night.

The foreman took a drink of the coffee and it roiled his stomach. I got bothered by what I saw.

Has the Kenmore boy been out to see you?

About what?

About finding out who that man was.

I talked to him yesterday when he came out to the vineyard, said the foreman. He wrote some things in his little deputy's notebook and that was it.

The elder, the one who had lost his wife to cancer five years ago, the one who never touched a drop because she had been a devout Baptist, who had never set foot in the liquor store even after he buried her, rapped his knuckles gently on the Formica tabletop. Mark my words, he said. Kenmore raised some smart boys, but you're going to be waiting a long time to hear anything about an old Mexican found in the fields.

Sounds like you're telling him to hit the bottle again tonight, said one of the men.

That's not what I'm saying.

If Kenmore's not going to come around to ask him anything . . .

Is that why you were drinking? the elder asked. You worrying yourself over a man you're never going to know? That no one is ever going to know?

The foreman couldn't bring himself to say what he had seen in the vineyard when dusk had arrived. They wouldn't believe him if he tried to describe the sensation that had overcome him, the feeling of words literally in his mouth, as if he had it in him to say something without thinking.

Drink if you want to, said the elder. I'm telling you to stay sober because Kenmore will want to talk to you again. You don't want people in town talking about how you turned into a big drunk just because you found a body out in the fields. This is a terrible world but people have held it together over more than you'll ever see.

One of the other men rose to his feet, sensing a lecture about to come on. He left extra dollar bills and slid them to the foreman, just enough for the coffee and the sweet roll. You drink as much as you want, he whispered conspiratorially to the foreman. Whatever you need to forget.

Nobody needs to forget, said the elder. If you all went to church on Sundays, you'd know what I was trying to say.

With all due respect, said the third man, rising to join his friend, you don't go to church either and reading a Bible at the kitchen table doesn't count for much. He patted the foreman on the shoulder. I can't do a sermon on a Monday morning. But you take care of yourself.

The two men exited and the foreman was left with the elder, the waitress standing at the register, wiping nothing down. The sweet roll sat uneaten and it occurred to the foreman that he had no idea how the bakery did on weekday mornings, with the churchgoers nowhere to be found.

I grew up in a small town in Arkansas, said the elder man after a time. My wife grew up about five miles from where I lived. Towns spaced out like they are here in the Valley, couple miles in between, fields all around. She came with me out here when her parents died in a car accident and she had no people anymore. That's what people did in those days. They went out to California. We raised a family out here, a boy and a girl. My boy died on the young side. Doing foolish things. But our daughter moved on out to the coast and had our grandkids before my wife passed.

I know it's been a while, said the foreman, but people still remember her.

That's my point, said the elder. You remember her. People knew her. I started coming to the bakery in my fifties, when my wife told me she thought I was spending too much time alone. She said it was good to get out and go have a conversation with people. Remind everybody that you're still around. You see what I'm trying to tell you?

The foreman looked blankly at him. I'm sorry, but I don't.

Do you think for a minute if I'd gone missing that people wouldn't notice? You're telling me you wouldn't worry just a little bit if I hadn't shown up on Sunday morning to drink coffee? I come here rain or shine.

You do, the foreman agreed.

This is a small town, the elder said. And you don't think it says something that no one knew that man? That you didn't know that man?

They sat for a while without the foreman answering him and the moment for pondering slipped right on past into a silence that felt like truth.

I'll tell you what, said the elder, it's hell on earth when you have to sit with the fact that nobody will miss you. That's what's tearing you up about that old man. Terrible thing to die lonely, without anybody knowing you passed.

The elder sighed and rose with great difficulty from the table. I have to get the day started, he said. He stared down at the bills. Will that cover it? he said, turning to the waitress.

It will, she said, though she was at the counter.

The elder took a long time walking out and after the door jingled shut, the waitress walked over to pour the foreman another coffee. Don't worry about the check, she said. He can pay me the rest tomorrow morning.

I'm sorry, he said, patting for his wallet. I left the house . . .

You look terrible, she said. You look ill.

I didn't sleep well last night.

Susto, she said. You know Spanish? You know what that is?

I've heard the word, but I don't know what it means.

She searched upward to find the right meaning. A scare, she tried. But in your soul, deep down.

Susto, the foreman repeated, and he wondered for a moment if he should tell her what he had seen and felt. He worried that she, too, wouldn't believe him, and then he worried that she would.

I just want to say, said the waitress, that Mr. Whittaker is very mistaken. We know who the old man in the field was.

We?

The neighborhood, she said. Our neighborhood. It was Don Facundo. He was the old man who lived at the last house at the end of the street, so everyone saw him coming and going. Facundo Nieves was his name.

Facundo Nieves . . . I've never heard of him.

He worked with the cattle farmers, not out picking the fields, so you wouldn't know him, she said. But we knew him.

Someone came through the door. The foreman heard the bells jingle and he could tell from the deliberate footsteps that it was an older person. The waitress went back behind the counter. A woman's voice, phlegmy and strained, asked for a loaf of bread and the foreman, with his back turned, could make out the faint clink of coins. She had bought the day-old Sunday bread. Gracias, Doña Lena, he heard the waitress say, a voice full of familiarity and knowing, and he heard the slow footsteps walk out, the bakery quiet again.

The waitress came back to his table. She sat down in the spot where the elder had been, the chair in a bit of sunlight, and he caught, for the first time, the name on her tag. Margarita.

Don Facundo rented out the house at the end of our street and had been living there for over twenty years. He had a wife and three children, but she wanted to go back to Durango. One day, she went to Mexico with the kids and never came back. He's been living alone ever since. But we kept our eye on him. We knew he was there.

Did you tell the Kenmore boy?

He hasn't come around to ask as far as I know. He doesn't know where to look. But you should tell him, she said, rising from the table. He'll listen to you.

140

Say his name one more time? the foreman asked.

Facundo, she said. Facundo Nieves. Nieves is snow, a funny name for a man from Durango, as he always said. But it snows in Mexico too. She reached for the untouched sweet roll. You should go to the P&A and eat something.

Thank you, he said. I think I will. Margarita waved to him as he walked out of the bakery and back onto the street that looked every bit as empty as it did on Sunday afternoon. The sun was bright. He drove up the street, wondering if Margarita knew anyone at the P&A, if she would ask after a man who had come in for breakfast and sat alone, a man whom the waitresses at the P&A wouldn't recognize. He drove past the large plate-glass windows but didn't stop. He drove past the liquor store, where the bored-looking clerk stood at the counter as he always did, oblivious to the fact that the foreman had thought for a moment about getting another bottle of whiskey. But there was work to do, empty stomach or no, and so he drove out to the small house he rented on the edge of town and got to it.

He had trellis work, checking the posts and the wires for breaks before the workers came out to strip and prune the vines in advance of spring. He walked out to the vineyard, the day bright and almost warm, the sun good on his hands. When he had to step under the vines to test a wire, he could feel the cold of the soil seep through to his feet. He went deeper into the vineyard, the work going quickly, even though he was hungry. The foreman turned every now and then and could see his small house in the distance, the air clear, and the sky open. When he bent down to inspect a post sagging at the anchor, his head rushed, and he had to steady himself before continuing. The days of working on an empty stomach were long over. It would have to be a short day. The sky held even bluer, even brighter. A bit of sweat broke on his brow and he swiped it away. He would have to break soon and head back to the house to eat. But it felt good to work, to not think about the old man who had a name now. Facundo, the foreman said aloud, out in the vineyard where no one could hear him. Facundo Nieves, he sighed, and held his sweaty face up to the blue sky, a small part of him hoping that a miraculous snow would come out of nowhere and alter the world, soothe him from what he had seen.

He was in the middle of the field, the house a little dot in the distance. Over there, the sound of the cars traveling along the county road, and he could see them, clear as anything. The few leaves that hadn't fallen from the vines fluttered in a light, cool breeze. Over by the house, some movement caught his eye, and he knew it was Kenmore's son coming out to speak to him. The foreman started walking back, bristling at the inefficiency of having to stop in the middle of a row. He compensated by double-checking his work as he started back toward the house. In the distance, he could make out the silhouette of Kenmore waiting for him at the end, but he kept his eyes on the vines, the posts, the wires, the leaves. He kept heading back until he got close enough to see that the silhouette was not Kenmore's son.

The foreman caught the whiteness of the shirt first and stopped. How could it be, out in the brightness of the day? He took one cautious step forward, but he knew what he would confirm if he headed any closer. He stood in the vineyard and looked this way and that, but he could see no one else and no one, he knew, could see him. The sky was so vast, accepting all the light. His loneliness struck him like a rattler lurking in the vines, swift and vicious, a small and hidden thing that he bypassed daily, unaware. The bewilderment came again, the half collapse in his chest, and he thought of the letter and the lines he'd written, unanswered. *I've been with you. I'll be with you. I want to be with you.* He felt himself break into understanding and he thought he could summon a question for Facundo Nieves. He could beg forgiveness for not having known him, some mercy to match his longing. He felt, instead, a bubbling directive. He opened his mouth as if to say something he had known all along. To his surprise, the feeling came in Spanish. He collapsed to his knees and anticipated all the things that had to be said, but only a single word came in his own tongue. *Dig*, it said, and under the bright blue winter sky, the foreman felt his hands push into the dirt. What do you want? he heard himself ask, though he could not stop himself. *Dig*, he heard again, from inside, and his fingers moved past the thin topsoil and into the colder, rockier layers underneath.

Former California and US
Poet Laureate, and coordi-
nator of the Laureate Lab—
Visual Wordist Studio at
Fresno State, JUAN FELIPE
HERRERA is a Capricorn,
cartoonist, and children's
book author. Winner of the
National Book Critics Circle
Award, his recent books
include *Imagine* and *Jabber-
walking*. He lives with poet-
partner Margarita Robles in
Fresno.

California Brown

JUAN FELIPE HERRERA

Zoot suit from San Ysidro

to the Klamath—wearing your drapes long cut coat
spaghetti belt flappy pants to the ankle
do not forget your calcos glossy pointed shoes
                          & your tando

fedora black or gray or cinnamon or blue—if you can spot it
& the chain—let's not call it a chain for the moment
hooked to your pants your tramos & of course
you gotta have the ranfla ready that sharpened Ford
rumble seat skeletal green or midnight border howl
flecked paint bloody streak that solar wheel you touch to turn
& your skirt fenders where are you going Brown?

There's a borlo up ahead
the East Los party—in the penumbra in between everything
        let's not call it a party let's call it

the place where you
become whole again
(I am not talking about the party)—
after that migrant long haul from Juarez or Juaritos to
El Paso or El Chuko or EPT lean towards Tucson or
Tuksón—meet up with Los Chasers then—wait my
time-space in this text is incorrect—in Juaritos
you become that Brown called a Pachuka or Pachuko

that nation-devourer why is it that
somehow you become infinite everywhere

let's get back to LA
to that Navy brawl they called the Zoot Suit Riots in '43
let's get back to now—you
                                        in Juarez again you
in Tijuana again you are in that muddy tent

all the way from Guatemala—for the moment
there's tear gas—there's the Thing Sky Piercer El Bordo
or we could say the border—and the brawl

there's no brawl
you could call it a cell
a detention camp a chain sewn around you it is also termed
Separation & the ranfla you could call it the border bus
in white & blackened windows—wait

we have not talked about your transcendence
we have not talked about the forces of power
ripped into your bones & flamed out of your face
we have not talked about how things have not changed
& your seat on that white bus blackened windows

we have not talked about how things have changed that
odd-shaped radio cracklin' wrapped around your shirt buckle

        So:
let's talk about you California Brown.

HEATHER SMITH is an editor at *Sierra Magazine* and a former Knight Science Journalism Fellow at MIT.

Eleven Short Histories of the Bison in Golden Gate Park

HEATHER SMITH

1

If you walk westward through Golden Gate Park in San Francisco, along John F. Kennedy Drive, and walk past the Victorian
cupcake of the arboretum, past the cement rectangle where people roller-skate in short shorts to a staticky boom box, past the
copper facade of the de Young Museum, past the waterfall, and
past the meadows where people gather for soccer matches and
family reunions and Renaissance fairs, you will find the bison.

The farther you move from the park's entrance, the more
the manicured landscape surrounding the park's main buildings
buckles and dissolves into something more improvisational.
The park's eucalyptus trees, steadfast in their determination
to kill every plant not themselves, let loose drifts of fragrant,
acid leaves. The hand of gardener is undone by the paw of
gopher and the smooth green turf laid down for the benefit of
soccer leagues is pocked with busy holes ringed with coronas
of freshly kicked dirt.

It is not a landscape that invites lingering, and the bison—or
buffalo, which is taxonomically inaccurate but which it still

somehow feels correct to call them—are easy to miss. To see the buffalo, you need to walk over to a chain-link fence about ten feet high—the sort that is usually placed around construction sites or very deep holes in the ground—and peer through. The bison look like brown, muppety haystacks. Here are things I have seen them doing: standing on the grass, lying on the grass, chewing.

The bison's own webpage, on the Golden Gate Park website, attempts to prepare the viewer for this possibility:

Overall, don't expect a grand show of movement and daring feats when visiting the bison. They tend to keep to themselves and really don't engage in any exciting activities. They appear in the standing position for most of the day and sometimes sit about. If you are lucky, one of the bison may slowly travel from the field to the corral.

Interesting Fact: Although you may not have the chance to observe, bison are known to reach speeds of up to 30 miles per hour.

On the review site Yelp, write-ups of the bison run next to reviews of local bars and noodle joints. The bison receive mixed ratings. "It pains me to not give the bison 5 stars," writes one poster, "but I can't in good conscience until I see them AWAKE."

"They aren't very entertaining and they refused to pose and run valiantly for me," writes another, "but nevertheless, it was cool . . . Star off for not giving me the photograph I wanted. And for the fact they look so sad."

Another posting leaves out the review altogether. "What the hell," it reads, "are bison doing in Golden Gate Park?"

2

The first bison arrived on February 12, 1891. Notice of its arrival appeared in the *San Francisco Call* the following day. It merited exactly one paragraph.

The Buffalo Bull.

The buffalo bull which was recently purchased by the Board of Park Commissioners arrived yesterday from Garden City, Kans., and was taken to the park menagerie. The beast is a splendid specimen, weighing nearly 1000 pounds. It cost the Commissioners $355, and the freight charges to bring him here amounted to $229.

That's it. Weight, cost, and splendidness.

Four days later, a more detailed portrait of the buffalo emerged, in an article about the eclectic assortment of animals (donkeys, llamas, elk, and pheasants) living in a pasture located to the east of the de Young Museum, near where the Academy of Sciences would later stand. The article is a fluff piece—breezily written descriptions of what the average visitor might find: a herd of "deer of all sizes, colors, and degrees of friendliness and intelligence"; a large elk who "can be very majestic when he chooses, but yesterday morning he threw aside his dignity and growled and grunted like a hypochondriacal dyspeptic. He . . . poked out his nose pathetically, as if craving sympathy"; and the buffalo, described as "the glory of the park menagerie."

The buffalo, named Ben Harrison after the then-U.S. President, was described as "a quiet, somewhat reserved, but well-behaved buffalo. Occasionally, however, he gets on the rampage and on such occasions his domestic arrangements are sadly

151

disturbed." The article went on to say that "the Park Commissioners expect soon to procure two buffalo cows who will lighten the hours of his confinement."

The day Ben Harrison arrived in San Francisco by freight car, another short article ran on the front page of the *Morning Call* about the other Ben Harrison—the President.

> **CALLED ON THE PRESIDENT.**
>
> **Mr. Harrison Has an Interview With the Sioux Chiefs.**
>
> WASHINGTON, Feb. 12.—The Indian chiefs now in this city called at the White House this afternoon and paid their respects to the President.
>
> The President pointed out the folly of their going to war with the whites, and made it very plain that if they made any more trouble they would be punished. He told them they must teach their young men not to be warriors, but citizens, and endeavor to earn their own living by some peaceful industry. The Government, he said, would protect and encourage every Indian who is disposed to be peaceful and industrious. The Indians then shook hands with the President and withdrew.

In 1800 there were an estimated twenty-eight to thirty million bison living on the shortgrass prairie between the western Mississippi and the Sierras. Less than a hundred years later there were about five hundred. In the final decades of the nineteenth century, the U.S. government had carried out a plan to exterminate the bison in order to force the last Indians outside of government control, a group of nomads living on the Great Plains, onto reservations.

The Indians on the Great Plains had been farmers and only occasional hunters a few generations earlier, but they had learned the dangers of staying put. The buffalo had become everything. Twenty buffalo skins made a teepee. Buffalo marrow, boiled out of cracked bones and then packed into a cleaned-buffalo stomach, was butter, and spread on everything. Another stomach made a water bottle. Strips of buffalo skin, twisted together, made ropes and bridles. Tendons became bow strings. Buffalo meat, pounded flat and mixed with salt and fat, kept all winter. Get rid of the buffalo, the thinking went, and you get rid of the Indians.

Not everyone thought this was a good idea. Nearly twenty years earlier, Representative Greenburg Lafayette Fort of Illinois entered a bill into Congress making it "unlawful for any person who is not an Indian to kill, wound, or in any manner destroy a female buffalo, of any age, found at large within the territories of the United States." "I am not in favor of civilizing the Indian by starving him to death," said Fort, in his opening address in 1874.

Ohio Republican James Garfield—who would be president of the United States in six years—disagreed, and so did the rest of Congress.

In 1876 Greenburg Lafayette Fort submitted the bill to Congress again. Again, it was shot down. The Texas Democrat John Hancock told him, "I hope sir, there is no humanitarian sentimentality that would induce legislation for the protection of the buffalo. If the theory upon which the Government is now treating the Indians is a proper one, and I am inclined to believe it is the best, the sooner we get rid of the buffalo the better it will be for the Indian and for the white man too."

As the buffalo Ben Harrison was being introduced to Golden Gate Park and the President Benjamin Harrison was meeting the Sioux, the last herd on public lands, a group of two hundred bison in Yellowstone, was being decimated by poachers. By 1901, there would be just twenty-five bison left in the park.

At the Red Cloud Agency in western Nebraska, hunters would prepare for the delivery of government cattle the way they once

153

prepared for the summer bison hunt. As the government cattle were released into a corral, the Oglala Sioux would hunt them down on horseback—or at least they did until 1897, when government authorities built a slaughterhouse and began distributing pre-butchered meat instead. The Oglala responded by setting the slaughterhouse on fire.

3

In April 1891, Ben Harrison the buffalo got married, in a meadow that, like all of Golden Gate Park, was a product of pastoral invention, crafted from horse manure laid on top of a shifting aggregation of sand dunes. The ceremony was timed to coincide with a visit from Benjamin Harrison, the President. BEN HARRISON'S NUPTIALS SOLEMNIZED AT THE PARK, read the headline, and the ceremony was presided over by the captain of park police. As the clock struck noon, the captain opened a crate containing a bison cow the city had shipped via train from a ranch in Wyoming. The female bison raced around the paddock frantically until Ben Harrison "gallantly ran out to meet her." At this, she quieted: "The appearance of her future lord and master calmed her tumultuous feelings. Both bride and groom appeared perfectly happy, and the crowd left them to spend their honeymoon among the trees of the inclosure."

4

It is hard to write historically about nature because nature doesn't care about history. Nature predates storytelling and will probably postdate it too. "When we choose a plot to order our environmental histories," the historian William Cronon has written "we give them a unity that neither nature nor the past possesses so clearly."

But even if nature doesn't live by stories, we do, and the stories we tell ourselves affect how we live with the other species around us. A little over a hundred years ago the government of this country virtually exterminated the largest land animal on the largest biome on the continent, one that roamed from Pennsylvania to the Sierras. And a little over a hundred years ago, my city held a wedding for two of them.

In 1870, before the buffalo were entirely gone, Red Cloud, the Chief of the Oglala Sioux (or, as they called themselves, the Lakota) went to New York to give a speech at the Cooper Union. "You have children, and so have we," he told the crowd through an interpreter. "We want to rear our children well, and ask you to help us in doing so." He asked that the Lakota be protected on the land they currently had and be dealt with honestly.

"It seems to us that this is not an unreasonable request," noted a reporter from the *New York Times*, "even though it docs come from a 'savage.'" The reporter continued, historicizing the event that had only ended a few hours before: "A few years more and the great Chiefs who yesterday stood before the New-York public will also have melted away, like 'snow upon the hill-side.' Their attempts to tell their own story to the white men, instead of allowing it to pass through all sorts of corrupt and adverse channels, will hereafter rank conspicuously among the historical events connected with the Indian race."

5

Here's another story:

Ten thousand years ago, the most recent ice age is ending. Humans cross over the Bering land bridge between Siberia and Alaska. On their way they might see horses for the first time—the horses have evolved in North America, but are striking out across the land bridge in the other direction, seeking their fortune. Homo sapiens continue migrating down into the Great Plains. Among the dwellers on the Great Plains at the end of the ice age are horses, camels, mammoths, mastodons, the American lion, the American cheetah, the dire wolf, the giant short-faced bear, and several species of saber-tooth cat. According to the fossil record, these species—after millions of years of evolution—seem to become extinct around the same time: ten and twelve thousand years ago, which is right around the time that Homo sapiens arrives. Some people think this is a coincidence. Some people do not.

B. bison, the smallest bison in North America, becomes the largest one by virtue of not dying. The gray wolf also survives, to become the bison's sole remaining predator besides humans. "In my mind's eye," writes Dale Lott in *American Bison: A Natural History*, "I see these two species walking silently together through a gray fog of extinction with larger predators and grazers dissolving into the mist around them. Apparently they were just small enough to get through."

The bison survive for another ten thousand years, evolving into symbiosis with the shortgrass prairie. Shortgrass actually thrives when it's being grazed—it has a deep root structure, which both supports the plant in terrible weather, and stabilizes the sandy soil of the prairie. It has a 6-1 protein to carbs ratio, which is convenient because bison, being huge, are all about the protein. The shortgrass feeds the bison and the bison eat up all the competition that hasn't bothered to develop a low-lying root structure.

The Homo sapiens have settled where the good farmland is. They plant crops in the spring, leave the village to hunt bison in the summer, and return in the fall to harvest the crops and store preserved meat. The horses were among the species that mysteriously went extinct, so the Homo sapiens catch the bison by chasing it on foot until it runs over a cliff, or by wearing a bison head and pretending to be a bison and leading other bison off a cliff, ducking behind a rock at the last moment.

This is not the most efficient way to kill a bison, but there are so many bison that it doesn't make much difference. Or rather: there are so many other ways that bison die that humans don't make much of a difference. Later settlers on the plains will be shocked at the bitter cold and the horrible scorching droughts and the chaotic weather patterns, and especially the effect that this has on their farming/ranching investments, but chaos is old hat to the bison. Bison have evolved to withstand temperatures of 110 degrees in the summer and 30 degrees below zero in the winter, and they did that by dying. They still die, all the time. They freeze, they starve, they fall through the ice. It's just that no one is there to write in a diary about it.

Sometime in the late 1600s, domesticated horses show up. Hernando Cortés brought them over in 1519, but it takes them a while to make it to the plains. In *Destruction of the Bison: An Environmental History, 1750-1920*, Andrew Isenberg recounts Cheyenne folklore collected by the ethnographic team Mariott and Rachlin:

> The Cheyenne are approached by the Comanches, who offer them horses, and their chief god, Masto, speaks through a priest and tells them that "If you have horses everything will be changed for you forever. You will have to move around a lot to find pasture for your horses. You will have to give up gardening and live by hunting and gathering, like the Comanches. And you will have to come out of your earth houses and

live in tents. . . . You will have to fight other tribes, who will want your pasture land or the places where you hunt. You will have to have real soldiers, who can protect the people. Think, before you decide."

The horses change everything, but then, so do smallpox, cholera, and increasing numbers of European settlers and traders. By the 1840s western plains nomads are bringing over a hundred thousand bison robes a year to the steamboats to sell. Travelers report seeing vast numbers of dead buffalo on the plains, skinned, with their tongues cut out. The tongues are, reportedly, delicious. The skins are not, but they turn out to be perfect belts for industrial machinery. The wheels of the industrial revolution will turn on bison. The Cheyenne and the Comanche will attempt to limit the full-scale hunting of the bison, the Blackfeet will participate in it, but the plains are also filling with teams of Europeans who have switched to the buffalo hide trade after being disappointed in the Gold Rush.

In 1870 the Kansas Pacific Railway arrives in Denver and in 1872 the Sharps Rifle Manufacturing Company develops the Sharps "Big Fifty"—a .50-caliber rifle that becomes the most common rifle used by bison hunters. It fires slugs weighing up to one pound. In 1872 the Atchison, Topeka and Santa Fe Railway reaches Dodge City, Kansas. Even before the railroad is completed in September 1872, the streets of Dodge are lined with wagons, bringing in hides and meat and getting supplies from early morning to late at night. Seven million pounds of buffalo tongue are shipped out of Dodge City, Kansas, in a single two-year period.

Between 1872 and 1873 the largest hide dealers in Dodge City, Robert Wright and Charles Rath, ship over two hundred thousand hides to Santa Fe.

I n the fall of 1873, Richard Irving Dodge wrote, in *Plains of the Great West*: "Where there were myriads of buffalo the year before, now there were myriads of carcasses. The air was foul with sickening stench, and the vast plain which only a short twelve months before teemed with animal life was a dead, solitary, putrid desert . . . The miserable animals, continually harassed, are driven into localities far from their haunts, anywhere to avoid the unceasing pursuit."

In 1874 Joseph Glidden, a farmer, businessman, and former teacher, in DeKalb, Illinois, receives the patent for barbwire—one of the obstacles to settlement of the West has been a lack of fencing to demarcate territory and cattle herds. At the time of his death in 1906, Glidden will be one of the wealthiest men in America.

The winter of 1881 is particularly bad for bison. There's a lot of snow that year, and the bison get caught in the drifts, making them particularly vulnerable to hunters. By 1883 the bison is nearly extinct. The plains are strewn with their bones. A. M. Bede, a county judge from Fort Yates, North Dakota, writes of those days in the northern plains: "The country out here used to look like a charnel house with so many skulls staring at a man, and so many bones that newcomers felt nervous, and, in some cases, could hardly plow the land."

Poor homesteaders and Indians scavenge for any bones they can gather, and sell them to sugar refineries or fertilizer plants for four to twelve dollars a ton—one hundred skeletons' worth of bones, give or take a bison or two.

In 1893, a railroad inspector interviewed by *Harper's* expounds further: "It is a mercy they can't eat bones. We were never able to control the savages until their supply of meat was cut off. We have had no trouble worth speaking of since 1883."

Some people kill the bison because it is fun: people go on safaris in the Great Plains. Bill Cody, aka "Buffalo Bill," makes his name organizing a buffalo hunt in 1872 for Grand Duke Alexei Alexandrovich of Russia. Buffalo Bill and the Sioux escort the Grand Duke and an ample supply of champagne through Kansas, helpfully pointing out bison along the way.

Others kill the bison because they cut into their profit margins: in 1883 the U.S. government hires a band of Sioux to slaughter around 5,000 buffalo near the Northern Pacific railroad line, out of fear that the bison could cause a train wreck. Trains have learned to watch for approaching bison, since herds can and do derail trains.

Telegraph companies kill bison too—bison, beleaguered by flies, scratch against telegraph poles until they fall over. Telegraph companies begin attaching bradawls to the poles, but that only makes it worse. Bison travel for miles to find a pole with a bradawl on it and battle one another for scratching rights. "The victor would proudly climb the mountainous heap of rump and hump of the fallen," reads one account in *Scott's Monthly Magazine*, "and scratch himself until the bradawl broke or the pole came down."

There are many stories at play about the future of the West. Not many of them are useful if you happen to be a bison.

6

The year was 1883. Theodore Roosevelt, a young New York state assemblyman, took a train out to the edge of Dakota Territory and hired a Canadian hunting guide. He really, he explained, wanted a buffalo head. The guide told him he didn't have much of a chance: bison were almost extinct. It took days of trudging through thunderstorms and sleeping in the rain before Roosevelt finally managed to shoot a buffalo. The guide looked over and saw Roosevelt run to the carcass and begin hopping and whooping in an improvised war dance. He reached into his pocket and handed the guide a one-hundred-dollar tip.

Roosevelt rode back to New York accompanied by the buffalo head wrapped in burlap. When he arrived, he took down the lion's head in his study, and put up the buffalo head in its place.

7

The first bison was born in Golden Gate Park on July 26, 1893 "looking like a calf, but with a veritable swelled head . . . it was amusing to note yesterday how readily and naturally the baby dropped into habits of her ancestors. The whole herd would win a prize in a contest for laziness by lying and sleeping—principally lying, as they sometimes seem too lazy to sleep." The *San Francisco Call* article went on to mention that the saddest animal in the park appeared to be a donkey named Billy, whose daughter, Mary, was "dying from reckless overindulgence in candy and sugared popcorn. Mary was a pet with the children with whom she was very friendly on account of candy," the newspaper continued, "but she is now reaping the sad penalty of excesses."

8

Today, accounts of the bison paddock in Golden Gate Park describe it as a conservation effort. Accounts then make it sound more than a little like a zoo.

I t was a zoo. Golden Gate Park had seals, an aquarium, kangaroos, zebras, and a bear pit that featured Monarch, both the largest and the last grizzly to be captured alive in California.

I n death, Monarch served as the model for the bear in the current version of the California state flag. He was moved to the San Francisco Zoo but returned, stuffed, and was exhibited at the California Academy of Sciences. In the early 2000s the Academy transformed itself from a warren of taxidermy into a sleek glass-lined blob of the future, complete with a green roof and a rainforest biosphere with live butterflies. It was at this point that the stuffed carcass of Monarch was moved to the basement, where it remains.

I n 1895 another bison was born, the fourth to be born in Golden Gate Park. A reporter visited the park and talked to John McLaren, the park superintendent, who declared himself quite elated at the success of the bison in the park. This population may in time, he said, supply the demand of those who visit the plains to hunt the bison.

9

In 1894 Theodore Roosevelt began collaborating with Madison Grant on the creation of the Bronx Zoo. The zoo, Roosevelt insisted, would have a buffalo paddock. It would breed the buffalo and release their offspring into the Great Plains and Rocky Mountains. Roosevelt's advisors suggested that it might be cheaper and more sensible to raise buffalo closer to their former habitat, but Roosevelt was insistent. The Bronx was going to repopulate the Great Plains, ideally in a decade or less.

The first herd of bison died, unaccustomed to Bronx grass. Workers in the park pulled up all the grass in the twenty-acre paddock and fed the second herd prairie grasses by hand.

10

In 2008 I walked out on Ocean Beach and saw that someone had arranged hand-painted wooden cutouts of the performers in Buffalo Bill's Wild West Show in front of the gray surf of the Pacific like a line of life-sized paper dolls posing for a photograph. They were a work of obsession—ornately, fanatically detailed, each one unique. I scanned the beach to see who might have made them and saw a man with a bushy gray walrus mustache. He was engaged in a civil, though heated, conversation with a woman in a Polarfleece beanie.

She was telling him that his art was disrespectful to Indians and he kept pulling on his cowboy hat, sticking his hands further into his brown leather jacket and telling her that no ma'am, it was a cruel world then and Buffalo Bill was a less cruel man in comparison and actually gave the Indians jobs and the self-respect that comes out of being able to live out your culture, even if you do that by performing for people.

I never found out how the argument ended.

11

Right before I left San Francisco, I took a friend who had just moved there to see the bison. She peered through the chain-link fence, unimpressed. Behind us, I could hear a small child whine, "Daddy! Why aren't the bison moving?"

"*W*hy are there bison here?" my friend asked.

I thought for a minute. I began to feel guilty. "I don't know," I said. "I just know they've been here for a long time. I guess I should know."

"Why," my friend said, slowly, "are *we* here?"

I knew how this went. It was a tradition in San Francisco. "A long time ago," I said, "when I first moved to the city, someone who had lived here a long time brought me here and said, 'Look! Bison!' And so I am doing the same with you."

ROBIN COSTE LEWIS, the winner of the National Book Award for *Voyage of the Sable Venus*, is the poet laureate of Los Angeles. She is writer-in-residence at the University of Southern California, as well as a Cave Canem fellow and a fellow of the Los Angeles Institute for the Humanities. Lewis was born in Compton, California; her family is from New Orleans.

Paramount

ROBIN COSTE LEWIS

There were six of us, but we paid
just for four. Before we reached the front,
Daddy would pull the car out of line
so Ritchie and Stevie could jump
inside the trunk. We'd smile and shush
right past the guard. I was five,
and still wore felt pajamas with the feet in.

•

The hefty steel speaker we hooked
over the passenger seat window.
Its knob and the static it sparked
when tuned towards the Paramount's
station. We saw all the movies there:
Cooley High, Coffy, Sparkle, Shaft. Perhaps
it was then that my longing first began
for mirrors, rhinestones and polyester.

•

Daddy's long tan Ford. Whenever we drove—
all six of us—down the Harbor Freeway on Saturdays
to visit Grandmother, I would roll down
the wide rear window and stick my head out
into the Santa Ana wind and make believe
it was a long river of water and I was
washing my hair with Wella Balsam.

•

In one scene, she wore a big gardenia
in her hair; the next she was tied up
on the floor in a white padded room,
jerking. A real story, at last. I remember
that deep prick of having sensations
for which I'd yet to learn any words:
acting, aesthetic pleasure, biography.
Yet there were other feelings I knew enough
to know I didn't need any words.

•

If my father could have heard what I was thinking
he would have made me kneel in the corner
with my face to the wall. She was too skinny
and dark to be that lady with the voice, stranger
than Christmas. Why couldn't she be fat
and yellow? And Billy Dee looked so smart
in his sky-blue fur coat, hair brushed down
hard and wet, I could smell the Murray's
dripping off the screen.

•

I can still feel the light of the projector
moving over my bird chest. I sat
between my mother and father.
My sister and brothers were in the back. Bodies
walked across me; cars drove up
and down my face; then wearing an opal
dress, she walked onto the screen,
and swam through the blue light
hovering all around me.

Gone in Sixty Sentences

RACHEL KUSHNER

Every time I've attempted to start this sidewinding medita-
tion on Matthew Porter's airborne muscle cars, cars that are
things and also backlit silhouettes of things, I end up scrolling the
new version of the old Autotrader online, and looking at models
of cars I've always wanted, and also their silhouettes.

If I had a hundred grand to drop right now, this morning,
which I don't, I could buy a 1969 Pontiac GTO Judge, mint. But
really it's not my style. A '67 GTO and its classy cigar-box lines is
what I always wanted. The '69 is a novelty item, like roller skates
or a leather shirt, and anyhow I get bored of the color orange.
I'd love a GTO but I don't need a Judge, even if there are certain
days—Tuesdays?—when I feel like I need a Judge.

For a Sunday drive I want a Stutz Blackhawk; doesn't even
have to be the one Elvis owned. I'll humbly accept some other
Stutz, but the more I research who owned Stutzes—Dean Martin,
Wilson Pickett, George Foreman, Muhammad Ali, Willie Nel-
son, and Barry White, just to cherry-pick from the longer list of
celebrity owners—I get mad that I haven't yet myself acquired
the pink slip for a Stutz. Even if I could afford one, there aren't
very many, and today none are listed for sale.

There's a 1965 Mercury Marauder, I always liked those. If the lines are a little square, the fastback makes up for it, although it's a car that has to have sport rims or forget it.

Why is 1965 the chicane through which all American car design went from curved to boxy?

Nineteen sixty-eight was another chicane, which led to puffy quarter panels, and even outright blimpage.

Sometimes I start to believe I want a Rolls-Royce, like a model from the 1980s. Today you can buy a 1985 Rolls-Royce Silver Spur for ten grand on Autotrader. I know nothing about Rolls models but if it doesn't come with pull-down teakwood dinner trays in the backseat the deal is off. Extras are important to me. The idea of a General Motors Lanvin Arpège perfume atomizer offered as a factory extra with the 1958 Cadillac Eldorado Brougham spritzes my spirit with something American that I can actually, for a moment, believe in.

I often want a 1961 Ford Starliner. That's something special to me, and it harkens back to one I saw for sale in Napa, California, in 1992. It was Wimbledon White, a stock Ford color I'm partial to. I didn't buy it. Say it: Starliner. Wimbledon White. That was the year I spent every weekend looking at cars. I ended up buying a 1964 Ford Galaxie, which I still own, but even after I bought my Galaxie I continued combing PennySaver and Autotrader and Hemmings and called numbers and dreamed of other cars. In 1997 I bought a 1963 Chevrolet Impala in Hendersonville, North Carolina. The night I bought it, a friend and I motored out to a drive-in movie theater in Waynesville, an hour south. We could hear cows lowing as we waited for the film to begin. Wish I still had that car. Had to sell it to pay for school, made a very large profit since it's a coveted year of a coveted model. The night before I sold it someone attempted to steal it from my parents' driveway in San Francisco. My neighbors saw my car in the middle of the street and knocked on our door. A guy had hot-wired it and was planning to drive away with the anti-theft club still attached to the wheel. He flooded the engine trying to give it gas and had to abandon on foot.

It's September as I write this, and the 2018 calendar my son got at the Pomona car show is opened to a 1971 Ford Mustang Boss 351. I've seen every muscle car a hundred times over. That was youth. This is now (middle age). I've given my copy of the *Standard Catalog of American Cars, 1946–1975* to my son, who can pore over specs like I once did. The '71 Mustang is shown parked in front of a tacky Italianate villa. The parked car versus the midair car is object instead of subject. A car flying through an intersection is the protagonist; that's clear. It knows the story and it is the story, even if the casual grace of electric wires, light poles, and traffic signals play their parts. Nothing like late-day light to put the city-sky infrastructure into relief: the light is half the charm of these magical images. The locations that Porter has chosen, too, are sweet, but maybe in part because they're familiar: some of them are in my neighborhood, or near it. He doesn't photograph famously steep Baxter Street in Echo Park, but his images conjure it. Cresting Baxter to get air is something LAPD motorcycle cops do at five a.m., when they figure no one is paying attention. They hit Baxter Street and court broken axles.

There are many iconic cinema stills of flying muscle cars, but the mother lode of the genre is from H. B. Halicki's 1974 film *Gone in 60 Seconds*, in which a Mustang Mach 1 hovers midair in a Los Angeles intersection after launching off a crash-pile it has used as a jump ramp.

The film's super-flimsy plotline involves the theft of forty-eight cars in forty-eight hours, each coded with a woman's name. The Mach 1, called "Eleanor," is the indisputable star and credited as such. Halicki financed, produced, directed, wrote, starred in, and did all of the stunt driving for the film. He was known as the Car Crash King, and he was also the Junkyard King who owned all ninety-three of the cars that were totaled in his movie, including multiple police cars, fire trucks, and even the garbage truck that drives right over a Dodge Charger. In my favorite scene, Eleanor the Mach 1 plows into a large sofa that's sitting in the middle of an alleyway, the sofa compressed and pulverized as the car commits to dragging the ruined frame from its undercarriage for several hundred feet.

There are other comical touches. Halicki evades police in a tow truck with a rear-facing Dodge Challenger, a mint car that later gets shoved in a compactor at a wrecking yard. Cornered at one point after a high-speed pursuit in the Mach 1, Halicki seems to assent to the police, as if the game is over. He puts his hands up at the officers' commands, multiple guns drawn on him from various angles. He keeps his hands up, but mashes the gas with his driving foot, complying and not complying, hands kept up as he blazes west on Ocean Boulevard and cops dive out of the way.

In other highlights, Eleanor the Mach 1 runs over a shopping cart full of groceries. A night scene at the long-gone Ascot Park speedway reveals the inspiration for the film's title, an announcement over loudspeakers for speedway guests to lock their vehicles or they'll be "gone in sixty seconds." A high-speed chase interrupts the Carson City Council's dedication of a new sheriff's department, a scene I favor because Carson is where, coincidentally, the best go-karting in Los Angeles can be had—or rather, the most scrappy and sketchy go-karting in Los Angeles. Another highlight is when Eleanor drives right into a Cadillac dealership, escaping through the service department.

But the heart of the film is a long and static sequence in a huge garage, as the camera slow-pans past every one of the forty-eight stolen vehicles: Rolls-Royces and Cadillacs and Lincolns, a Plymouth Barracuda, a Corvette Stingray, a Manta Mirage, car after car, some rare, some not, all gleaming and still. They are part of the plot but real—actual cars that Halicki owned (and which, in real life, he'd acquired dubiously). A woman named Pumpkin sits behind a desk, the superego in the room, leaning back. She has big hair I mean really big—amazing hair, and long nails. The studs on the collar of her denim shirt wink at the camera, her Malibu-tan hands tented in rumination, although maybe she's thinking only of money, or of nothing at all. Either way, I love her. The actress who plays her is named Marion Busia, and apparently she is now, as you read this, a real estate agent in Rancho Palos Verdes. This is not disappointing. I'd settle for nothing less.

Joined to the theme of destroying cars is a fetish for cars but also other stuff. Halicki's belt buckles are different in every scene, and never subtle. He's got a lot of sunglasses, bell-bottoms, and briefcases. Several wigs and an artificial mustache. Various styles of slim jim, for opening car doors. An array of hats and deerskin driving gloves. He was a collector. I heard he later acquired his own Goodyear Blimp but I'm having trouble verifying that.

H. B. Halicki died while filming a sequel to *Gone in 60 Seconds*. A telephone pole was clipped by a wire meant to pull a water tower into a parking lot full of cars, and the telephone pole hit Halicki and killed him.

Time passes. People die. They become real estate agents. Car collections get auctioned. Classics become more valuable, and rarer, and also forgotten, and thus, to some, less valuable, and that's good, and also sad. The light stays the same. Or rather, it is always changing.

REYNA GRANDE is an award-winning author, motivational speaker, and writing teacher. As a girl, she crossed the US–Mexico border to join her family in Los Angeles, a harrowing journey chronicled in *The Distance Between Us*, a National Book Critics Circle Award finalist that has been adopted as the common read selection by over twenty schools and colleges and fourteen cities across the country. Her other books include the novels *Across a Hundred Mountains*, winner of a 2007 American Book Award, and *Dancing with Butterflies*, and the non-fiction *The Distance Between Us: Young Readers Edition*. She lives in Woodland, California, with her husband and two children.

My Mother's California

REYNA GRANDE

When I was four-and-a-half years old, my mother left me in Mexico, along with my older siblings, to come to California and be reunited with my father, who had left two years earlier. When she'd announced her departure, the first thing I asked was, "How long will you be gone?"

"Not too long," she replied.

But "not too long" turned out to be "never" because she was never the same mother to me after she crossed the border. The little girl in me is still waiting for my mami to return.

When she arrived in Los Angeles in January 1980, my thirty-year-old mother found a job at a garment factory trimming threads off freshly sewn garments. She made fifteen cents per garment, the threads clinging to her clothes like spiderwebs. All day she stood, scissors in hand, in an airless room full of industrial-sized sewing machines and steam presses. She hated that job. She felt trapped, suffocated. In Mexico, she'd been an Avon lady. She loved walking around the neighborhood from house to house, displaying her merchandise and catalogs, chatting with her friends. On weekends, she made candied tamarind pulpa, coconut popsicles, lime-flavored gelatin, and bags of freshly popped popcorn. She'd stroll through the streets, tray and basket in hand, selling these treats. In Los Angeles, she missed the freedom of working outside, setting her own hours, being her own boss. She missed la chamba, the hustle, of working in sales.

Two years after she arrived, my parents split up. My siblings and I were still waiting in Mexico to be reunited with them. In May 1985, when I was nine-and-a-half, my father returned to Mexico to bring me and my older brother and sister to live with him in Los Angeles. Through most of my childhood, I saw my mother once or twice a month. My father had left her for another woman, and my mother, in turn, left her children for another man. My father and stepmother could raise us as they saw fit without any interference from her.

My siblings and I grew up in Highland Park in Northeast L.A., which back then was a working-class Latino neighborhood with a serious gang problem. But having come from a poverty-stricken area of Mexico—Guerrero, the second poorest state in the country—Highland Park was a huge upgrade from what we'd left behind. The dirt roads of my childhood were replaced by wide, paved streets that seemed to go on forever. Instead of shacks made of sticks and cardboard like the one we called home in Mexico, the streets were lined with real houses made of thick stucco walls and shingled roofs. Although we were still impoverished by American standards—my siblings and I slept in the living room on a sofa bed, our sleep punctuated by gunshots, ambulance sirens, and the whirring of police helicopters in the distance—the solid walls of our one-bedroom duplex on Avenue 50 separated us from those sounds, and I felt protected in a way I'd never felt in Mexico.

My father, a maintenance worker with a third-grade education, spoke little English. We were undocumented then, and he told us he'd brought us to this country so that we could get an education, have careers one day, be homeowners, have money for retirement. These were his dreams for us, and he demanded excellent grades and perfect attendance. He wanted us to have the American Dream 2.0. He wanted our lives to be completely different from the lives we'd left behind in Mexico. We were in California now, and we needed to look forward, not back.

My mother was the opposite of my father. She had humble aspirations, not lofty dreams. She was content with what little she had because no poverty in Los Angeles could ever compare to the real poverty she'd left behind. As long as she wasn't *that* poor, she was happy. My father yearned for more and passed that ambition on to his children. "I didn't bring you here to end up being nobodies," he would often say. "We didn't risk our lives crossing the border so you would end up as failures."

My mother left her job at the factory and returned to being her own boss—she became a vendor at local swap meets. Because she didn't drive, her husband quit his job ironing clothes, and they both worked the swap meets: in Rosemead on weekends, in San Fernando on Tuesdays, in Santa Fe Springs on Wednesdays and Fridays. Thursdays they'd restock their merchandise at the wholesale shops in L.A.'s Toy District. They gave up their stable, if low-paying factory jobs for the risky business of selling Avon, Jafra, Mary Kay products, and seasonal items like silk roses and teddy bears for Valentine's, cheap plastic sandals in the summer, toys at Christmastime.

"Look at your mother," my father would say. "That's no way to live. Selling at the swap meet doesn't provide a stable income, you don't put money toward retirement, you get no health benefits." The more he criticized her, the more we, her children, criticized her, too. We worked harder at school, vowing not to follow in her footsteps.

Still, we would go see her. We entered another world when we visited her in downtown L.A. My mother's neighborhood near

179

Skid Row made us wonder if we were still in California and not in a third-world country like the one we'd left behind. Walking from the bus stop on Spring Street to her house on San Pedro Street, we navigated through all the homeless people spread out on the sidewalks and avoided the prostitutes standing on corners. The streets reeked of urine and marijuana. Piles of trash crunched under our feet. Plastic bags of all colors floated around us in the wind like miniature parachutes. We hurried to our mother's one-room studio and crammed into it, squeezing into the spaces between her furniture and the mountains of boxes in which she stored her belongings. Her home, with its shared bathroom and kitchen, was infested with roaches and mice, and it smelled like skunk. My mother supplemented her earnings by recycling cans and bottles. After the swap meet closed for the day, while her husband loaded their wares back in their van, she would pick up the cans and bottles scattered on the ground or dig into trash cans with her bare hands. The cans and bottles would sit in black trash bags in a corner of her apartment, feeding the roaches and stinking up the place, until she had enough to make a trip to the recycling center worth her while.

As my siblings and I came of age in California, we assimilated more and more into American culture. We spoke English fluently. We learned the nuances of the American way of life. We listened to Madonna and Depeche Mode, dressed up as superheroes, ghosts, and Greek goddesses on Halloween, watched *Small Wonder* and *Married with Children*. By the time we reached junior high, we had surpassed both our parents' educational achievements. My brother played soccer. My sister did modern dance. I joined the marching band and performed in Disneyland's Christmas Fantasy Parade and the Pasadena Tournament of Roses Parade three times.

As time went on, we understood our mother even less, and our worlds shifted away even more. We began to reject our mother and everything she represented. To our Americanized eyes, she was a symbol of what we didn't want to be—a working-class, uneducated, non-English-speaking immigrant. The more we were educated in U.S. schools and the more we assimilated, the more we internalized the disdain American society has for someone like my mother. My siblings and I spoke English all the time, and consciously and unconsciously, we excluded our mother from all our conversations and eventually, our middle-class American lives.

"Why don't you go to night school and learn English?" we would suggest to her. My mother would shake her head, her eyes terrified at such a suggestion. "El inglés no se me pega." *English doesn't stick to me*, she'd say.

"We aren't speaking about a piece of chewing gum," we would say, "but a language that takes effort and sacrifice to learn."

When she complained about the pitiful sales at the swap meet, we would suggest that she learn to drive. "That way you can drive yourself and your husband can get a stable job. Then at least one of you could have a steady income."

She would be even more scared of such a suggestion. "¿Y si me mato?" *And if I kill myself?* She insisted that her husband keep driving her to the swap meet.

In 1996 I went to study at the University of California, Santa Cruz, six hours to the north. When I told my mother I was leaving, she said, "Ahí nos vemos." *See you later*. Not *Take care, call me if you need anything*—the words I'd longed to hear from her. We didn't have that kind of relationship. She wasn't the mother who said motherly things, and I wasn't the daughter who was supposed to long for such things anyway. This is what I told myself as I drove up Interstate 5.

When I arrived in Santa Cruz, I felt as if I had been given access to another, better version of California—a fairy-tale version. It was an idyllic place, the campus nestled in a redwood forest overlooking Monterey Bay. Every morning, the first thing I saw when I opened my eyes were the world's tallest trees. As I walked to my classes, I would pass deer foraging for breakfast, or see banana slugs crawling on the forest floor. I would look at the sparkling water of Monterey Bay, feeling more than lucky. My world was expanding, and with it, my place in it changed. In Santa Cruz I met my first vegetarian and vegan friends. It was my first time hearing the words tofu, soy, and wheat germ, my first time eating alfalfa sprouts and split pea soup. It was there where I met my first lesbian, gay, and bisexual friends. It was also my first time being a minority student in my classes, which were full of blond-haired, blue-eyed students. When I shared these experiences with my siblings, they thought I had moved to another country, not another part of the state. To my mother, Santa Cruz sounded like another planet.

In Santa Cruz, everyone was into protecting the environment. When it rained, some students danced naked in the forest pretending to be fairies and worshipping the redwoods. They tied themselves to trees and rose up in protest when the campus administrators announced the construction of new buildings. We were all supposed to do our part to protect the environment and recycling was a must. Even our food waste was recyclable— destined for something called "compost." My mother dug into trash cans with her bare hands to fish out cans and bottles and drove around downtown L.A. to pick up cardboard and sell it by the ton at the recycling center—to make extra money to pay her rent, not for the altruistic purpose of saving our planet.

I majored in creative writing and film and video. An assignment in film class was to make a five-minute documentary about

182

something we wanted to learn more about. I chose my mother as the subject of my film. I wanted to know more about this woman, the biggest enigma of my life—my absent mother. So I went down to Los Angeles with a camera borrowed from school to spend a weekend with my mother documenting her life as a swap meet vendor.

All the other seats in her van, except for the two front ones, had been removed to make room for the merchandise. I found myself wedged between crates of Avon deodorant and boxes of hair polish, the camera pointed at my mother while I prayed we didn't get into an accident. I would surely die, if not from the accident, then from being buried alive under all the merchandise. It was the crack of dawn, but the Star Lite Swap Meet was full of activity, all the vendors pulling up to their spots, putting their booths together, unloading their merchandise. Through the camera lens, I watched my mother doing what she loved— arranging and rearranging her merchandise and finding just the right way to display it, talking to all the customers strolling past the booth, getting their attention by making small talk, having them smell a perfume or letting them sample the silkiness of a hand lotion.

Through the camera, I bore witness to my mother's love of selling. It didn't matter that she was on her feet all day, skipping a meal or forgoing a trip to the bathroom so as not to miss a sale. I felt bad for her when people walked away having made no purchases. I watched her face beam with happiness and pride when she did make a sale and—with the bills still in her hand—made the sign of the cross and thanked God for helping her.

As dusk settled over Los Angeles, with the silhouettes of palm trees in the distance, we drove back to her tiny apartment, the van a little less full of merchandise, me a little less suffocated, less ignorant.

After dinner that night she put on her favorite music and through the camera I captured her dancing to "Juana la Cubana," a cumbia that she loved because her name is Juana and, though she isn't Cuban, felt the song was written just for her. In the editing room at UCSC, I watched my mother's face flash across the computer screen again and again. I felt closer to her than I ever had.

I had to screen my edited film in class. I was nervous, ashamed even, to show such an intimate portrait of my mother. What would the students and teacher say? What would they think of her? Of me? I shook those insecurities off because I realized that through my film, I had brought my mother back with me to Santa Cruz, into my California.

I got an A on my project, and I was glad that the students and my teacher got to see what I had seen for the first time through the camera—not a woman beaten down by her poverty, but rather, a woman whose humble aspirations filled her with gratitude for a life that was a tiny bit better than what she'd escaped from.

When I graduated from UCSC, I went back to Los Angeles because, to my dismay, I couldn't afford to live in this better version of California. Santa Cruz was home to wealthy retirees, people with trust funds, and workers from Silicon Valley. There were few good jobs available. I had worked at the Santa Cruz Boardwalk selling hotdogs and ice cream cones to supplement my student grants and loans, but I couldn't work there after graduation. I didn't cross the border to end up selling hotdogs for a living, I told myself.

I returned to Los Angeles, said goodbye to the redwoods and the deer, the wharf and the boardwalk, the surfers and the hippies, to try my luck as a writer in the city where I had come of age.

Though it was a difficult road, I managed to accomplish all that my father had dreamed of—I had a college degree and a promising writing career. I eventually owned my own home and began putting away money for retirement. All these things have given me access to yet a different California. My writing opened the door to the literary community of Los Angeles and beyond. I read from my work at the Los Angeles Times Festival of Books, the largest book festival in the country and yet I'd never even heard of it in the fifteen years I'd lived in L.A. I read at the Mark Taper Auditorium at the beautiful Los Angeles Central Public Library, a mere ten minutes from my mother's home but in the nice part of downtown, which I hadn't known existed. I read at Vroman's Bookstore in Pasadena, Skylight Books in Los Feliz, Barnes & Noble in Santa Monica. I presented my work in California cities I'd never visited or in some cases even heard of: Mission Viejo, Santa Barbara, Delano, Camarillo, Idyllwild, Point Reyes, Santa Maria, Arcata, Carlsbad, Merced, Chico, Half Moon Bay, Red Bluff, San Jacinto, Taft.

While I was crisscrossing the state reading from my books, my mother moved to Pico-Union, one of the last remaining low-income communities adjacent to a gentrified Downtown L.A. She lived less than a mile from a four-star hotel, L.A. Live, and the Staples Center, on the other side of the 110 Freeway, which—like the U.S.-Mexico border—divides the haves and the have-nots. Due to declining sales, she gave up the swap meets and began to recycle cardboard full time in addition to cans and bottles. Businesses in downtown called her to come pick up their cardboard at the end of the day. With knife in hand, she'd slit the masking tape of the boxes, carefully flatten them, and throw box after box in the van. When it was full, she and her husband would drive to a recycling center on Slauson Avenue in South Central to sell the cardboard, getting forty to fifty dollars for their effort.

185

"That's not even minimum wage," I once pointed out.

She shrugged and answered, "In Mexico, I would be making five dollars a day."

Whenever I found the time to visit her, she'd tell me stories about her world. She told me about a restaurant parking lot in Pico-Union from where buses take the locals to gamble in a casino on the way to Las Vegas for as little as twenty dollars round-trip. She'd go whenever she could afford a day off. "They even give you forty dollars in game tokens and a meal voucher to get you more excited about the trip," she said. She told me about the friends she had made, such as a housewife who sneaked out of the house when her husband left for work, took the bus to gamble the grocery money, and made it back before her husband returned. Sometimes my mother won, but most of the time she lost.

"I can't believe there are buses waiting to take you to a casino," I said incredulously. "Especially in an area where people can't afford to gamble."

So then she told me about a woman from El Salvador who, for thirty dollars, could take you down to San Diego to visit the Saint Jude Shrine. "They even give you free medallions of San Juditas," she said.

She told me about her friend's son who was a drag queen and danced at the local nightclubs imitating Selena. How one night his friend, another drag queen, had been lured into a restroom, doused in gasoline, and set on fire. She told me about the time she and her husband gave her brother-in-law a ride to LAX, leaving their rickety truck on the curb. They went inside to help him with his luggage and use the restroom, and when they came out fifteen minutes later, their truck was surrounded by six police and TSA vehicles and a tow truck. They arrested her husband, towed the truck, and left her stranded at the airport. "I didn't know you couldn't leave your car at the curb," she said. There was no point in my mentioning the repeated announcements outside the terminal telling you to not leave vehicles unattended. All those announcements are in English.

When my daughter was little, I was asked to be the keynote speaker at an annual education conference in San Jose with five thousand educators in attendance. I asked my mother to come with me so that she could help me with my daughter. The conference had provided a booth at the exhibit hall where I spent all day signing books and talking to educators about my writing and my experiences as an immigrant child in California schools. I introduced my mother to every teacher who came to my booth. At one point, my daughter got antsy, and I asked my mother to take her around the exhibit hall where vendors were selling teacher supplies and materials. Half an hour later, I saw my mother walking toward me down the aisle, with a huge plastic bag in one hand and my daughter's hand in the other.

"What do you have there?" I asked her, wondering if a vendor had given her a sample.

She opened the bag so that I could see the many cans and bottles it held. Her face beamed with joy when she said, "The trash bins are full of these! I couldn't fit them all in. I need another bag!"

I wanted to die from humiliation, but then I realized that while I had wanted to bring my mother into my world, she had brought her world into mine. If I wanted to have any kind of relationship with my mother, I would need to accept that. So I did. And I have.

My mother is sixty-nine years old now. She still doesn't speak English. Still doesn't drive. Is still living in a one-room studio in Pico-Union and recycling cardboard and cans and bottles. Although my siblings and I have offered to move her into our homes and take care of her, she refuses. She is not at home with us. My siblings and I have given her thirteen grandchildren—all born in California. Unlike us, our U.S.-born children are all native English speakers. Most of them can't even speak Spanish, can't speak to their abuela Juana without the help of Google Translate.

I am no closer to knowing my mother than I was when I was a child. There will never be a day when our worlds will align, when we can live in the same California, dreaming the same dreams. When I feel the distance between us is insurmountable, I think of the time I followed her around with a camera, making a documentary film of a day in the life of Juana, my mother, the stranger. We will never be co-stars in the same film, and I might always be on the outside looking in on her world, seeing her through the camera lens in a way I cannot see her with my naked eye.

CATHERINE BARNETT is the author of three poetry collections, *Into Perfect Spheres Such Holes Are Pierced, The Game of Boxes,* winner of the James Laughlin Award from the Academy of American Poets, and *Human Hours,* which won the 2018 Believer Book Award for Poetry and was a finalist for the T. S. Eliot Four Quartets Prize. Her honors include a Whiting Award and a Guggenheim Fellowship. She is a member of the core faculty of New York University's Creative Writing Program.

Ultimate California Highway 1 Road Trip

CATHERINE BARNETT

Yes, perhaps like yours now my father is old.
He looks at me through agatey eyes
with a layman's dread, I cut his meat for him,
play some early Stones and ask him to read Frost
because I don't want him to pour another Tanqueray.

Back out of all this now too much for us,
back when he could repair anything,
it was as if he'd made us solely so we could stand there
and hold the screws and listen to the Accutron
humming on his wrist.

We marveled that the watch didn't tick, you could see
clear through to its insides, it would work, he told us,
in any gravitational field, and we could see it glow
even as we sped down Highway 1 at night when the cliffs
dropped all no-man-fathomed to the Pacific and we begged him

slow down but the radio played on
—Time, time, time is on my side, yes it is—
and he sped up, said he was following the taillights
just ahead of us and that when they started to fall
he'd know it was a good idea to turn the other way.

TOMMY ORANGE is the author of the *New York Times* bestselling *There There* (Alfred A. Knopf), winner of the 2018 Center for Fiction First Novel Prize, finalist for the Pulitzer Prize in fiction, and longlisted for the 2018 National Book Award for Fiction, the Aspen Words Literary Prize, and the 2019 Carnegie Medal for Excellence in Fiction. It was deemed a Top Five Fiction Book of the Year by the *New York Times*, won the John Leonard Award for Best First Book, and was nominated for the NCIBA Golden Poppy in Fiction in 2018.

Copperopolis

TOMMY ORANGE

O n my days off, I walk the narrow blacktop roads of an area
called Diamond Twenty in the small town of Copperopolis.
We're in the foothills of the Sierras now, just barely still in what
can be considered Northern California. The sun's right above me,
pressing on the back of my neck. I reach back and cover it—keep
my hand there. It's the middle of the day, in the middle of summer,
which out here means it's hot as hell. I'm just coming back from
one. A hell. Or I'm still in one and I've gotten so used to it I started
calling it something else. No, this isn't hell, it's just fucking hot.

The heat here is dry and mean and everywhere. It crushes,
seeps, floats up in waves like smoke from the pavement—gets
into the brain. Slows thinking. I pass under the shade of an oak
and look down at my shadow, which is joined by the shadow of a
tree, so mangled by or mingled with branch shadows it becomes
a new thing, a shadowed object like and not like me or the tree,
the blending of images only possible where light can't be.

The shine of gold in the tall dead grass makes me think of the
people who came to these hills for gold. The rush to get it. And
then thinking of that time, thinking of those miners, makes me
think of Indians—who would have been here and been seen as:
in the way. I'm thinking of Native people here because I am one,

not full-blood but enough. We Natives are always looking for our presence in the absences. I look up on my phone whether there were ever Native Americans in Copperopolis. There's a small entry on an abandoned website about signs of human settlement dating ten thousand years back. Human remnants, it says. This makes me think of remains and how we use that word to describe people who haven't remained at all but left what time didn't get at all the way. I look up as if to get out of the gloom of that thought and see turkey vultures circling what must be something dead or dying nearby. I think about how things must stink worse in the heat. There's a big field of tall dead grass the vultures are circling above. The stalks of yellow move a little from a hot wind that, instead of cooling me, just reminds me of how hot the heat is. I find that I am swaying a little like the grass. I look down and watch my mangled shadow sway.

My four-year-old son Alex isn't old enough to know to be afraid of me the way the rest of my family is afraid of me. He still runs up to me when I come home and I bend down and he holds my big head in his arms. He's just learned to say I love you. He knows what it means to say it and uses it sparingly so that it keeps its meaning. As for my ever-understanding wife, Anne, we haven't talked about what happened very much because when we've tried, something between us opens up too wide for us to know how to speak across it. My mother- and father-in-law, and my sister-in-law and her two girls, they either talk about me like I'm not there, or they don't talk about me at all. Never mind talk *to* me. I'm a haunt they're afraid to be afraid of in front of— because of what it might do to me. I don't blame them. I wouldn't wanna talk to me either.

I'd tried for a voluntary exit before my time had come with a razor. Voluntary exit is too clinical or noble-sounding a euphemism here of course. Before my time had come isn't right either. Time and its length, the one we're given, is an elusive thing. There are exits everywhere for those of us who—actively or not—look for them. A train or approaching bus, twenty-two too many drinks, a sharp object. Anywhere. Much less common are entrances. Ways in. Like the day we had our son, there in the hospital on my knees holding the bedrail and listening to the machines and my wife's breathing; there was paper constantly being printed out that showed the contractions, their size and length, like we were measuring earthquakes. There was something that made sense to me about how acute the pain seemed to be for my wife. Why that was part of birth. Like a blow to the body from within. A magical wound from which a human boy came out. Things were good for the first several years of his life. Everything he did was a miracle. Sure he was incapable. A mouth. But I didn't know what love was before he came. Not that kind of love anyway.

Before Copperopolis, those first few years after he was born, I was still telling people I was a poet. And then to the expected follow-up question, No, but what do you do for a living, I'd say: videographer, which wasn't a lie, but it wasn't exactly true either—I hardly made a living at it. I'd been ready to sign a significant contract with a Native nonprofit to produce promotional videos for their website. Then that job, and a psychotherapist position my wife had lined up at the same organization, fell through at the last minute—after a sudden tribal leadership change.

When we moved in with my wife's family in Copperopolis I'd just been released from the hospital after going at my left wrist with a razor in the bathroom I was supposed to be cleaning in order to move out of our house in Oakland. I'd thought about suicide plenty before trying it—as it goes. It was the razor's angle in the bathroom, that little blade on the sink, square and flat against it like a self-destruct button I'd just then realized I could press. So I pressed it in deep then across. A dark purple circle appeared in the middle of my vision as I went to the ground. Later that spot would return, only white and not dark purple—the bright white of stars away from cities in a new moon sky, or like the sun looks with your eyes closed after having stared at it too long. When I was on the way to the hospital, I felt untouched by the dark purple spot, and yet maybe about to enter it at the same time. Levitating above its grasp—its gravity.

When my wife found me on the bathroom floor she told her mom, who was there to help us clean and move out, to take our son for a walk in his stroller. It was time for his nap anyway. The ambulance ride seemed buoyant to the point of pleasant before I passed out from losing too much blood. I don't remember any of what happened in the hospital. When I came to my wife was rolling me out to the parking lot in a wheelchair. I felt refreshed, born again, as if into a new life.

I got a job as a sandwich artist at the local Subway. It's the first time I'm being paid and acknowledged as an artist. The Subway is in a sort of shopping complex designed to look like an old-fashioned town like maybe from the fifties. Except everything looks brand new. There's a giant clock tower in the center of the town square everyone calls new old town.

I've recently taken to sucking on pennies and contemplating bank robbery. The pennies because there was an especially shiny one brand new out of a roll I broke to make smaller change for an impatient man with a sandwich I'd just made in his hand, lightly slapping the sandwich against his palm like a cop's baton, like if I didn't hurry he'd hit me with it. As he left I popped the penny in my mouth and sucked on it. It didn't taste like I thought it would. It tasted good to me. Thoughts of robbing the local bank came to me after I made a cash drop for the first time the other day and noticed there was no bulletproof glass between the customer and the teller. I didn't know they still had banks like that. Robbing a bank didn't seem crazy when I thought about it. It seemed reasonable. I need to provide for my family more than I need the discounted sandwiches and day-old cookies I get to take home for free. My son loves the cookies and says it wrong like the Cookie Monster says his own name wrong on Sesame Street. *Cooky*.

In the new life everything seems allowable. The star-white hole is there every time I close my eyes. I've started to think of it as a cell. I've been thinking if I could split the cell something important might happen. I close my eyes more now, fascinated by the details I can sometimes make out inside the hole. It sort of shimmers at its edges. Or the edges blur if I stare too long like it's reacting to my staring at it. My co-worker Sam caught me with my eyes closed and accused me of sleeping on the job.

"Late night?" he said, smiling and lifting his eyebrows like people do to suggest you got into trouble or something.

"No, I was—" I started. He was laughing. "I get headaches and it helps when I clench my eyes shut."

"Oh," he said, his smile gone. He went to the back to make more bread.

I'd requested for my green name tag to say Thomas, which is my author name, Thomas Blaine, but my manager told me they—Subway—liked to use shorter names on name tags. So it says Tom on my name tag. I didn't know if this was to save money on letters or because shorter names indicate a casual kind of friendliness and familiarity.

Do I take putting sandwiches together as seriously as I do my poems? The scaffolding is similar. You begin the build in order to begin to build the order. What kind of bread? Toasted? No two sandwich orders are the same. Variance is the constant. Of course poems aren't asked for or ordered. And how do you build a life? My life had felt like it was building to something that came apart, which I'm now attempting to rebuild behind sneeze-guard glass.

I'm lying in bed awake because I can't sleep. It's too hot. There's no AC here. It doesn't cool down at night at this point in the summer. I'm with my wife and son. We just have a sheet over us. I think they're asleep but then hear them both shift in bed in a way that feels to me like they're awake. I don't know though and don't want to wake them if they're asleep. They might be awake thinking the same of me.

"Tom?" my wife says. She can always tell when I'm awake.

"You can't sleep either," I whisper.

"It's that damn fly," she says, with real, actual hatred in her voice. I haven't noticed the fly.

"Me too mama," our son says. So he's been awake too. All of us lying here in silence. Something about it is so sweet and sad at the same time. I start crying without meaning to.

"What happened to Dada?" our son asks his mom.

"I don't know, maybe he really loves flies," Anne jokes, and this makes the boy laugh harder than I'd have expected. We all laugh and Anne gets up and turns on the light, carefully stepping around the room listening and looking for where the fly might land. I wipe my tears and sit up, looking for the fly too.

"There!" the boy shouts and points to the mirror, where half a dozen flies are squashed from earlier in the day. My wife is an excellent fly hunter. You have to be still then swift—without hesitation. She gets the thing and it doesn't squish but gets knocked against the glass then falls to the ground. She steps on it and I see the boy in my periphery look to me for a reaction to the death of the fly.

"It's okay Dada," he says. "Flies don't live long anyway."

I smile at him in a way that tells him I'm not sad about the fly. It goes silent after that. Something about not living long anyway. Something about it being okay to die because of a shorter life makes me and his mom remember.

I look up on the internet how to rob a bank without a gun. I watch a YouTube clip about a guy who robbed twenty banks by just writing a note, and learn that bank policy requires that they give over the money, be compliant, no questions asked even if no gun is present. I write several drafts of the kind of note I might write. *This is a bank robbery. Put ten thousand dollars in the bag and no one gets hurt*. I analyze the note. Wonder at its faults. I want it to be plain and clear what is happening and how much money I need. But this: no one gets hurt. There's something beautiful about the idea of no one getting hurt. Also delusional. I want to strike that part of the robbery note and save it for a future poem called "No One Gets Hurt."

This is a ~~bank~~ robbery. Put ten thousand ~~dollars~~ in the bag ~~and no one gets hurt~~ or else. I can't help but question this: or else. A threat as vague as it is trite. And this else, else isn't specific enough, else can be so much else. Do I need to declare this a robbery? I research more about bank policies, about gunless robberies. There is a strict adherence to nonviolence being the most important possible outcome even if no gun is present. Sometimes customers don't even know what is happening while a robbery is happening. Bank policy and training ensures there is no scene or risk taking. I need brevity and clarity.

~~This is a bank robbery.~~ I'll shoot if you don't ~~put~~ give me ten thousand ~~dollars in the bag and no one gets hurt or else~~. I read

199

the finalized note out loud: *I'll shoot if you don't give me ten thousand*. It's terrible.

I t's the night before I'm going to attempt the robbery. We're all eating dinner together. Someone's put on old-sounding country or bluegrass. The way everyone is smiling at first makes me suspicious, like they're trying to make me feel better. We're having homemade Chinese food. Anne's dad is Chinese—grew up in Hong Kong.

The kids are all laughing at something on YouTube. Anne's parents are in the kitchen. She catches my eye and smiles at me in a way that we sometimes smile at each other to say I love you without having to say it. We clink our glasses of rosé. When she gets up to go help in the kitchen, I wonder about whether maybe I was making it up all along, that they didn't want to talk to me, or that they think I'm too fragile. Maybe it's just that we're new to living together in the same space. They've let us stay here in their home, they cook and clean for us. The feeling doesn't last. Clarity never does. I go back to thinking about the money. What it could mean. I never consider jail time, or getting caught. My plan is to say it was for a book of poems I'm working on, I'll tell them I'm researching. I've even written some poems to show as proof alongside my notes for the robbery. The book will be about stealing, and greed, and hunger for gold, about how this whole country is based on theft of land, and how much that all has to do with this region, this gold country.

I can't sleep again. Alex and Anne fell asleep watching a movie out in the living room. My eyes are closed. I stare at the white light. Figures and shapes start to appear inside it, and I wonder if this is me falling asleep, or getting a deeper understanding of the hole's insides. Had I torn something open in me? Stared at a strange star too long, while I was wherever you go that memory can't come back from, in the hospital, after losing all that blood. I clench my eyes tighter and what's inside the hole is the hospital room. It's Alex and Anne playing in the chair next to my hospital bed. They're playing a game where he hides something and she pretends not to know where it could possibly be. It's the game where he tells her it's magic with a mischievous smile like we both know it's not but let's pretend you don't know. The rest of the family comes into the room. Everyone we're living with now. Everyone I thought forgot about me. I feel stupid, and selfish. I try to focus harder on the hole, see the scene, but just as I do, it all goes away and the hole is just white again.

My wife comes in carrying our son. He's asleep. She lays him down between us.

"I was gonna do something really stupid," I say. And there's a pause. She's wondering if I mean something else. Do something really stupid *again*. She's wondering if she even wants to have this conversation. What am I asking her to carry?

"It's not that," I say.

"What then?"

"It's nothing."

"What?"

"I'm not going," I say.

"You're not going to what."

"I said I'm not *going*," I say.

"To do something stupid."

"I mean, I'm sure I will."

"But not *that*, again."

"No."

"Good," she says. "We need you here."

"What are we gonna do?" I say.

"Things'll change. They always do," she says.

"Not all change is good."

"Well when it seems it can't get worse the odds are better."

"True."

"Let's get some sleep."

"D'you ever see the image of the sun when you close your eyes even if you didn't look at the sun?"

"What are you talking about? You mean like the floaty things you see when you close your eyes too tight or jam your fists into your eyes?"

"No, this doesn't float, it stays right in the middle."

"In the middle."

"Yes."

"Okay, well, you can go up to the Indian Clinic if you're worried about it."

"I'm not worried."

"Well maybe you should be."

"Thanks."

"I'm kidding."

"I was gonna rob the bank."

"What?"

"With a note."

"You're tired," Anne says.

"I couldn't get it right. Everything I wrote down was awful," I say.

"You've been writing again?"

"I guess I have."

High Windows

GEOFF DYER

When Philip Larkin saw "a couple of kids, etc. etc.," he knew this was the "paradise everyone old has dreamed of all their lives." He was thinking of sex—Larkin was always thinking about sex ("wanking at ten past three")—but if he'd been living in California and writing fifty years later he'd have been thinking not just about Tinder but marijuana. Has there ever been a better time to smoke pot? It's so great, you don't even have to *smoke* it. That's what stopped me infiltrating the cool crowd at Oxford in the 1970s: having to smoke those revolting, tobacco-stuffed, English joints over which a tiny lump of hash had been ritually crumbled. I tried a couple of times but always felt nauseous because of the tobacco, because I'd never smoked a cigarette. It was only after college when I discovered pipes and bongs that I managed to get stoned, but while these useful accessories did enable me to achieve that mythical grail—at once all-pervasive and oddly elusive—the taste was revolting and my throat was left feeling like a scalded cat's, like a cat with a sore throat. But yeah, I got the hang of it and smoking pot became a joy, enhancing every aspect of my life, including work. There were plenty of occasions when I thought I couldn't write something and then, while stoned, an idea wafted into my head. Every experience could be enhanced by being stoned except the ones that were diminished by it: listening to music (almost a hundred percent success rate), sometimes reading (poetry mainly), having sex (if one could remain focused), eating certain foods (as long as they had no potential to become revolting), walking in nature, visiting art galleries, sacred sites, or war memorials. Even getting stoned could be enhanced—by getting more stoned. I always got stoned at parties, it made me wittier, only rarely made me think that I might be thinking that I was wittier than I thought I was, thereby opening the door to an infinite feedback loop of self-inquisition. I could even handle taking the night-bus home after parties, the slur of lights through the window-drizzle, the perpetual lurk of London yobbery.

And then, as skunk came first to dominate and then entirely monopolize the market, I lost the appetite for it. I liked skunk for a while, for the totality of immersion, the *Gesamtkunstwerk* effect, but then it became a conduit to paranoia, dread, and what seemed like a premonition of traumatic head injury—though even this had a positive side as, in the nick of time, I prized a story called "Skunk" out of the rubble of skunk-paranoia and skunk-dread.

At the age of fifty-five, I moved to Los Angeles where I looked forward to getting back on the horse and resuming my life as a pot smoker. As a gesture of commitment I invested in a state-of-the-art vaporizer, glamorous and silver-sleek, looking and packaged as if it were designed by a hipster offshoot of Apple. And there was no need to buy pot from dealers—something else I'd come to dislike—as one could register for a medical card. This process was frankly farcical but, having told the "doctor" that one was having trouble getting to sleep or staying awake or that one's slippers were the wrong size, it was pleasant to take one's card to a dispensary and be advised by a consultant who was often not the best advert for marijuana use, in order to have a properly curated high even if the high ended up being one that one didn't actually care for. Things got even more convenient a few years later as the need to visit a medical dispensary was itself dispensed with. A branch of MedMen opened up on nearby Lincoln Boulevard in Venice. Then another branch opened even nearer by on Abbott Kinney. That's when Larkin's line about paradise really hit home. I passed this always-busy store almost daily, on the way to do or buy something else, even though Abbott Kinney is full of stores no one in their right mind would ever buy anything from and every time I walked up Abbot Kinney all I ever did was lament the passing of Axe, a restaurant I'd first eaten in years before I moved here, remarking to my companion at the time that this was the best mashed potato I'd ever eaten, though this may have been influenced by the fact that we'd got incredibly stoned somewhere miles away and the drive to Venice had been so nerve-shredding that I was, at some level, relieved to be alive and able to eat anything, let alone this utterly sensational mashed potato. Walking past MedMen the first few times I was surprised that they had chosen big ugly red lettering for the storefront design. I'm guessing it was to get as far away as possible from all of the associations of traditional pot use even though pot culture has generated an aesthetic that extends well beyond *The Fabulous Furry Freak Brothers* and Bob Marley T-shirts. Although the MedMen sign (red) connotes anything *but* marijuana (green), once inside you can describe exactly the kind of marijuana experience you want, which, in my case, is always the same: clarity above all else, but not *just* clarity.

"Clarity accompanied by laughter," I clarified the first time I stepped inside this new frontier of narco-retail. "Free-flow of ideas. All-round enhancement of the senses. Ability to inhabit even the most demanding passages of Beethoven's late quartets.

Laughter. No tiredness or dopey feeling, no heaviness and no next-day fogginess either. That, young man, is the kind of high I am in the market for." And the respectable-looking young man I said this to claimed he could make it happen.

"Buddy, we'll get you rocking out to the *Grosse Fugue*," he said. MedMen has exactly the products to do this and anything else one might wish, the multitudinous strains with their fun names all broken down and itemized either as sativas or indicas. And so I would get whatever was recommended but always, eventually, whatever had been chosen ended up making me heavy-headed and the longed-for clarity would give way to unwanted fogginess. The experience was made-to-measure but it never quite fit. Even if a bespoke suit fits perfectly that doesn't mean the person stuck inside it feels comfortable. I gravitated toward the sativas but they made me anxious, while the indicas made me sluggish and the hybrids made me anxiously sluggish or sluggishly anxious. Either way it was never quite right. Despite all the subtle varieties of high promised by the impressive roster of pots on offer there was always one consistent effect, namely that after a while they all made me wish I was un-stoned, and so the intervals between getting stoned grew lengthier and the conditions in which I could attempt breaking this marijuana drought became more stringent. It was important that there had to be no social interaction whatsoever. If I was going to a concert, if I had collected my ticket and knew exactly where I was sitting—had, ideally, already rehearsed the route from ticket booth to seat before stepping outside again—then I could quickly have a couple of hits on my sleek vaporizer before taking my seat and immersing myself in Beethoven's A minor String Quartet (op. 132) at the Broad Stage in Santa Monica or sink into a performance by the Necks at the Blue Whale or the evening of jazz-metal by Burning Ghosts all the way across town at Zebulon (where there *were* no seats). These successes aside, it was only fifty-fifty whether gig-going was enhanced or diminished by getting stoned. Sometimes I could lock into the music for a while (Gillian Welch at the Orpheum) before drifting off (Stars of the Lid at the Regent) and mainly what I would drift into was thinking about whether I would rather not have been stoned, whether the music had merited getting stoned or, in the case of Zubin Mehta conducting Brahms' Fourth with the L.A. Phil—too frail to stand, he basically just waved his wand from a chair—if we are being utterly frank, merited coming to at all. The standing ovation at the end was a sort of get-well-soon expression of collective goodwill, designed to get the old boy back on his feet—or at least off the stage so we could get in our cars and listen to Brahms at home.

In tandem with my increasing reluctance to get stoned or, more exactly, my relief when I'd thought about getting stoned but had opted not to, two potentially contradictory tendencies made themselves felt. First, with evidence of the Green Rush all around, a rapidly escalating sense of regret that I'd not got a financial stake in the booming business of legal marijuana. Second, a gradually escalating hostility to marijuana culture generally. I came to dislike the smell wafting everywhere in Venice, wafting from the boardwalk to Abbot Kinney, wafting from the ocean to the inland empire, possibly as far as Oklahoma, like some THC iteration of the Dust Bowl. There's no getting away from it. Everywhere reeks of marijuana, marijuana that is far too strong and rots people's brains. It's far too strong and it's difficult to resist the conclusion that smoking this mind-rotting pot is rotting people's brains, making the mentally unhinged even more unhinged and further deranging the already deranged. It's not just that it's far too strong. Increased strength might be taken to mean that less is needed to create the desired effect but even a small amount creates a fundamentally different effect,

209

an effect that is the opposite of desirable. Changes in degree become changes in kind.

Which brings me, kind of, to changing lanes. One of the reasons I always think twice—*twice*? More like fifty times!—before getting stoned, before deciding not to, is the driving. It's not just that being stoned impairs my ability to drive in L.A. Right from the start just being in L.A. was enough to impair my ability to drive. I found driving here nerve-shredding anyway but being stoned also made *being* driven nerve-shredding, especially since so many other people were driving while stoned, driving while their ability to drive was impaired, making it more and more dangerous and more and more nerve-shredding, so that I'd always be calling out "Careful!" or "Watch out!" to my driver (my wife) who claimed that these constant and unprovoked exclamations of alarm actually made us more accident prone, so I'd force myself to remain silent as we approached—as we did with astonishing regularity—the latest flashing-light apocalypse of a crash-site on the I-10, prompting me to think back to our London life, to how relaxing and safe it was to get the tube from Ladbroke Grove to Baker Street and then walk down to Wigmore Hall to hear the world's premier quartets and soloists, and it seemed incredible that, in all the years we'd lived in London, we'd gone there precisely once, to what turned out to be such a disappointing recital of something by someone that all I could think about was the crippling lack of legroom.

But it's not so much fear that's the issue; it's a propensity for confusion or, more precisely, what I fear is the confusion induced by getting stoned. I used to have an excellent sense of direction, I used to *pride myself* on my superb sense of direction, but marijuana has shredded wherever it is in the brain that deals with navigation, geography, and orientation and I often struggle, these days, to get my bearings. I blame it on marijuana because that is preferable to the alternative, which is that I am starting to show signs of Alzheimer's and it's possible that this underlying fear—of Alzheimer's—is contributing to the lurking readiness to become anxious and unhappy if stoned. I'd need an MRI to confirm these hunches but one thing is for sure: the main part of my brain that marijuana has damaged is the part that responds favorably to marijuana—and there's a reassuring side to this too.

There are people who still like to get high in their sixties but in many ways it's a young person's game, getting high. I take solace from the fact that a lot of people my age share my deepening aversion to marijuana, a process that is the opposite of the addict's agonized withdrawal from hard drugs. I drink less than I used to even though I still *love* beer and wine, it's just that drinking makes me feel so bad afterward that I'm always keeping an eye on how much I'm putting away. Pot is not like that at all. It's not that we still enjoy it but reluctantly accept it's having a harmful effect. What's involved is a gradual acceptance that we no longer like something we've had a hard time accepting we no longer like. Unlike tennis, for example. Oh tennis, I still love tennis and everything about it. I love cycling past the moronic stores selling vapes and bongs on the boardwalk, through the miasma of pot wafting from the stoned skatepark, down the stoned cycle-path alongside the stoned ocean, all the way to the lovely courts themselves, near the basketball court where so much pot is being smoked that we always try to avoid court 5. Court 5 is so close to the basketball court that it's like playing tennis in a giant open-air bong, but this unwanted adjacency of tennis and marijuana reminds me of the glory days back in London when, if I got stoned at a party in the evening after playing tennis in the afternoon, I'd end up replaying certain points in my head and if a friend I'd played tennis with earlier that day was also at the party we'd both relive certain crucial passages of play and it was glorious, obviously, like being a pro player back in the days when they'd all go out partying together at Studio 54 after matches. Anyway, that's all in the past now. I still love tennis but I just don't like marijuana anymore and at some level I can scarcely even remember what it was like when being stoned lit up the world, releasing the latent glow of things. It's difficult not to feel, like Wordsworth, that there has "passed away a glory from the earth," which is inevitable in Cumbria but which is not at all the way to feel in California, the land of glory, one of the last places on earth where the glory fades each day, where everything glows, where the blue sky that shows nothing—though whether sky this blue should be counted as nothing remains a moot point—is nowhere and is endless.

MAGGIE MILLNER's poetry
has appeared in the *New
Yorker, Ploughshares, Gulf
Coast, ZYZZYVA,* and elsewhere. She lives in Brooklyn, New York, where she
teaches in the Writing Program at Rutgers University
and is at work on her first
book of poems.

Monterey

MAGGIE MILLNER

Evenings, I would sit
on a moldy, high-back couch
and watch the light outside go mauve, then die.

The neighbor's house was strung with discs of mirror
that turned in wind, blinding us
when the sun was right, or throwing phantom orbs
the cat would hunt
across the wall.

Those years were shapeless, unperfumed,
a tintering of salt and beaten air. Winter looked identical
to summer, which gave the dim impression
of a stilled planet, of a planet
to which the worst had already happened.

It was also a time when stars were back in fashion,
not knowing their names or the physics of them,
but using them for augury or just diagnosing
personality traits. Many turned to stars because they felt jilted

or unpersuaded by Western science, which had by that point
made most other knowledge irretrievable,
but some just said, "It's fun, it's only fun.
You don't have to believe in anything."
I couldn't see the fun.

Still, I startled when the chart said I was flirty
and contrarian, obsessed by hair. Just that week
I had received a regrettable haircut, which energized in me

a passion for hats. A helmet was a sort of hat,
and I wore one every weekend when I bicycled
to the abandoned military base, where bits of missile
nosed out of the beach and ice plant
splashed the dunes with rust and green, the colors

of my fear. Ahead of me between the bluffs
would tromp the man I loved, a stalk
among sargassum, tacking west. Or else behind me
if I pedaled fast, or next to me if talk or some dispute
were underway. Our fights, I thought, were very rare,
though he found them very frequent,
it was a question of thresholds.

Sometimes we would fight about how much we fought,
facing each other in the little apartment
we shared by the harbor, frothing up
the atmosphere between us with our hands.
During PMS, I'd say outlandish things:

I feel like a spayed cat, I feel like a woman
trapped in a painting that depicts her
as a virgin, but she's not a virgin, she's not even
a woman all the time.

It was the West, its lassitude and gorse.
It was the soft land ending as soon as I got used to it,
and the light, exhausted, spinning itself always

into gold. This was just before the era
of overt misinformation, or perhaps that era's undetected
dawn, and for a while I suspected
that the world was an invention of my mind.

This made it difficult to advance at all
across the world, or make the bed, or taste
the fragile cod
the wharfmen hawked.

Looking out over the cliffs,
the man would say the names of fish and succulents,
the processes by which the beach
had cleft itself so steeply from the crag.
A tern flew by.
The sun came through a slotted spoon of cloud.

I've come to think that land was like my interest
in my life: hidden, for a time,
beneath a sheet of sand and dread.

Then, gradually, I began to see it.
I began to actually see it.

SHOBHA RAO is the author
of the short story collection
An Unrestored Woman
and the novel *Girls Burn
Brighter.* She moved to the
United States from India at
the age of seven and cur-
rently lives in San Francisco.

THE O RING

SHOBHA RAO

The television cart had a squeaky wheel. Lava heard it—squeak, squeak, squeak, squeak, crying out on every revolution like a drunken rat—as Mr. Jolliett rolled the cart down the hallway and into the classroom. All the kids waited. Evan sat behind her but she knew he too must be tense, excited; even the cool kids blinked into the morning sun, looked with new wonder at the snow-covered Sierras. It was first period at Oakhurst High School, and the Challenger was scheduled to take off in twenty minutes. A teacher was going up. Every high school in the country would be watching, Mr. Jolliett had said. Lava didn't doubt him. A teacher! Who knew who could be next? At first there was only snow on the screen. Mr. Jolliett changed the channel. Adjusted the antennae. They saw the launchpad. The two rocket boosters, the red silo of the external tank, the orbiter. The class waited, the sun now blanketing the bald, low hills, the deer grass and fescue shining like wild fur. Thick white stripes began moving horizontally across the screen. Mr. Jolliett smacked the side of the television. It settled back into the image. The voice-over. And then the countdown began. Ten, nine, eight. The engines flared. The class held its breath. Seven, six, five. Lava looked at the glistening hull. Imagined the astronauts strapped into their seats, smiling. Four, three. She saw the motel. The way they would see it from space: a tiny dot, or more likely the mountains would be the dot, and the Pacific would have the depth of a spoon, still and blue, no, gray probably, and no bigger than a tongue. Two, one, and there was Evan's coat, the one that had brushed her arm this morning—their lockers were next to each other's—and that black coat, the thought of it cradling his body, was unbearable to Lava in the way the thought of outer space was unbearable: both so impenetrable, weightless; polished obsidian, the odor of musk.

And liftoff. *Liftoff*.

The class cheered, their eyes glued to the screen. Mr. Jolliett beamed. The sun now reached through the windows, slid along the floor, and scythed their feet at the ankles. Lava pivoted, snuck a look at Evan, but his eyes, along with every other pair of eyes, were on the screen. On the bone-white body. Rising and rising and rising.

L ava had moved to Oakhurst, California, the Gateway to Yosemite, at the age of five. Her parents, Raghava and Maithili, ran the only year-round motel in town, the Sequoia Inn. They arrived in winter, in January of 1976. Her father was a civil engineer, but he took over the twenty-room motel along Highway 41 after a college classmate, Gopal, had visited Raghava and Maithili at their home in Visakhapatnam, a maritime city on the Bay of Bengal, and regaled them with tales of all the opportunities in the States, specifically in the motel business. What's a motel, Raghava had asked. "Aré, can't you tell? It's just like a hotel, but better. America is full of them. You can't go a kilometer without running into half a dozen of them. Look at me. I started with one, five years ago, and now I have three. Three!" And then he'd laughed, a loud and robust and incongruous laugh—incongruous because it was such a plump laugh from such a thin man. That's what

Lava thought at the age of four (when Gopal first approached her parents), that his laugh was *plump*. And not quite right. Plump and not quite right like a watermelon laugh coming out of a string bean body.

When they arrived early the next year, Lava hardly knew any English, so on her first day of school she sat in a corner of the brightly colored room and looked at each of the letters of the alphabet. She was fluent in Telugu and knew some English, short sentences and a few phrases, but she was too bashful to speak them. One boy in her class came up to her and said, "You don't even know your ABCs, do you? My mom says I knew mine by the time I was two. You're slow, aren't you? I can tell you're slow." The teacher, when she called Lava's name, pronounced it *lava*, and she didn't have enough English to correct her. When she told Amma that night, she said, "Tell her it's pronounced luv-ah. Tell her it's 'love' with an A." Still, she was mostly confused those first few months. And not always with regards to language: when the only black boy in her class, whose name she didn't know, handed her a pink paper heart one fine morning, she didn't know what to do. He'd made it, she could tell, and his paper heart was joined by other pink and red paper hearts, given from boy to girl, but why? On the card was written:

From: Thadeus

To: Love with an A

Yet another mystery on a warm spring afternoon in late April when the entire class filed out of the school onto the lawn and stood in a circle around the head janitor, who was holding a sapling. "My name is Doug," the man said, almost shyly, "and this here is a beech tree." His thick, chapped hands held the beech, a fist around its swaying trunk, as Lava sometimes held her father's finger, and then he stood it upright, raised his shovel and began to dig. The children watched in awed silence. Why,

221

Lava wondered. The scent of earth drifted up from the widening hole. A worm wiggled out. Lava saw the sweat forming on the sides of Doug's face. So he was planting a tree. But why the fanfare? Once he lowered the sapling into the ground, all the children gathered closer. Each raised a handful of dirt and flung it into the hole. It was all so solemn. Like a funeral. The hole, the lowered beech, the springtime quiet. Even the birds seemed discomfited. It was only at the very end that the teacher clapped and sang out, "Happy Arbor Day, children."

So it was called Arbor Day.

When she told her parents about it that evening, her mother beamed and said, "You know I studied botany in college, don't you, Lava?"

"What's botany?"

"Trees," her father chimed in proudly. "Your mother studied trees. And grasses. And the most beautiful flowers." Lava thought of the color green, she thought of gummy sap. At this point, her father glanced at Amma and winked. He said, "She was sitting in one, you know. When I met her."

"A beech tree?"

"No, a tamarind tree."

Amma blushed. "Don't tell her all that, Raghu. She's too young."

Nanna laughed. He raised Lava onto his lap. "You remember a tamarind pod, don't you? Long, smooth like bark. Your amma was sleeping on one of the branches. Imagine! I saw her arm dangling down and I thought it was one of the tamarind pods! Her schoolbag had fallen to the ground. I was afraid someone might steal it, but I didn't know whether to climb up and wake her, or call out. I was afraid she would fall too."

"What did you do?"

Amma smiled.

222

"A pretty girl. Sleeping in a tree. What could I do? I sat down at the base of the tamarind tree and I waited. I waited and waited. It was almost sundown when your amma finally woke up. She looked down from her branch, saw me holding her schoolbag, and you know what she said?"

"What?"

"She said, 'What time is it?' I looked at my watch and said, 'Quarter to five.' And your amma's eyes widened, she jumped down, grabbed her schoolbag and ran off, yelling, 'I've missed my tea.'" Lava's father started to laugh. "That was when I fell in love with her. That's when I thought, I want to marry that girl."

Within the first year after they arrived, the Sequoia Inn started having financial troubles. First, the boiler broke down. Gopal Uncle helped. He gave Amma and Nanna the money to have it replaced. "Nothing doing," he laughed, when Nanna said he'd pay it back by month's end. "What's a little something between family?" He looked straight at Amma and smiled. By the end of the second year, the motel was losing most of its off-season customers to the Bridal Falls Inn down the street. They had recently opened after a renovation, with HBO *and* a free buffet breakfast included, and hardly anyone booked at the Sequoia after the end of the summer rush. Gopal Uncle stepped in again. "Look here," he said, "we can set up a payment plan. No interest." He waved away their gratitude as if it were a pesky fly. "Good people. Nothing harder to find. I know that Falls owner. A bastard. Bridal, ha! Rents to pimps, takes some of the cut. No morals. None." Her parents, in order to save money, began letting the rooms go. The bedspreads needed to be replaced—most of them, in both the smoking and the nonsmoking rooms, were pocked with cigarette burns. Amma said, "They're dark enough, no one will notice." Every night, one guest or another would call the front desk, complaining that their

SHOBHA RAO

television or their air-conditioner or their shower wasn't working right. They let Lina go too. She was a vestige of when Gopal Uncle ran the motel, and she would come in on the weekends and during the busy summer season to help them clean the rooms. Do laundry. She kept to herself, and one Sunday evening in November, Nanna caught her trying to pry open the cash register. She said it was all mucked up and she was only trying to clean it. The money was all there, but they let her go anyway.

By middle school, Lava had made two friends. There was Molly, who was short and serious and looked like a mushroom with her dark brown, bowl-cut hair. She had such bad asthma that she was often out of school. Pippa was her other friend. Pippa's dad was British, and she told Lava that he'd been born in India, and though she was nice enough, she once told her, after Lava asked what marmalade was, "It's *jam*. Don't you know that? Of course you don't. My dad says Indians eat with their hands. Do you? He says you can take the savage out of the jungle, but you can't take the jungle out of the savage." Pippa asked about her name. "It would've been cool if they'd actually named you lava. That would've been so rad." I guess, Lava said. "Think about it," Pippa said. "You'd be named for that stuff spewing out of volcanoes!"

"Magma."

"Right, magma. It can burn anything. It's like, it's like, the coolest thing ever! And it's right there. The whole time. Just sitting in the volcano, waiting for us to forget about it. And then, boom!" Her arms shot into the air and made a circle. Even Molly laughed.

The years tumbled by. Lava started doing her homework in the lobby, and one April afternoon she looked up into the quiet greening of the Sierras and the bright blue sky, with crows circling in the distance, and saw Gopal Uncle's white Mercedes pulling into the parking lot. "Amma," she called out, "Gopal Uncle is here." Amma came out of the back office where she'd been sorting the morning's credit card slips. She stood behind the front desk. Lava stared at her. She'd seen her only minutes ago, and yet this woman was unrecognizable. Her face had gone ashen, the gray-yellow of a ship lost at sea. Its hull is breached, Lava thought; she laid her pencil down.

They heard the car doors open and close.

Her parents had made the payments at first, and they had often been invited to Sunday dinner and Saturday lunches at Gopal Uncle's house. His wife, Rajini Auntie, had made all kinds of dishes Amma didn't make: pallau rice studded with peas and cumin and crisped onions, pakora with fresh chilies and fennel, and tiny cocktail samosas, so small you could pop the entire golden-brown triangle into your mouth. She'd once even roasted a whole head of cauliflower, helmeted with a thick, delicious mixture of turmeric and tandoori spices. But once Lava's parents started falling behind on the payments—missing a month here and there, sending partial payments—the invitations to lunch and dinner stopped. Gopal began showing up unannounced. Sometimes he'd bring his son, Ashwin. He went by Ash, and both he and Lava went to Oakhurst High School. Ash was older; a junior while Lava was a freshman. They lived twenty minutes outside of Oakhurst, in a four-bedroom house overlooking a pond and a thick grove of trees. "What kind are they," Lava had asked her mother, standing at their French doors. "Blue ash," she'd said. "Strong enough that they use it in tools."

"That's why they were named for me," Ash had laughed, not looking up from his Atari.

The lobby filled, bloated as soon as they walked in. Gopal Uncle looked at Lava, said something about her being a good girl for getting her homework done, and then he glanced around the lobby. He didn't look at Amma, not at first. In fact, he seemed to be taking his time, almost holding off, savoring the hum of the coffee machine in the corner and the drone of a distant television. The cool of the gold and diamond watch against his wrist.

"Go on," he said, turning to Ash. "Go upstairs with Lava. Help her with her homework."

"But Dad—"

"I said, go."

Lava gathered her notebook and pencil, and Ash plodded out of the lobby. Her mother said, "I can wake Raghu. It'll just be a minute. It's almost time for him to get up, anyway. Lava, go wake up Nanna."

It was then that Gopal Uncle finally looked at Amma. He smiled. "No, no need, Maithili. No need at all. Why disturb him? I just want to take a quick look at the books. You can help me with that, can't you? You know where they're kept I'm sure. I think I'll call you Mai. May I? You see how nice that sounds? May, Mai, My. What do they call that? What do they call that in English?"

"A homophone," Lava said.

"That's it. Such a smart girl. So pretty." He looked lovingly at her, as if she were his own daughter. "What more can you ask? Smart, pretty. She takes after you, Mai. I like that: Mai. Go on," he said to Lava. "Find Ashwin. Finish up your homework."

Ash was in the grassy area just past the last room, staring out at the road. A semitruck drove by. The grasses along the road bent their heads back and looked at the sky. When Ash saw her, he said, "Hey, you have any beer? Cigarettes?" Lava shook her head. "Let's go up to your room," he said.

"My dad's sleeping," she said. "He's midnight to eight."

He seemed not to hear. "Let's go."

The stairs to the apartment were in the back of the motel, and Lava followed him up. He pushed the door open and stood in her living room, still wearing his shoes. She could hear Nanna faintly snoring. The refrigerator started up. She got a glass of water and looked out of the little window above the sink. "You coming?" Ash called. He'd found her bedroom, which was the open door. He flopped onto her bed as if it were his own. And in his reclined body, in its carelessness, Lava saw again Gopal Uncle's gold and diamond watch, his white Mercedes. "You don't even have a TV in here?" No, she said, without apology. He pulled her pink stuffed bear from under his head and threw it into the air. He caught it. Then he threw it twice more. "Do you know Evan Daniels?" she said.

"Say what?"

"Evan. He's on the basketball team."

His expression brightened. "You like him, don't you?" Then he looked at her, his eyes narrowed, mischievous. "Hey, Lava, take off your top."

"*What?*"

"Your top. Just for a second."

"No way. Why would I? That's stupid."

"Come on. It's not like I like you or anything. I won't touch 'em."

Lava turned as if to leave the room.

"Come on. You owe me."

"Huh?"

"You broke that lock, remember? When you guys were over."

She'd forgotten about the lock. It had been months ago, one of the last times she and her parents had been invited to dinner. "Only because the lock stuck. How was I supposed to know it would snap like that?"

"Yeah," Ash said, putting the stuffed bear back behind his head, "well, my dad had to spend two hundred dollars to get it fixed. He was pissed. Remember? I covered for you. Said it was a faulty lock."

"It was."

He shrugged. "Anyway, take it off. I can tell him, you know. I can tell him the truth."

"Go ahead," she said, feeling defiant, feeling Nanna in the room beside hers.

"You have two hundred dollars?"

Lava was silent.

"Come on. Just a peek. What's the big deal?"

Fine. She lifted her T-shirt without taking it off and then yanked it back down again. She wasn't wearing a bra.

"Fuck that," he howled, "I didn't see shit."

"Shut up!" Lava listened for her father's snoring. And then she lifted her T-shirt again and held it there. Ash's expression didn't change. "You ever notice how an Indian chick's nipples look like McDonald's hamburgers?"

Her mind went blank. Like a leaf or a stone. In her blankness she forgot to bring her shirt back down. That's what bothered her more than anything: that she'd let him look for a second or two beyond what he had demanded. It seemed a greater error than all the others. She would remember it for the rest of her life, that her shirt had stayed, she had stayed; she had stayed her shirt. Then he said, "Yeah, I know Evan. He's a prick."

Did the Sequoia's financial problems worsen? It was hard to say. Things happened: An ambulance was called once because a little boy had a seizure; late one night, one man pulled a gun on another and the police showed up. In the spring, there was a drug bust in one of the rooms but they didn't find anything. Mostly, the days went by and nothing happened. Amma and Nanna barely spoke anymore but Nanna was up all hours, during his shift and after, going through their accounts and scheming ways to increase revenue. Maybe we can put in a pool, he said, and Amma retorted, And the money for that? "You need money to make money—that's how the world works, Lava," he said with a sigh. For a few weeks he was giddy, thinking the loan application he'd put in with the farmers' credit union would be approved, but in the middle of summer, they told him it was denied. The collateral was insufficient, the letter said. "Insufficient? Insufficient," he railed. "As if their measly loan is worth more than my Sequoia." That was the thing. The new thing that Lava noticed. Instead of calling it the Sequoia, or simply "the motel," as they always had, Nanna had taken to referring to it as *my* Sequoia. She couldn't understand it.

Gopal Uncle offered them another loan to tide them over until next summer's tourist rush. This time with interest. By now, Lava understood that he wasn't helping them out of the goodness of his heart. And that there had been a kind of payment all along. How did she know? It was the years. It was the afternoons. It was the parking lot, the weight of it; Lava bore it like a cloak around her neck. "What's the difference between a hotel and a motel," she'd asked Gopal Uncle once. "Ah," his face had lighted up, fuller now, not at all drawn, shrewd and sharp and laughing, "there's only one, Lava," he'd said. "In a motel, cars can park in front of the rooms. Directly in front. In a hotel, no. Not possible."

Was that all, Lava remembered thinking. Was that it? Did such a small thing really need a whole new word?

She'd come home from school and see the white Mercedes regularly now. To her, it seemed a coffin, unto itself and whole and nothing but itself. It was always during Amma's shift, always while her father was sleeping before his own. She could no longer even look at Amma. She obviously couldn't tell Pippa or Molly. And her only thought, the thought that consumed her, an obsessive protectiveness: keep Nanna from finding out. Nanna. She saw him sitting at the base of the tamarind tree. She saw him in a citadel, sleeping, and she was his guard, defending his silence, his innocence, his sleep. It was his Sequoia, after all, no one else's, and she understood, in the way she understood the human heart—it took so little, almost nothing at all, to pierce it (she averted her eyes every time they passed a McDonald's)—that Nanna could bear it, had enough strength to bear it, *only* because he didn't know.

Amma, she hated; she'd betrayed them both. But Nanna. Nanna would sleep. She'd make sure of it.

Lava began cleaning rooms on the weekends. She was fifteen, and no one asked her to do it, but one Sunday, as she walked past the western wing of the Sequoia, she saw the cleaning cart outside room 4. She knew Amma must be inside and avoided her. She also knew there was another cleaning cart in the storage room, next to the back stairwell. The one Lina had used. She wiped off the cobwebs, loaded it with cleaning supplies, and started on the eastern wing. There were people staying in rooms 17 and 19, but 11 and 12 and 15 were dirty. She started with the bed in room 11. She pretended Evan had slept in it, his blue eyes, moist with weariness, closed against the moonlight. The bathroom was piled with wet towels. He'd used every single one, strewn across the floor, hung from the shower rod; she even found one in the trash. The drain was blocked with a mound of hair, not the same shade of brown as Evan's, but close. She wouldn't look at the toilet. Not yet. The sink had dried phlegm stuck to the side. She could smell him, even though he'd left hours ago. He'd left the heat on too high. An empty whiskey bottle. A piece of paper, crumpled, with a phone number on it. She nearly called it. He'd used all of the cheap lotion and most of the shampoo. The bar of soap had a strand of hair stuck to it. Wadded up tissues. The toilet wasn't so bad. She put her Walkman over her ears and tried not to look. She didn't care. It was Evan. His hair and his stink and his eyes like lamps.

Then the next room. And the next. Every room was his.

After she cleaned and did her homework, the rest of her weekends Lava spent wandering. Outside of Oakhurst, into the hills, along the dirt roads. There was a stand of trees she'd never seen, crowded around a tumbling creek. Moss on the round stones, the brightest green, and what were those, wiggling there? Small fishes, minnows maybe, and Lava nearly dived in after them, though the water was only ankle-deep. But cold. Colder than air. Her toes grew numb and she wished it higher, the numbness, the filmy embrace. The canopy of leaves shook above her and she shook with it, feeling the edges of her body, its perimeter, become no perimeter at all. Where once there was gold, there was now a girl. She came across a dead possum on the road. And countless pulped jackrabbits. Field mice by the dozens. Along the ditches, she sometimes saw birds bathing, avoiding the discarded plastic bags and cans and tires and clothing choking the thin, polluted waterway. In spite of the filth, the birds clacked joyously, preening and sunning themselves as if on a riviera.

She roamed the county roads, and she roamed the ones in town too. She snuck into Logan's and no one asked her age. She didn't order anything; she watched some men play pool and studied the jukebox and sat on a barstool and then left. A man asked her into an alley once, when she was standing on a corner waiting for the light to change. It was broad daylight and she knew what he wanted. So what? He was old, but he wasn't half ugly. He kissed her against the brick wall of the bank and all she knew was the taste of tobacco and the beer on his breath and the squishy towel damp of his lips. It felt like she was cleaning one of the smoking rooms. But then he put his hand under her shirt and she felt his hardness against her stomach. She thought of plums, the moss on round stones. She said, "I'll scream," and he let her go with a look of longing and disgust. Another time, a Ford Pinto pulled up and a man asked if she wanted to go see the drive-in movie theater. Nothing's playing, he said, just to see. There isn't one near here, she said. Yes, there is. Get in, I'll show you. So Lava got in and he drove on 41 but then he turned off the highway. He was not much older than her, and he didn't look like anyone she'd ever seen before. He was brown too, with a low forehead and black eyes and black hair. His knuckles were scabbed over. He said his name was Jessie and he was in the Paiute tribe, and she thought he was lying, but maybe he wasn't because there, after five miles or so, was an abandoned drive-in. It had a wide dirt lot for cars and then the towering screen on which probably nothing had played in years. Jessie pulled the car up to face the screen and then he turned the engine off. They sat in silence, staring at the enormous white rectangle. Birds lined the top and squawked at each other and then they all flew away. Jessie said, "If we had a baby, it would be half-Indian and half-Indian." Lava laughed and laughed. Eventually he said he had to get back on the road. Where to, she asked. Oregon, he said, wanna come? He was joking, but she wished that he wasn't. She wanted him to touch her, but he didn't do that either.

After the Challenger disaster, school let out early. There seemed nothing else to do. The school buses pulled up but no one got on them. The kids with cars lingered in the parking lot. Mr. Jolliett's class had sat in stunned silence. Everybody staring at the TV, at the thick plume of white smoke splitting into two plumes. Barbarian clouds, spinning senselessly, away and away and then toward Earth. And the tiny speck of debris. Was that it? Was that bit what held the astronauts? One of the girls began to cry, and Mr. Jolliett blinked and blinked and then he raised himself up. Soon afterward, the PA system announced that school was dismissed for the rest of the day.

Lava, standing at the top of the steps by the main entrance, saw her classmates wander around the parking lot, lost as dogs. Without scent, without even the slightest wind to carry hope, the fragrance of distant feasts. She was transfixed, imagining, with shame, the plop plop plop of the pieces as they fell into the Atlantic, mutilated and mad and white-tailed. She turned at the sound of the main door. Evan. He had his gym bag, and his hair was tousled, as if he'd changed in a hurry. Maybe he had; he'd been wearing jeans but now he was wearing red baggy basketball shorts and a loose T-shirt, and his body in the morning sun seemed to her like granite statuary, stumbled across in a corner of a neglected garden, chiseled, unaware, immaculate, and self-possessed even when forgotten, even when draped in ivy and lichen.

He saw her looking. He said, Hey. Lava froze. She thought she should say something about the space shuttle, something eloquent, something that would link, like an embrace, their sorrows. "Sad, isn't it?"

"What?"

"On TV. The Challenger."

"Oh. Yeah." He eyed the parking lot, clearly waiting for someone. "You guys watched it too?"

Lava looked at him. Such a little thing. Almost nothing could pierce the heart. "No, we're—I'm in Mr. Jolliett's class too."

He waved to someone. "Cool." He bounded down the steps. Lava watched him. The school buses pulled away, and then the parking lot emptied. It was nearly noon, and Lava began the two-mile walk home. When she neared the motel, she saw the white Mercedes. Her chest clenched, hard as a fist. She approached slowly. She walked past the lobby, expecting it to be empty, but there was Nanna at the front desk. What was he doing up? She raced inside. "Nanna," she said.

He looked up. His face, too, tightened in some way. "What are you doing home? Why aren't you at school?"

"What are *you* doing? This isn't your shift."

He shrugged. "Amma needed help," he said. But there was the white Mercedes. The solidity of it, the assault of it. When she turned to him, he averted his gaze and bent abruptly over the filing cabinet, as if fiddling with one of its drawers, and Lava went suddenly dizzy. She swayed, or maybe it was the Sequoia that swayed, and then she sank into the brown sofa in the lobby. She knew. She knew now. There was no need to protect him, there never had been. She closed her eyes. They warmed with rage, with helplessness. She no longer wanted to be love with an A, she wanted to be the other. The one that erupted, that destroyed everything in its path.

"Are you sick? Is that why you're home?"

"No," she said, her voice trembling, "the space shuttle."

Her father shook his head. "I heard," he said. "So sad." Lava nodded, though she could no longer separate the sad from the tragic from the disastrous from the lamentable from what was simply life. "It's always the same," he said. "Bridges, buildings, any structure, edifice. Something small destabilizes it, and then it's done. Nothing can save it. It's always the smallest thing. A detail. I bet that's what it'll be. The smallest thing."

Was it the next week? Or the week after?

Amma was in the kitchen. Lava had just come up from cleaning rooms. Amma said, without turning from the stove, "Thanks for doing that. Never even asked you to."

"It's alright. No big deal. I just put on my Walkman."

"What do you listen to?"

"Whatever." And then, after a moment, because there was no longer anything left to hide, "I think of a boy I used to like."

Her amma laughed. "So do I," she said.

Lava wanted to cry out. Instead she said, "What boy?"

And Amma, gathering in her voice all that was lost and lonely in the world, said, "Don't you know? The boy under the tamarind tree."

NATALIE DIAZ was born in the Fort Mojave Indian Village in Needles, California. She is the author of *When My Brother Was an Aztec* (Copper Canyon Press, 2012). Diaz is the recipient of a Lannan Literary Fellowship, a Princeton Hodder Fellowship, a PEN/Civitella Ranieri Foundation Fellowship, and in 2018 was named a MacArthur Fellow. She is enrolled in the Gila River Indian Tribe and teaches at Arizona State University in Tempe, Arizona, where she is the Maxine and Jonathan Marshall Chair in Modern and Contemporary Poetry. *Postcolonial Love Poem*, her new collection, will be published in March 2020.

Bodies Built for Game

NATALIE DIAZ

Before each of my basketball games, from rec league to high school, my mother told me, Knock 'em dead, as I walked out the door. Even after I moved across the country to Virginia to play Division I basketball, she ended our pregame phone calls with the same phrase, Knock 'em dead. She never said, Good luck.

I didn't learn how to read poetry, how to let poetry into my body in a physical and emotional way, until my basketball career was over. It makes sense if I consider how much basketball needed and took of my body—it is a sensual and intuitive game, a relationship of movement and space, momentum, timing, a defiance of the body's socialized limitations, a corporeal inquiry that shapes the imagination. The game itself exists within and also creates the conditions of futurity. Yes, basketball is a game of the future! On defense, you must think two steps ahead of the ball or your opponent, toward what has not yet happened but could. On offense, you must vision every opportunity that might occur and then risk entering into that unknown, taking what the game offers you, or demanding it give you something else, conjuring a pass or a move that didn't exist until you arrived there in its perfect moment, prepared and lucky.

237

Basketball also gave me my future, leaped me from the desert rez I was born on and into my life. At this point in my life, I have played basketball longer than I have not—I played basketball longer than I have done anything else. In the game was where I was always the most possible. In the game was where I had the most future. It was where I learned to imagine what I might be capable of.

The intense physicality of both basketball and poetry have at times made me ecstatic. A good shot is called "touch." On a rebound, you locate your player and "put a body on her." A poem too can make you realize your body in a way that doesn't require you to break it or to perform the stories and fears U.S.-America has always projected onto women and men of color—though every page is white, the language of poetry itself is made of dark figures, inked bodies of sound, building, aching, reaching out, all up and down the page.

Though I was early to basketball and late to writing, the two have a long relationship, an entanglement that is my lucky inheritance.

Poet and rapper Tupac Shakur starred in the movies *Above the Rim* and *Poetic Justice*.

In his own gesture of justice—justice for his body and that of other straight, white men—poet Charles Bukowski wrote a letter to the editor of the *New York Quarterly*, complaining, "In our age, the only safe target for the writer is the white heterosexual male." He continued, "Nobody protests. Not even the white heterosexual male. He's used to it. Also, things like 'White men can't dance,' 'White men can't jump,' 'White men have no sense of rhythm,' etc." He wrote that letter in 1992, the same year the movie *White Men Can't Jump* premiered. Prior to the movie and Bukowski's self-proclaimed victimhood, we always knew the statement was true—white men have never needed to dance, or jump, or have rhythm to be afforded the privileges they offer to and accept from other white men.

In the basketball flick *Finding Forrester*, Sean Connery plays Forrester, a writer who mentors or saviors a young black basketball-star-become-writer.

Kareem Abdul-Jabbar spent a season as the assistant varsity basketball coach of the Alchesay Falcons. Alchesay High School is located in Whiteriver, Arizona, on White Mountain Apache or N'dee land, N'dee meaning "the people." What originally brought Abdul-Jabbar to N'dee territory was research for a book about a black cavalry regiment nicknamed Buffalo Soldiers who had been stationed at Fort Apache. He later wrote a book about his experience, *A Season on the Reservation: My Sojourn with the White Mountain Apache*.

Poet Jim Carroll was a high school basketball star at Trinity in Manhattan. His experiences there, including his addiction to heroin, led to his writing *The Basketball Diaries*, a book later adapted to film.

Poet Marianne Moore taught the phenomenal multisport Native and Olympic athlete Jim Thorpe at the Carlisle Indian School, officially the United States Indian Industrial School. Thorpe played basketball, as well as football, baseball, and track and field. Moore however preferred baseball and was known as an avid fan.

John Edgar Wideman, author of the memoir *Hoop Roots*, was All-Ivy League forward at the University of Pennsylvania. I played against his daughter, Jamila Wideman, in the 1997 Women's NCAA Final Four. She was Stanford's point guard, and I was a 1-2 guard for Old Dominion—we beat them in the semifinals. Though I didn't meet John Edgar Wideman in person until twenty years after that game when we judged a writing prize together, he had been in the stands watching his daughter, which meant, in a way, he and I had met before. Before either of those meetings, I met Wideman in a different way and with more at stake—I met him in the many pages he wrote about brothers, about his brother, and in my mind about my own brother. The way he held his brother on the page, a brother some might call "bad," gave me a place to love and hold my own bad brother. It was a tough lesson—I can sometimes love my brother best on the page, in a poem, better than I can manage to love him in real life.

Spike Lee knows basketball is holy—he created Jesus Shuttlesworth in the movie *He Got Game*, played by real-life baller Ray Allen. It was Jesus Shuttlesworth who said, "Basketball is like poetry in motion, cross the guy to the left, take him back to the right, he's fallin' back, then just 'J' right in his face. Then you look at him and say, 'What?'"

My mother had eleven kids. If we'd all survived, we'd have been a soccer team. We are nine now, enough for a baseball team. But in the Southwest fervor of pavement and blacktop, where temperatures can exceed one hundred and twenty degrees, basketball is currency, is credibility, especially on the rez.

Writer and philosopher Albert Camus, no stranger to sports, was on a soccer team—goalkeeper for the Racing Universitaire Algerios (RUA) juniors. He said, "After many years during which I saw many things, what I know most surely about morality and the duty of man I owe to sport and learned it in the RUA."

I lived years on a court, in the driveway, at a park, in a gym, on a bus or plane to or from a game, drilling, sprinting, stretching, watching film, attached to an electrical stim machine, in an ice bath, in a season—preseason, in-season, postseason, off-season, next season. My brain, my muscles, my emotions have been shaped by my life as an athlete, in the way each triggers or smooths, attacks or defends. It's hard to comprehend "sport" as "game" when you've been built by its rules, triumphs, failures, and wagers, as I've been built. I am the game's machine. I am its apparatus as much as it is mine.

I frequently dream basketball. In a recurring dream, my college coach, Wendy Larry, calls me back to play for her. She and I didn't always get along. She thought I was wild, and I was. I didn't understand her motives or mind games yet respected her authority—feared it sometimes and resisted it other times. I loved basketball too much in those years, and I played through many injuries for her, injuries that might have caused another player to sit out. Part of the wildness in me was an eagerness for a fight, for a challenge, for a reason to put my body up against another body and see what might be at stake, what I might win or lose.

I gave my coach my body to break down and build back up, to push toward ecstasy—in the form of a spin move and jumper with a release so high not many could stop it, or in the sound of the band's trombones and drums, the applause of a crowd of strangers, with my teammates in a congratulatory huddle, a win—even the ecstacy of failure and losing, which made me feel more alive and whole, a dissatisfaction and ache as close to desire as anything else I've touched.

During my NCAA career, inner-city student-athletes were discouraged from going home over holiday and semester breaks—to keep us out of trouble. My teammates' inner-city and my rez meant "trouble" to our coaches. These undesirable places were our homes and apparently also meant desirable basketball, since we were all on full-ride scholarships. So when my grandfather died, I couldn't go home to my desert for his funeral.

For the record, trouble did happen. Neighbors called the cops to my sister's house the night before the funeral. One of my brothers went to jail, the others attended Mass the next day with gouged or blackened eyes and busted lips. My family mourned together while I ran the point for a new offense in our practice gym three thousand miles away. I was angry—a convenient mask for my grief back then. I let the new play break down again and again, on purpose, until I had to run suicides as punishment.

A few weeks after the funeral I wasn't allowed to attend, I caught an elbow in practice that severed the infraorbital artery beneath my orbital bone and eye. I grabbed my face and fell to my knees. My teammates crowded around. As I lifted my head, one teammate screamed—it was an ugly, painful injury. I had a concussion, and my bloodied black eye lasted the entire season. I didn't cry when it happened but my tear duct was injured upon impact and wept on its own. That year, basketball was the way I mourned.

I have learned, now that I no longer play competitively, basketball was always my way through grief. A suffering as much as a pleasure. A fine balance of control and the wilderness of my feelings.

Athletes learn to read the body, another's body, like a text—and there is a way of learning one's own body as intimately as if you had written yourself into your own flesh. It is an art to tell the body's story not with words but with itself, as if movement and touch were the only language. And it is a power to imagine having a story to tell about what is possible with what gift you've been given, and then to think, "Watch me tell it."

In a 1998 interview in the *Atlantic*, John Edgar Wideman was asked what the bodies in his work revealed. He replied, "All my life I've been very aware of my body. I have always used it as a gauge of things. When I look at a person and I see their body, that's the beginning of knowledge about them. Furthermore, I respect the body."

In the 1997 Women's NCAA Championship at the Riverfront Coliseum in Cincinnati, my team, the Old Dominion Lady Monarchs, faced the Tennessee Lady Vols. We had beat Wideman's Stanford in the semifinals two days before, and I'd had a strong game. The championship was a different story. We blew a lead that turned into a 12-2 Lady Vol run, and Tennessee beat us with a final score of 68-59.

Days after the game, newspaper reports came out about Tennessee coach Pat Summitt's husband, R. B. Summitt, having yelled racist remarks to one of our international players. We had heard him during the game—he was sitting behind our bench. Once it was public, the Summitts apologized to our coach, who relayed the information to our team, and it wasn't mentioned again. But it was something that stuck in me, that two white female coaches smoothed over this white male's transgression toward my black, African, female teammate, my center, my target in the post, my high-post pick-and-roll, my sister.

I tried to research this incident in print many years later, and I finally found one or two articles quoting R. B. yelling, "Go back to Mozambique!" though I remember him screaming, "Go back to Africa!" as do some of my teammates, and screaming it more than once. What was the intent of this edit? Was saying "Mozambique" less violent? As if it simply referred to geography, a city like any other city? A place one might travel from and then return to, as in, "Go back home." In my memory, he yelled, "Go back to Africa!" and he, Coach Summitt, and my coach explained it by saying he got "caught up" in the heat of the game.

In a 1998 *Sports Illustrated* article about Pat Summitt a year after the incident, focus momentarily shifted to R. B. and his behavior. The reporter wrote: "Sure, sometimes he goes off the deep end in the heat of action and yells things at opposing teams that she wouldn't, but Pat can live with that. She knows what it is to enter another realm during a game"—"another realm" being the place R. B. Summitt went, a place where it is okay to scream at a black woman competing in a sport to go back to Africa, or, according to someone else's memory, to go back to Mozambique. And not only Coach Summit lived with it, we all did.

A thletic fandom is one of the most beautiful and horrific human conditions. It can join a group of strangers in a bond of loyalty or love akin to family; all for a team, all for a game. Fandom is also one aspect of sports I trust least. It doesn't take long for fans to revert to Colosseum-like behavior. The only thing worse than a man overcome with anger or inadequacy that he masks and channels toward another body, or a man given an arena-sized mirror in which he appears victorious over another body, is a group of men under those same circumstances.

In 2015, at a hockey game in Rapid City, South Dakota, it was reported that a group of fifteen white men in a VIP area poured beer on the heads of several Lakota children and their chaperones from American Horse Middle School, while yelling, "Go back to the rez!" Only one man was charged. The magistrate judge who acquitted him said this in the verdict: "The Court concludes that Defendant's actions of spraying beer were the result of an excited reaction to a very important score in the Rapid City Rush hockey game."

In 2010, a group of mostly white, mostly unathletic-looking, male Cleveland Cavaliers fans burned LeBron James's jerseys and T-shirts when he left the team to join the Miami Heat (and win a few championships). "Witness is real!" a man hollered as one after the other white man fed his LeBron shirts and jerseys to the flames. The historical and racial implications of this action didn't seem to cross their white minds—if it did, it didn't matter, because U.S.-American hunger and hatred, and white men's assumptions of power and property, have never abided by logic and rarely demand introspection. The game, especially one they are not playing in, becomes a place where they can act like gladiators, or worse, emperors.

In George Orwell's "The Sporting Spirit," published in 1945 while Britain was at war with Hitler and the Axis powers, he asserted, "Serious sport has nothing to do with fair play. It is bound up with hatred, jealousy, boastfulness, disregard of all rules and sadistic pleasure in witnessing violence: in other words, it is war minus the shooting." Sports were a great mobilizer for Hitler, and the young athletes who competed for Germany in the 1936 Berlin Olympics, behind the symbol of the eagle and the swastika, would be called to join the Hitler Youth less than a year after their participation in the Games.

In U.S.-America, where Native Americans are killed by police at a higher rate per capita than any other race yet volunteer for the military at a higher rate per capita than any other race, and black and Latino men and women are being killed by law enforcement with seeming impunity, we begin to understand that the games we play are part of a larger social structure. A war that began hundreds of years ago.

When I followed both stories—the white men dumping beer on the Native kids' heads at the hockey game and the mostly white men burning LeBron's jerseys—I recalled a passage from

Orwell's *Animal Farm*: "The creatures outside looked from pig to man, and from man to pig, and from pig to man again; but already it was impossible to say which was which." Athletics can bring out those animals, though I doubt athletics created them. Instead, I have come to believe that athletics are also structures of racialized and gendered diminishment, and it has caused me great stress to consider this at the same time I consider how athletics made me who I am today, who I am still becoming.

In 2015, Thabo Sefolosha played for the Atlanta Hawks and was known to guard LeBron James during matchups with the Cleveland Cavs. There is a video on YouTube of LeBron crossing-up Sefolosha in a game from 2014: LeBron dribbles once to the right, then crosses and loses him left. The cross-up was so brutal, Sefolosha tripped and fell. The highlight reels announced LeBron "broke Sefolosha's ankles" with that "nasty" cross.

So before going on to meet the Golden State Warriors in the 2015 Finals, when the Cavs met the Hawks in the Eastern Conference Championship, Sefolosha should have been defending LeBron. Instead he was on the bench, out with a season-ending injury sustained a month before. On the morning of April 8, 2015, Thabo Sefolosha had his right fibula, or his ankle, broken when a white police officer came up behind him after an altercation at a nightclub and swept his leg out from under him. He required surgery and missed the rest of the postseason and playoffs.

LeBron never got another chance to break Sefolosha's ankles that year—the NYPD did. The Cavs swept the series, or the NYPD swept Sefolosha.

In *The Stranger*, Camus wrote, "It was as if that great rush of anger had washed me clean, emptied me of hope, and, gazing up at the dark sky spangled with its signs and stars, for the first time, the first, I laid my heart open to the benign indifference of the universe . . . To feel it so like myself, indeed, so brotherly, made me realize that I'd been happy, and that I was happy still. For all to be accomplished, for me to feel less lonely, all that remained to hope was that on the day of my execution there should be a huge crowd of spectators and that they should greet me with howls of execration."

Isn't Camus describing the game in its purest form? Isn't this what fills your chest when you're at a park after dark shooting elbow jumper after elbow jumper with only the stars and planets keeping score, and more and more stars appear because you can't miss—yes, you are making the stars light up—and nothing exists outside the concrete court, not your shut-off electricity, or the rifle reports in the middle of the night, no brother who thinks spiders are crawling on him, no coyotes crying at the edge of the rez, not your friend's dad stumbling the alleyway with a needle dangling from his arm or the fact that your cousin will overdose soon—it's just you, you triumphant, and teammates hoisting you on their shoulders, carrying you out to the parking lot, down the high school hill, over the railroad tracks, along the Colorado River, past the stand of mesquite trees and their glowing yellow beans, off into the bright dune fields of your desert, while the fans of the opposing team jeer and curse your jump shot?

Or maybe Camus meant something darker, like in 2017 when Boston fans threw peanuts at Baltimore Orioles center fielder Adam Jones and called him "nigger" multiple times during a game at Fenway Park. Or the way Jeremy Lin was treated, whether he played well or poorly, because fans couldn't get over their projections onto his body and race, or because they thought his body and race didn't belong in the NBA. Or darker still, like the beating two Los Angeles Dodgers fans gave to a San Francisco Giants fan after a game at Dodger Stadium in 2011. Their victim was left brain damaged and now requires twenty-four-hour care. One of the perpetrators was overheard saying, "Fuck the Giants. That's what you get" as he kicked the victim in the head.

I met Grace Thorpe at a nuclear protest in my desert town, Needles, California, located in the southwestern sliver of the Inland Empire, on land that is important to my Mojave people—reservations are attractive places for white people to dump and hide poisonous things. In the minds of most Americans, Native lands have as little value as the Native body. Grace Thorpe was an activist, and she was at my home rez, Fort Mojave, as part of a coalition to help fight a nuclear waste dump in our desert. My Elders told Grace I was soon off to college on a basketball scholarship, and she began telling me stories about her father, Jim Thorpe. I had never heard of him. He was a Sac and Fox and attended Carlisle Indian Industrial School like some of my relatives had. He played professional baseball for the New York Giants and the Boston Braves. He helped cofound and played in the NFL. He was the greatest ~~Native~~ American athlete.

Carlisle was run by Captain Richard H. Pratt, later a brigadier general. In describing Pratt and his wife, Marianne Moore—a canonical American poet I have been expected to study and acknowledge as a master—said this about them: "They were romantic figures, always dashing up with their horse and carriage, and they were intelligent and cultural. But General Pratt was so monumental no one could dare approach him to tell him one approved of the work he was doing."

An oft quoted excerpt from a speech Pratt gave at George Mason University in 1892 tells about the work he was doing: "A great general has said that the only good Indian is a dead one, and that high sanction of his destruction has been an enormous factor in promoting Indian massacres. In a sense, I agree with the sentiment, but only in this: that all the Indian there is in the race should be dead. Kill the Indian in him, and save the man . . ."

In the 2016–2017 season, the NCAA reported 0.3 percent of its male athletes and 0.5 percent of its female athletes were "American Indian/Alaskan Native." I didn't know any Native collegiate athletes when I began to dream of a place other than my reservation, didn't even know any Natives in college. When I was a kid I saw Dawn Staley and the Burge twins play for the University of Virginia in an NCAA tournament game on television, and suddenly, I knew I could make it there, even though I wasn't yet sure where that place was.

Robert Griffin III, or RGIII, played for the Washington Redskins. He had an awesome first year, then was hampered by numerous knee injuries, including a torn anterior cruciate ligament or ACL. It was a disastrous equation from the start—a black body wearing a representation of a fragmented Native body in the form a Redskin's helmet. It's a historical problem, or a long division problem. Both bodies divided/broken by X; where X = wealthy white men = American sports.

The brown body, the non-white body, poor body, female body, queer body, disabled body has always been measured by what it can bear, what it can endure of pain and ecstasy. But whose pain? Whose ecstasy?

The spectacular body of color. How it swings from a rope. How it breaks when swung at. How long it can hold its breath or a bullet. How it handles a virus, a blanket, sterilization. The fearful and fascinating body of color. How close it can be to animal in its spectacle and glory, in its grief and mourning.

249

Sports is the intersection and the collision. The performance of the brown body on a court, a field, around a track, for the entertainment, financial gain, projection, and validation of the white body. Sports are often the appetite of the rich white men who own them, who sit in the box in suits and ties while the brown and black bodies fly and break and sweat and glow. Yet how many young brown and black girls and boys are out in the streets, beneath the streetlamps, enacting what they view as heroic, supernatural, destiny, and possibility—sticking their tongues out like Jordan while they jump from the free throw line, tossing imaginary chalk up into the air like LeBron, or pulling up for a Steph Curry three from too far out? I was once one of them.

Sports also feed and pique the appetite of the average person, the not-agile, the not-able, the not-*gifted*. In the Colosseum of Rome, people crammed in to see the bestiarii—mostly slaves or criminals—fight to the death against bears, elephants, jaguars, cheetahs, and boars. Audiences craved this, and emperors gave them more and more spectacle. It is believed certain species were wiped out because of mass slaughter performed in the Colosseum, not to mention the slaughter of the bestiarii themselves—even if a bestiarius managed to win against one animal, chances were another would be sent out to fight, on and on, until the bestiarius was finally failed.

In a game where RGIII suffered a concussion, the Redskins reported instead that he was "shaken up." Redskins head coach Mike Shanahan stated he didn't know about the concussion diagnosis until after the game, which is why RGIII returned to the field. Whereas, the Redskins head trainer said the concussion was confirmed "two to three minutes" after it occurred. In fact, the Redskins were fined twenty thousand dollars for violating the safety protocol. After a week off, RGIII returned to play. Many thought it was too soon.

Shanahan formerly coached the Denver Broncos. At Denver, he once sent running back Terrell Davis back onto the field after Davis had been kneed in the helmet, suffered a migraine, and lost his vision. Shanahan sent him back onto the field even after Davis told him, "I can't see."

Mike Shanahan knows what all white coaches know—there is value in a brown or black body, the way it takes and takes and takes what it is given.

RGIII broke. And they loved it. They loved calling him weak.

I've existed in a separate space of gender—not masculine or feminine, not even queer. I was all athlete—a 1-2 guard, a wing, a scorer, a defender, back of the 1-3-1, ball handler on the break, cutter in the triangle, expected to be strong, to take up space, to lean forward, *una guerrera*. Today I get called "Sir" all the time, especially in airports. At a gas station in Searchlight, Nevada, on the way from my rez to Las Vegas McCarran Airport en route to a poetry reading, a man grabbed my arm as I walked into the women's bathroom and said, "Dude, you almost went into the ladies' toilet. Ours is over there."

My mother was waiting outside in the car, and when I told her, she said, "It's just the way you hold yourself."

"And how exactly do I hold myself?" I asked, a little defensively.

"Like you belong there," she answered, "Like you know how to take care of yourself in a way that will let you stay there."

"Yeah," I replied, "but you don't have to be a man to do that."

Taking and holding space has always been natural to me—boxing out, setting screens, showing big on the baseline, knocking down cutters, flashing the lane, finishing a layup

251

through a foul, even the way I walk into a gym or a room. I suppose I learned spacing the way most Native, brown, and black people do, the way most queer people do, by being defensive. In college, I was known for my defense, regularly guarding the other teams' best guards. And I first learned defense on the rez.

When we played Smear-the-Queer, our cousins and friends intentionally threw the football to my little brother John or me. We were mixed, and lighter complexioned than they were, and this was our penance. This was also one of the ways we learned to be fast.

When John's legs slowed, when I heard him sucking air, when the pack began to catch him, I raced to the front and let him pitch me the ball; the pack chased me instead. They didn't catch me often—their pudgy boy bodies hadn't hardened yet, and I was more agile, even stronger at that age. Times I wasn't fast enough or tired before they did, their knees, elbows, feet, and fists crashed down on me, and I found myself at the bottom of the heap of our bodies. They pressed my face into the yellowed grass and dirt, the way I would learn to press their faces into the grass and dirt when they had the ball, hollering out, "Smear-the-Fucking-Queer!" This was also one of the ways I learned not to cry.

Here is the second half of the earlier-referenced quote from John Edgar Wideman's 1998 *Atlantic* interview: "It's one thing to be smart and quick-witted, but can you back it up? In the world that I grew up in, if you said something, if you acted in a certain way, you had to back it up—and that meant being physical. It didn't mean you had to win all your fights, but it meant you had to be willing, with your body, to back up what you were saying. I trust the body. I trust pleasure, I trust pain." What Wideman is expressing is a constellation of my relationship to my body and sports—how one often leads to the other, how in some ways my body has depended on sports to become itself, to know what it fears and desires.

I n the summer of 2016, the National Book Foundation held a fundraiser called "The Other NBA: The most storied basketball game in literary history." The matchup was billed as "award-winning writers against publishing powerhouses." I agreed to play, even though I hadn't run a full-court in years. I ran half-court pickup games with some scrubs at the Princeton YMCA a few weeks before the game, in half-assed preparation.

I had planned on taking it easy, jogging a little, maybe being a passer—however, at a certain point I found myself hurtling toward a loose ball I'd deflected. A female publisher from the other team moved toward the ball too. Something in me snapped, not in a disruptive way, more of a falling-into-place way, like a memory rushing through me. A memory of myself. It happened quickly: I was back. I was the body I'd been built to be. Next thing I knew I stood over where she lay on the ground, where I had knocked her, the ball in my hands, looking down court where I hit my wing on the fly with a bullet of an outlet pass.

I saw it in the others that afternoon too, those who had the game in their blood. We all unraveled and became those locked-away parts of ourselves. Mitchell Jackson, author of *The Residue Years* and *Survival Math*, missed a handful of three-pointers until he found himself, deep behind the arc, where he lifted again and again, unleashing and draining triple after triple. The air was something else for him—gravity couldn't hold him because he was beyond gravity. Dwayne Betts, poet, lawyer, activist, was half locomotive and half butter as he throttled and slicked through the lane for easy buckets. We were all out on the hardwood, returned to the cities of our bodies, doing what we were built to do on the busted courts of our childhoods, among our friends and enemies. And, of course, we won. This was our inheritance—these bodies, these games.

What often draws me to people is the way they move, especially if they move with the game in them—a series of long lines, neck to shoulder, torso, arms and legs, a certain lean, a glide, a grace. It is a movement I recognize and gravitate toward when I encounter other athletes in a crowd, in a room, at an awkward post–poetry reading party or writerly gathering—a smooth swagger and muscularity that puts me at ease.

Borrowing James Baldwin's term, my body was my "gimmick"—it is what got me off my rez. My brother's body was also *his* gimmick; it is what he burned down trying to escape. I sometimes wonder why it was me and not my brother who got "the gift." How easily it could have been me with pipe burn blisters on my fingers, and my big brother snapping his wrist to rattle a jumper through the rim to a crowd's applause. The most shameful thing to ever cross my mind is that I don't know if I would change this if I could—if I would trade his life for mine, my winnings for his losings.

As it was in Baldwin's days, in many non-white and poor environments today there are two dreamlike and spectacular paths toward mobility: entertainment and sports. Only very few of those who buy into this dream will ever reach elite levels in either entertainment or sports, though the glimmer and opportunity seems to be enough. If you can see your life reflected in someone who has "made it," the notion of a way out, even if it never arrives, is enough to keep your body moving toward a future. To move toward a future is to move away from a lot of choices that might end you early.

My strong body, my obedient body, my body that found its gimmick early: run and run and jump and jump. Maybe my gimmick on the page is the same—isn't the brown body the body I come back to and offer you—my own body, my brother's body, my lovers' bodies. Or maybe I'm trying to trade in this gimmick for love. Maybe I can, maybe I can't.

I've pushed my body beyond what I thought were its limits, and I've had my body pushed beyond where most bodies can go. Isn't one game or another—from memory or from some future— always calling? In my dreams, when Coach Larry asks me to take the floor for her, I always say yes. The body's demise happens in many ways. The dreams usually end the way my real-life basketball career ended—tearing my left anterior cruciate ligament (ACL), medial collateral ligament (MCL), and my meniscus.

I have a crafted and earned intimacy with my body. I know and trust it differently than a non-athlete can. It's the way I make sense of the world, a lover, a book, the earth—put my hands on/ in them, see how I can open them or be opened. I touch them, looking for whatever energy I might become in that touching. There is nothing I am more confident or vulnerable in than my own body. You know the body differently when you break it, whether the breaking is your own or someone else's.

Even though most sports commentaries are politically numb and historically ignorant, it is true, in a sense, when announcers say, "The Natives are restless." They say this more frequently when talking about the Kansas City Chiefs, the Cleveland Indians, and the Washington Redskins. It is no secret—the Natives haven't been able to rest for hundreds of years.

After re-injuring his knee in a game between the Redskins and the Ravens, RGIII went back onto the field without the team doctor checking him. Shanahan okayed his reentry to the game. Only a real body needs a doctor, and RGIII's was not a real body. He was a dark machine. A body of dusk and sinew must go and go until it cannot.

The patellar tendon functioning as my current ACL is called an "autograft" because it came from my own body. *Harvest* is the word the doctors use—my patellar tendon was *harvested* from my body. Harvesting is associated with Natives, maybe because of corn and cornucopias, or Thanksgiving and Indian summers. My tribe's casino has a Native Harvest Buffet. Most of my brothers worked there during high school.

Some missing or deceased persons' bodies or body parts are found in such diminished shape they can only be identified by the serial numbers of the surgical hardware implanted in their bodies from reconstructions and replacements.

Coach Larry taught us, "Defense is the best offense." If memory is passed down in DNA, I learned defense centuries ago, from my ancestors, from all they defended themselves and our people and land against.

From a CNN article with the headline WHO'S MOST LIKELY TO BE KILLED BY POLICE?: "In fact, despite the available statistical evidence, most people don't know that Native Americans are most likely to be killed by police, compared to other racial groups. Native Americans make up about 0.8% of the population, yet account for 1.9% of police killings."

Natives between the ages of eighteen and twenty-four have a higher rate of suicide than any other ethnicity, and Native women have the highest suicide rate of other female ethnicities in the U.S. Is suicide considered defensive or offensive?

What will my DNA give to my children? Poetry? My long arms and relentless defense? My sadness? My anxieties? Will their bodies know to sweat when they are pulled over, to be still, to relax and not resist as they are bent into an impossible position?

In *Hoosiers*, Coach Norman Dale, played by Gene Hackman, tells his team, "I've seen you guys can shoot but there's more to the game than shooting. There's fundamentals and defense." I agree—defense is the best offense, unless offense is the best offense. I am tired of defending. This page is a kind of offense.

Jaylen Brown, the Boston Celtics' number three pick in the 2016 NBA draft, was called "too smart for his own good" by a conveniently (and typically) anonymous NBA executive. Brown is an intelligent man, plays chess, plays piano, learns languages, all the things that make him dangerous to a system that requires a black or brown body to perform its physicality but not its mentality or emotionality.

In a 2018 interview with the *Guardian*, Brown said he knew the NFL wouldn't let Colin Kaepernick back in after his peaceful protests before NFL games, explaining, "That's the reality because sports is a mechanism of control. If people didn't have sports they would be a lot more disappointed with their role in society. There would be a lot more anger or stress about the injustice of poverty and hunger. Sports is a way to channel our energy into something positive. Without sports who knows what half of these kids would be doing?"

It was sports, however, that gave Colin Kaepernick the platform that has slowly begun to chip away at the well-known facade of the NFL and other professional sports leagues. He chose the lives of black men and women and children in the United States over his space on an NFL roster. He took a knee to protest a country—a country that takes more than a knee, a country that takes entire lives, here and in other countries across the world, in order to maintain its system of white power and control.

Before Kaepernick, Mahmoud Abdul-Rauf of the Denver Nuggets made the same wager. Remember him? It was 1996, the year I graduated from River Valley High in Mohave Valley, Arizona. He had converted to Islam a few years before and decided to stretch or stay in the locker room for the national anthem because, as he once said, the flag was "a symbol of oppression, of tyranny."

This was the same year sportscaster Billy Packer referred to the Georgetown Bulldog Allen Iverson as "one tough little monkey." In defense of Packer's comment, people mentioned how Packer had supported the Black Coaches Association. Mike Patrick of ESPN added: "We need to get past the words and look at the intent, and I know Billy Packer has no racist intent."

Today, just like in 1996, nobody is "racist." Not in academia, not on a police force, not in the White House, and certainly not in sports. There is no real "racism" anymore; there is only the "offense" brown and black people take at innocent gestures and words used by white people. We might as well quit using the antiquated word "racist," retire it from our lexicon, since it no longer applies to anybody. Instead, we prefer to use words like "misunderstanding" and "miscommunication," or as Packer did back in 1996, we "apologize profusely."

Jaylen Brown pointed out that it is common for reporters and fans to expect athletes to remain quiet about political events, often saying things along the lines of: "You should be happy you're making X amount of money playing sports. You should be saluting America instead of critiquing it."

James Baldwin, whom many U.S.-Americans quote lately—though I wonder if they are actually reading him—once said, "I love America more than any other country in this world, and, exactly for this reason, I insist on the right to criticize her perpetually."

In 2017
approximately 70% of the players in the NFL were black; approximately 75% of the players in the NBA were black; approximately 68% of the players in the WNBA were black. How many black head coaches or owners are there?

In reference to protests by professional athletes during the national anthem, in particular those in the NFL, Trump addressed a rally in Alabama: "That's a total disrespect of our heritage. That's total disrespect of everything we stand for."

I have often had these same sentiments when I consider American Empire. Much of what *American* stands for, and arguably all of its "heritage," is disrespectable. My father, who built me a four-foot-high hoop so I could reach the basket when I was a child, is from a family of Mexican and Spanish immigrants. He fought in the Vietnam War and almost died when a missile hit his bunker. He continues to suffer that war in many ways. My little brother John, who was always my first pick, my on-the-ball screener, my in-bounder in hundreds of two-on-two games on indoor and outdoor courts all over our rez and small desert town, is still haunted by his participation in the Afghanistan war. Neither my father nor my brother are seen as fully human and are denied basic dignities in many ways. No mythology of a flag, of a colony, of an empire will change that. The United States will sacrifice my brothers' and sisters' bodies on a battlefield in the same way they will sacrifice them in an agricultural field or on a field of play, or on any street of any city or town in this country.

Captain Pratt, founder of Carlisle Industrial Indian school, the man Marianne Moore so admired, in that same speech he gave at George Mason University way back when, also said, "We make our greatest mistake in feeding our civilization to the Indians instead of feeding the Indians to our civilization."

The U.S. is certainly that for many of us—a feeding, a consuming, a hunting ground, an appetite for and a lessening of our bodies.

At Denver, before RGIII was even in college, Shanahan coached John Elway, a white quarterback, who played his entire career without an ACL. Possibly, Shanahan equally disrespects black and white bodies—but I don't buy it. That season I watched Shanahan try to break RGIII. Finally, I watched him succeed. I watched the black body fall.

At the 1912 Stockholm Olympics, Jim Thorpe's shoes were stolen. He won one of his two gold medals competing in a borrowed shoe and a shoe he found in the trash can. In the photo taken after the race, the two mismatched shoes are noticeable—one is too big so he has extra socks on that foot.

My siblings and I shared shoes as kids. Five of us are within a six-year range of ages—John, Desirae, Gabrielle, Belarmino, me. We played in different divisions for the city rec league, took turns with a single pair of shoes. It was embarrassing.

Is this why we played so hard? To forget everyone saw us poor, in our bare socks, waiting for our turn to wear the shoes? I distrusted kids with fancy shoes, so I worked hard against them, ran faster, stole the ball every chance I got, until eventually I was better—I was the best.

There is a terrible structure of goodness in the United States that is designed to be unattainable for most non-white

Americans, most poor Americans, most immigrants, most queer, most disabled bodies. We are taught early to be good, to behave, to be quiet, to not take up space, to be invisible. Maybe this is why we gravitate toward sports—a place where we can be good. Not an equal playing field, as we have seen, but as close to one as we get. It's the gimmick Baldwin was talking about—sport/game—our way up and out from under the thumb or boot of our nation's power structures.

The attributes that make us lauded on the courts, on fields, in rings are the same attributes that make us hunted and killed off the courts, off the fields, out of the rings—quickness, fight, aggressiveness, unwillingness or inability to quit, pride and shame, strength, quick thinking, fearlessness, the way we know and own and carry our bodies, the grace, the muscle of us, the beauty and shock of our brown and black and exotic bodies gleaming in motion.

Like bulls we are. When yoked, we are beautiful. When refusing to be yoked, we are wild and whippable, butcherable.

As we've seen throughout time, the combination of athletic prowess, intellectual complexity, and autonomy, as well as human sensuality is threatening to white America—Tommie Smith and John Carlos standing shoeless and raising their gloved fists in protest on the podium at the 1968 Mexico Olympics, Kareem Abdul-Jabbar boycotting those same Olympics, Jackie Robinson not singing the national anthem, NBA and WNBA players protesting with T-shirts they wore in warm-ups even before Colin Kaepernick's peaceful protest rippled then exploded across the NFL. The brown or black athletic body coupled with intellect is dangerous, defiant even, to empire. It challenges the idea of the master and the beast, of the fans and their spectacle.

261

T habo Sefolosha testified that the NYPD officer who came up behind him that night and swept his leg out from beneath him said, "With or without a badge, I can fuck you up."

T o repair my torn ACL, the middle third of my patellar tendon was used along with bone fragments from each end. A surgeon drilled tunnels in my bone to thread the tendon through, then screwed the bone fragments and tendon into my tibia and femur, where my ACL used to be.

If I'd had an allograft, it would have come from a cadaver.

In Mojave, we burn our dead—transplanting tissue from a dead body into mine wasn't an option for me or was an option I considered troublesome. In fact, if I'd done the entire procedure the Mojave way, I'd have had a small funeral pyre for my ACL, sent it off to the other side so it would be waiting for me when I passed on and over. Now, it's possible I'll arrive to the afterlife without an ACL, and if so, I'll have to have this surgery all over again after I die.

B ecause I am a Native woman born on the reservation, I am more likely to be assaulted, raped, or disappeared, and to die as a result. According to the Department of Justice, in 2009, when U.S. Attorney General Eric Holder was briefed by the FBI that one in three Native women are physically assaulted in their lifetime and on some reservations the murder rate for women is ten times higher than the national average, he couldn't believe the statistics. He asked his team to fact-check the numbers.

According to the U.S. Office of Juvenile Justice and Delinquency Prevention, "Native girls are 40 percent more likely than white girls to be referred to a juvenile court for delinquency; 50 percent more likely to be detained; and 20 percent more likely to be adjudicated." Another disturbing report, by the National

Women's Law Center, concludes: "Girls who spend time in juvenile detention facilities are nearly five times more likely to die before age 29."

A United Nations document titled "Sport and Gender, Empowering Girls and Women" reports that female athletes show "increased self-esteem, self-confidence, and a sense of control over their bodies." According to the UN findings, sports also foster "positive changes in gender norms, giving girls and women greater safety and control over their lives." There are myriad articles and studies that claim I am less likely to be in an abusive relationship because I am an athlete.

If the statistics of me being assaulted, raped, and disappeared as a Native woman meet head-to-head with statistics that say I am less likely to be abused and will have greater safety because I am a female athlete, which statistics will win?

And if I lose that matchup, if my body is found the way most murdered Native women's bodies are found throughout the Americas—discarded, decomposed, on a rarely traveled tract of land, at the bottom of a canyon or riverbed, in pieces, and by accident because police aren't looking—it is quite possible that my body will be difficult to identify.

If my body is difficult to identify, then the titanium screws in my knee will become significant. The authorities will interview my family, look through my medical records and those of other missing Native women. They will see that I had surgery on my left knee. They'll check the left knee of the found body for signs of a fractured tibial condyle, for titanium screws and their serial numbers. If it is me, if it is my Native, female, queer, athletic body that they find, basketball will not have saved my life—but it will have saved me from being added to the thousands of missing Native women in the Americas.

The king of Sweden called Jim Thorpe the world's greatest athlete the week he won those two golds for the U.S. Track and Field team. The next week, Thorpe had to return his medals according to Rule 26 of the Eligibility Rules of the International Olympic Committee. It was discovered he'd received a small amount of pay from two semipro baseball teams.

It was about rules, they said, not about his Nativeness. Rule 26.

Twenty-six is a bad number for Natives. A deck of cards has twenty-six red cards and twenty-six black cards, but really all the cards are white. On the twenty-sixth day of December, 1862, Honest Abe Lincoln, the Great Emancipator, ordered the hanging of thirty-eight Dakotas. He *ordered* them to be hanged. The periodic table is an *ordering* of elements. Twenty-six is the atomic number for the element iron. The word for iron or metal in the Mojave language is also the word for bullet. Because this is how iron or metal first came to us, like bullets still come to us, through our bodies. In twenty-six years I will still have played basketball for longer than I have not played it.

I had a lateral X-ray taken of my left knee, and it looked like there were two .22 caliber rounds lodged in me, except for the deep threads of the titanium screws.

Even though the International Olympic Committee (IOC) presented Jim Thorpe with replica gold medals, they snuck in some fine print that allowed them to not enter his actual records back into the Olympic books. It's as if he never participated. They have erased him, as has always been their way with Natives.

I would buy a ticket to watch the 6'7" Sefolosha take that 5'7" officer, *with or without a badge*, out onto the court and work him, school him, take him to the rim, break his ankles, *fuck him up*.

A few years before leaving the Redskins, when asked to describe his relationship with Coach Shanahan, RGIII replied, "Heartbreaking."

W riting is an extension of my body. I am seeking the body on the page, even the broken body, even the ecstatic body—even the broken *and* ecstatic body. I am looking for a new field for the body to run in. I am looking for a field where the body might be struck down. I am looking for a field where the body might rest or hide or flee or reap or build a house or set a fire. The body doesn't want solace—the body wants to be possible.

The page has never solved my troubles, but the page has let me know them better, let me know the body of myself better through those troubles. Maybe.

I never thought much about what my mother meant all those times, before all those games, when she told me, Knock 'em dead. Now, I think she meant, *This isn't just a game for you. Don't let them hurt you, even if it means hurting them first*. I think she meant, *Live*. It's funny how a game can teach you that.

JAVIER ZAMORA was born in
El Salvador and migrated to
the United States when he
was nine. He is a Radcliffe
Fellow at Harvard Univer-
sity and has held fellowships
from the Lannan Foundation,
the Poetry Foundation, and
the National Endowment
for the Arts, among other
places. His first book, *Unaccompanied*, was published
by Copper Canyon Press in
September 2017.

Columbine

JAVIER ZAMORA

I'd never seen one like it: the flower
with its many orange cups. Dad drove me to Yosemite
the second month in this country.
He didn't know the name of it. I didn't know the name of it,
only that I loved the cups & that
they reminded me of the hibiscus
outside the glassless window I'd left months ago.
I hadn't started school yet. There were many things I didn't know,
    English
the most important. Didn't have friends.
Entire days spent inside the apartment
memorizing words, reading bilingual picture books,
comparing *couch* to the picture, to the couch
in my parents' living room. In the news,
earlier, much earlier, before I arrived in June: headlines
I could not read. Could not understand. Parents
shared a fear I'd never known. Though
I'd seen guns on the way up here. Though
there had been war; I did not know the way to school yet.
The names of highways that would show me blooms.

NAMWALI SERPELL is a
Zambian writer who teaches
at the University of California, Berkeley. She won
the 2015 Caine Prize for
African Writing, received a
2011 Rona Jaffe Foundation
Writers' Award, and was
selected for the Africa39, a
2014 Hay Festival project
to identify the most promising African writers under
forty. Her first novel, *The
Old Drift*, was published by
Hogarth/Penguin Random
House in 2019.

Take It

NAMWALI SERPELL

Yeah. So, this was back when he was scrounging around between Berkeley and Oakland, the borderland there like a tease. He was fourteen then, still a yard rat, still garbage diving with Adeline. He was tall for his age but she was taller. Skinnier, darker. She taught him to check the recycling bins first: if there were scraps, at least they'd be contained. Less rotten.

Adeline. She said her name with the hauteur of a drag queen, eyelashes swooping down and brushing back up like palm fans for the Queen of Sheba. But she got it from a street sign, because she was always hanging round that one corner by Ashby BART. She'd stand there in her garbage-bag poncho, with her 7-Eleven cup. (She'd caught him pissing in it once and nearly torn his earlobe off.) She'd hold it straight ahead, chanting at the commuters. *Care to share care to share care to share.* Cheerful in its way. Sometimes he'd find her squatting on the sidewalk, clothes torn, blood strung over her thighs and crudding her nails. Whimpering. *Could somebody help could somebody could somebody.* Just another kind of song, but it spooked him.

It was like everybody around there was inside out. Bedrooms laid out in storefronts, bathrooms where-the-fuck-ever. The crazy you're supposed to keep inside always on the verge of bubbling

out. The townies were saner but hella snooty. Mostly white—
or tattoo-gray—sprawled on the sidewalk outside Rasputin or
Amoeba, playing their own music on boomboxes, leering at the
Cal students skittering past. He limited his dealings with them to
weed and made survival alliances with the older folk. Lox, who
lived in the cave of the Berkeley BART stairwell. Black Jesus on
Sproul. Mexican Jesus on Bancroft. Adeline.

At night, he'd peel away from her and sneak alone into this
spot on Stuart Street. The back garden was overgrown. Lofty
grass, wildflowers, an apple tree in the corner pummeling a shed
with fruit. There was a ruin of a brick oven in the middle, framed
by two cacti that looked like an old couple: a thin man with reaching limbs and a fat woman with spiky curves, both tangled with
spiderwebs that aged them. The house itself was being renovated.
When the sun fell, he would hop the rickety back gate and camp
out next to the oven, its bricks still warm from the day. He'd
curl around his stuff and crash till dawn, slipping out just as the
construction workers pulled in. The only bother with sleeping
there was the cats, who stalked him unafraid, then scampered
at his slightest move, their burnished eyes like marbles rolling
off into the dark.

It was September, a warm East Bay night, cloudy enough to
muffle the chill and halo the moon. He'd been asleep for a couple
of hours when the sounds came over the fence: ricochet laughter
and every once in a while, a pistol-shot shout. It was coming from
the neighbors', a three-story house with velvety brown shingles
and lime green trim. He'd seen them and they'd seen him—both
sides staring as if across a moat—but they'd never spoken.

He listened to the conversational fuzz growing over the night.
Another shout. He crept over to the weathered fence between
the yards, too janky to keep out anything but kindness, and
peeked between the slats. It was a party. A bunch of people were

standing around on the patio behind the neighbors' house, red Solo cups in their hands. They were all wearing white or . . . he peered closer, then startled back. What the—? He drew close. They were naked.

He shifted to the next gap in the fence to catch another angle. That's when he saw the girls. A heavy heat swept into his crotch. The closest one was thick, a fedora casting her face in shadow, her breasts bigger than her head, the nipples like soft-spreading stains. The girl beside her was sickly-thin, her pubes triumphant, almost windswept. Behind them, some dudes were wrestling—or pretending to. He looked for hard-ons but it wasn't easy to tell, what with the blotchy skin and the shadows and the shreds of costume—a chain here, a hat there, a cloak. A laugh fizzed in his throat but he felt oddly at peace. The variety of bodies was comforting, like remembering exactly where you'd put something that you thought you'd lost.

The back door to the neighbors' house opened and a backlit shadow sauntered out holding a speaker, Bob Marley murmuring alongside. *Come on and stir it up.* The dudes started to jerk and hitch their limbs. *Little darling.* The girls raised their liquid arms, singing in unison, their notes splattered around the true melody. *C'mon baby.* He shifted from slat to slat, staring. It wasn't like porn, exactly. It was more like the zoo—the same quiet watchfulness. He could have spent the whole night just looking, marveling at the legs and hair and skin.

But then someone saw him. Someone saw, through the crack in the fence—a gap the width of a finger—the coin-sized eye of the kid who'd been sneaking into the yard next door for three weeks straight, no problem. The girl gasped. She shrieked. When she pointed, he ran off to crouch behind the brick oven.

A clunk shut Marley down. The party frayed: naked guys clamoring at the fence, trying to see over it. Naked girls screaming "ohmygod" through giggles. Half a minute later, the back gate to his yard chuckled open. He tensed.

"Come out, come out, wherever you are," a deep male voice sang. Then a clean whistle.

"Shut up, Pete," a girl muttered. "*Hello?*" she called. And again: "*Hello?*" Her voice came closer, low and swarmy. "Where *are* you?"

The hinges of the gate snarled.

"Listen," the girl called out. "My name's J. You're safe. You can . . . *ow*, fuck."

He peeked out. The moon was behind the clouds but he could see the girl standing on one foot, her other ankle netted in her fingers, hair curtaining her face. As she brushed off whatever had jabbed her sole, the moon soaked through and turned her skin silver. She lowered her foot and tossed her hair over a shoulder easily, casually. She was wearing an eye patch and at the sight of it, the beat of his fear shot to his crotch and pulsed there, dumb as a bell.

"Hey," she said directly to him.

His muddy sneaker was in full view. He pulled it back behind the oven again.

"Come," she insisted. "Join us." She was smiling. There was a gap between her front teeth. A guy stepped forward from behind her, his cheeks and his chest painted with streaks of red, his eyes narrowslits. J glanced over, then turned back to say, almost apologetically:

"You have to take off your clothes, though. Party rules." She flashed the gap at him. "You can leave 'em in the kitchen." She pointed over the fence at a glowing window. "Come."

And so he did, spellbound by the unlikelihood of it. He met her at the gate and she escorted him across the driveway to the back door, the whole party seeming to shift on its axis to look. She left him inside the kitchen, smiling slyly but with eyes averted when she closed the door behind her, as if he were the naked one. He blinked around, scoping the food-smeared dishes in the sink—barbeque, looked like—and the bulky brown grocery bags scattered over the floor. He crouched and opened one—it was stuffed with clothes. Here and there between the bags were neat little pairs of shoes. It reminded him of kindergarten, and he realized he remembered that: going to kindergarten. The fridge grunted and began to hum.

He took off his jeans and sneaks and sweatshirt, moving quickly to keep from smelling himself. He grabbed a paper bag from the flat stack on the counter and was stuffing his clothes inside it when the back door flung open again. He jumped and crossed his hands over his crotch like a soccer player. An Asian girl wearing only a translucent mermaid's tail shuffled past him, careening over to the sink, where she puked sobbingly over the stack of dirty dishes, then staggered into the house beyond the kitchen. He glanced down at his skin, the planes of him rough with goosebumps. Then he breathed, turned, and stepped out into the sea of pastel.

At first, he eased his way in from the side, heading toward a tree in the middle of the patio. It had displaced two concrete slabs and was buckling the others around it. Standing under its moon-mottled shadow, he watched. The party's voice had thickened with talk and laughter and Marley's plaintive croon. He caught the eye of an athletic looking girl wearing a slanted belt and a ruffly collar—no shirt, just the collar. His dick was still bobbing before him like a docked pit bull's tail and he covered it with his hand, then changed his mind and tried to play it cool. The girl pressed her smiling lips together as her eyes flitted off.

He turned his attention to the girl beside her, who had only one hand. She was dancing too fast and he stared with dread as her hook began to slide off. Fingers blossomed from underneath.

273

She shoved the hook back on impatiently. A costume. He looked around for a while, gathering, until all of the costumes finally clicked into a coherent theme: *Pirates*.

And then J was at his side, with her gappy smile and her shine and her eye patch, which made more sense now. She handed him a Modelo and introduced him to a dude with a stuffed parrot on his shoulder and a handlebar moustache. The guy was vaguely brown. Chicano? Indian? J said something about embarrassing herself.

He smiled at her. "I don't care."

And he didn't, because she was here. J was more *here* than anyone else at the party—more *here* than anyone he'd ever met—but maybe that was just because she didn't talk to him like he was fourteen. Her sheer presence was already wicking people off the crowd, guys and girls seeping close, their costumes clashing with the traces of their real, clothed lives. A grass bracelet. Colored thread in a braid. A glinting toe ring. The music changed to Solange and J yelled, "Yasssss!" and danced away again. The people around him gangled and swung, baring their armpit hair, which looked and smelled like mold. He shuffled a little, cowed by an enthusiasm that sizzled and swelled and then, after a while, receded as the music evaporated into some floaty Björk-y song and the smell of pot drifted into the air. He leaned against his tree and tracked J as she wandered around the naked party, taking tokes like she was picking wildflowers.

He took one himself from a sweet-faced boy wearing only a septum ring and a shell bra, who swung by the tree and gave an air-kiss to a white couple, both dark-haired and wiry. They each took hits of the spliff, too, then continued their hazy argument.

"Uh, no, the intestine is definitely the largest organ."

"Think about it. The intestine *also* has skin, so if you add it all up . . ."

"Skin isn't an *organ*, Megan—"

A fat dude with a strategically placed holster interrupted them.

"Guys, what do you think this place would go for now? With this real estate market?"

"The housing bubble's gonna burst," the girl said, taking a drag from what smelled like an American Spirit. Who were these people? They seemed too old for Cal but too young to be homeowners. Without clothes, it was hard to stack them in the money shelves in his mind.

"But *when*?" the fat dude was pleading, scabbard dancing. "I can't take it anymore!"

"Probably when the Big One comes."

"Dude, the tech-bros are gonna flee like rats the second they feel a tremor." The wiry dude shoved his glasses up. His dick was at a comfortable half-mast, kinda big for his size.

"This place has become so fucking unlivable."

"Uh"—the girl glanced over again—"Didn't *we* do that?"

The fat dude frowned. "Who you mean *we*, sensei?"

He moved away from them then, wading toward the party's center. After a while, the churn of dancers broke up, spinning off into couples and trios. Voices strained over the music. The sex in the air felt stronger. He caught sight of J across the party, her eye patch like a hole in the head and before he knew it—he was high now—he was walking toward her. When he reached her side, she smiled, the gap between her teeth like some charming inner dimple.

"Heyyy . . . uh, hey." She swayed to greet him and then fell forward, her knee's impact against his thigh too hard to be intentional. He put a hand on her shoulder to steady her. Her skin was as soft as old cash. His gulping heart could have swallowed him whole. Then the tall dude beside her turned—it was the one from before, with the streaks on his face and chest—and gave a low grunt. Two other big dudes turned as if on command, shoulder muscles drawing a wall up around them. He stepped away from them, his vision laddering like a stocking.

The tall dude laughed, the red paint on his cheeks cracking. "I'm just messin' with you, man."

"Pete, *staahp*." J giggled, her palm sliding sloppily off his arm.

"What?" Pete shrugged.

"Stop being a *dick*," she said, half her mouth smiling.

"You can take it, right?" Pete said to him, then stuck out a fist. He blinked at it, then cautiously bumped it.

"Yeeeah!" Pete's eyes pulsed wide, then narrowed again. "See. That's my *boy*!"

"*Peeet*." J's giggles were bubbling over her words now, dissolving them as she began to laugh harder, and still harder, her face growing incredulous that she couldn't stop laughing. Tears wetted one pink cheek. A stoner's blind alley. He wished he could join her there.

"*Ka mattay! Ka mattay!*" Pete suddenly yelled.

The crowd around them muttered backward like a spray of water. Encouraged, Pete leaned forward and yelled louder, in his face now: "*Ka ora, ka ora!*"

"Yo man, what the fuck?" He instinctively stepped back, right onto someone's foot.

"Watch it!" the girl yelped.

He looked at her, grit grinding between their skin as he stumbled off.

"Watch out!" the girl said this time, or again.

"Sorry." He turned away, feeling his dick sticky against his thigh, soft for the first time since he'd arrived. Pete's head was tipped back with laughter but when he brought it down, he rolled it in a subtle neck-stretch and his pecs clenched briefly, once, like a wince.

276

"Look, Pete, man"—he shook his head—"I'm not tryna . . ."

"What?" Pete interrupted, dipping goofily toward him, eyes bright and flat.

J's giggles had finally fizzed out. She was frowning, biting her lips.

"Guys, guys, guys," she murmured to her collarbone, to her hapless breasts.

He felt the sudden impulse to grab her by the jaw and slap her serious. Instead he fit his teeth together and willed himself to look up and lock eyes with Pete, who was still smiling, chin ever so slightly raised, his boys on either side like shadows under a spotlight. They all breathed, panting in the night. Some techno song zipped and rattled around them like a trapped horde of flies. His ears and neck were staticky and hot. His eyes stung.

He shut them. He felt himself slide, then shuffle off sideways. Time to go. He turned and, ignoring the clamor behind him, weaved his way through the crowd, moving toward the kitchen door. The closer he got, the more impatient he got. He pushed people aside, skin brushing skin, daring them. But no one stepped to him, no one squared up. Just eyes itching up his back as he walked into the kitchen. He shut the door. The party burst to life behind it—laughter and a panicked joy and that terrible fucking music.

Hands buzzing, he rifled through the bags on the floor until he found his clothes—they smelled even more rank for having been mashed up together. He put them on and crumpled up his paper bag. He paused and looked around, his eyes washed clean. Then he smoothed his bag open again, whipped it through the air with the sound of wings. He squatted over the scatter of things on the floor and began to fill it up.

Yeah. Wallets, loose change, keys: all the stuff that goes in the plastic bin before you pass through a metal detector. Y'all don't even know. With all the efficiency and thoroughness that

Adeline had taught him, he ransacked those Berkeley Bowl bags, leaving them curled open on the floor like the empty nests in *Alien*. Y'all don't know who I am, do you? Eight cell phones, two necklaces, three iPods, a baggie. And from a bag labeled with a swooping black "J," a bracelet—a silver cuff that he decided to keep as a souvenir. Y'all have no fucking idea. He took it. He took all of it. And he ran.

Contributor Notes

Rabih Alameddine is the author of *I, the Divine*; *The Hakawati*; *Koolaids*; *The Perv*; *An Unnecessary Woman*; and *The Angel of History*. *An Unnecessary Woman* was a finalist for the National Book Award in 2014 and winner of the prestigious Prix Femina étranger. His most recent novel, *The Angel of History*, won the Lambda Literary Award.

Catherine Barnett is the author of three poetry collections, *Into Perfect Spheres Such Holes Are Pierced*, *The Game of Boxes*, winner of the James Laughlin Award from the Academy of American Poets, and *Human Hours*, which won the 2018 Believer Book Award for Poetry and was a finalist for the T. S. Eliot Four Quartets Prize. Her honors include a Whiting Award and a Guggenheim Fellowship. She is a member of the core faculty of New York University's Creative Writing Program.

Frank Bidart is the author of *Metaphysical Dog*, *Watching the Spring Festival*, *Star Dust*, *Desire*, and *In the Western Night*. He has won many prizes, including the Wallace Stevens Award, the 2007 Bollingen Prize, the National Book Critics Circle Award, and, for *Half-Light-Collected Poems 1965–2016*, the National Book Award and the Pulitzer Prize.

Elaine Castillo was born and raised in the San Francisco Bay Area, where she graduated from the University of California, Berkeley, with a degree in Comparative Literature. *America Is Not the Heart* is her debut novel, and was named one of the best books of 2018 by NPR, *Real Simple*, *Lit Hub*, the *Boston Globe*, *San Francisco Chronicle*, *New York Post*, *Kirkus Reviews*, the New York Public Library and more. It has been nominated for the *Elle* Award, the Center for Fiction Prize, the Aspen Words Prize, the Northern California Independent Booksellers Book Award, the California Book Award, and Italy's Fernanda Pivano Prize.

Jaime Cortez is a writer and visual artist based in Northern California. His fiction, essays, and drawings have appeared in diverse publications including the anthologies *Kindergarde: Avant-Garde Poems, Plays, Stories, and Songs for Children*; *No Straight Lines*; *Street Art San Francisco*; and *Infinite City*, Rebecca Solnit's experimental atlas of San Francisco. His debut short story collection will be published by Grove Press.

Natalie Diaz was born in the Fort Mojave Indian Village in Needles, California. She is the author of *When My Brother Was an Aztec* (Copper Canyon Press, 2012). She is the recipient of a Lannan Literary Fellowship, a Princeton Hodder Fellowship, a PEN/Civitella Ranieri Foundation Fellowship, and in 2018 was named a MacArthur Fellow. She is enrolled in the Gila River Indian Tribe. She teaches at Arizona State University in Tempe, Arizona, where she is the Maxine and Jonathan Marshall Chair in Modern and Contemporary Poetry. *Postcolonial Love Poem*, her new collection, will be published in March 2020.

Geoff Dyer is the award-winning author of many books, including *But Beautiful*, *Out of Sheer Rage*, *Zona* (on Andrei Tarkovsky's film *Stalker*), and the essay collection *Otherwise Known as the Human Condition* (winner of a National Book Critics Circle Award for criticism). A fellow of the Royal Society of Literature and a member of the American Academy of Arts and Sciences, Dyer lives in Los Angeles, where he is writer-in-residence at the University of Southern California. His latest book is *'Broadsword Calling Danny Boy': Watching* Where Eagles Dare. His books have been translated into twenty-four languages.

Jennifer Egan is the author of six previous books of fiction: *A Visit from the Goon Squad*, which won the Pulitzer Prize and the National Book Critics Circle Award; *The Keep*; the story collection *Emerald City*; *Look at Me*, a National Book Award Finalist; *The Invisible Circus*; and most recently, *Manhattan Beach*, which won the Carnegie Medal for literary excellence. Her work has appeared in the *New Yorker*, *Harper's Magazine*, *Granta*, *McSweeney's*, and the *New York Times Magazine*. She was born in Chicago and raised in San Francisco and lives in New York, where she serves as president of PEN America.

Reyna Grande is an award-winning author, motivational speaker, and writing teacher. As a girl, she crossed the US–Mexico border to join her family in Los Angeles, a harrowing journey chronicled in *The Distance Between Us*, a National Book Critics Circle Award finalist that has been adopted as the common read selection by over twenty schools and colleges and fourteen cities across the country. Her other books include the novels *Across a Hundred Mountains*, winner of a 2007 American Book Award, and *Dancing with Butterflies*, and *The Distance Between Us:*

Young Readers Edition. She lives in Woodland, California, with her husband and two children.

Former California and US Poet Laureate, and coordinator of the Laureate Lab—Visual Wordist Studio at Fresno State, **Juan Felipe Herrera** is a Capricorn, cartoonist, and children's book author. Winner of the National Book Critics Circle Award, his recent books include *Imagine* and *Jabberwalking*. He lives with poet partner Margarita Robles in Fresno.

Rachel Kushner is the bestselling author of *The Flamethrowers*, which was a finalist for the National Book Award and the Folio Prize, and a *New York Times* Top Ten Book of 2013. Her first novel, *Telex from Cuba*, was also a finalist for the National Book Award. Her latest book is *The Mars Room*, a finalist for the National Book Critics Circle Award.

Robin Coste Lewis, the winner of the National Book Award for *Voyage of the Sable Venus*, is the poet laureate of Los Angeles. She is writer-in-residence at the University of Southern California, as well as a Cave Canem fellow and a fellow of the Los Angeles Institute for the Humanities. Lewis was born in Compton, California; her family is from New Orleans.

Yiyun Li is the author of six books, including a recent novel, *Where Reasons End*.

Lauren Markham is a writer focusing on issues related to youth, migration, the environment, and her home state of California. Her work has appeared in outlets such as *Guernica*, *Harper's*, *Orion*, the *New Republic*, the *New York Times* and *VQR*, where she is a contributing editor. Markham is the author of *The Far*

Away Brothers: Two Young Migrants and the Making of an American Life, which was awarded the Northern California Book Award, the California Book Award Silver Medal, and the Ridenhour Prize.

Anthony Marra is the author of *A Constellation of Vital Phenomena* and *The Tsar of Love and Techno*. Reservations to Trattoria Contadina can be made at 415-982-5728.

Maggie Millner's poetry has appeared in the *New Yorker, Ploughshares, Gulf Coast, ZYZZYVA*, and elsewhere. She lives in Brooklyn, New York, where she teaches in the Writing Program at Rutgers University and is at work on her first book of poems.

Manuel Muñoz is the author of a novel, *What You See in the Dark*, and two short-story collections, *Zigzagger* and *The Faith Healer of Olive Avenue*, which was shortlisted for the Frank O'Connor International Short Story Award. He is the recipient of a National Endowment for the Arts fellowship, a Whiting Award, and three O. Henry Awards. His most recent work has appeared in *American Short Fiction, Glimmer Train, The Southwest Review, ZYZZYVA*, and *The Best American Short Stories 2019*. He has been on the faculty of the University of Arizona's creative writing program since 2008.

Tommy Orange is the author of the *New York Times* bestselling *There There* (Alfred A. Knopf), winner of the 2018 Center for Fiction First Novel Prize, finalist for the Pulitzer Prize in fiction, and longlisted for the 2018 National Book Award for Fiction, the Aspen Words Literary Prize, and the 2019 Carnegie Medal for Excellence in Fiction. It was deemed a Top Five Fiction Book of the Year by the *New York Times*, won the John Leonard Award

283

for Best First Book, and was nominated for the NCIBA Golden Poppy in Fiction in 2018.

D. A. Powell is the author of five collections of poetry, including *Chronic*, winner of the Kingsley Tufts Poetry Award, and *Repast: Tea, Lunch, and Cocktails*. *Useless Landscape, or A Guide for Boys* received the National Book Critics Circle Award in Poetry. He lives in San Francisco.

Shobha Rao is the author of the short story collection *An Unrestored Woman* and the novel *Girls Burn Brighter*. She moved to the United States from India at the age of seven and currently lives in San Francisco.

Greg Roden is a photographer and filmmaker. He won the *San Francisco Bay Guardian*'s best photo essay in 1998 for his black and white photo series, "Driven: Portraits Behind the Wheel," made while driving a cab in San Francisco in the early days of the Internet. Nominated for a James Beard award in 2012 for the TV series *Food Forward* on PBS, Greg received an Honoree Webby award in 2018 for his short film profiling photographer Danny Wilcox Frazier. He recently teamed up with writer and journalist William T. Vollmann on a film project titled "No Bad Takes," to be released sometime in the not-so-near future. He (sometimes) lives in Emeryville, California.

Namwali Serpell is a Zambian writer who teaches at the University of California, Berkeley. She won the 2015 Caine Prize for African Writing, received a 2011 Rona Jaffe Foundation Writers' Award, and was selected for the Africa39, a 2014 Hay Festival project to identify the most-promising African writers under forty. Her first novel, *The Old Drift*, was published by Hogarth/Penguin Random House in 2019.

Heather Smith is an editor at *Sierra Magazine* and a former Knight Science Journalism Fellow at MIT.

Matt Sumell is the author of the critically acclaimed collection *Making Nice*, which he is currently adapting for Warner Brothers Television. A graduate of the University of California, Irvine's MFA Program in Writing, his short fiction and nonfiction have appeared in the *Paris Review*, *Esquire*, *Electric Literature*, *Noon*, *McSweeney's*, *One Story*, *ZYZZYVA*, *Lit Hub*, the *Guardian*, *Publishers Weekly*, and elsewhere.

Héctor Tobar is the Los Angeles-based author of four books, including the novel *The Barbarian Nurseries*, and the nonfiction book *Deep Down Dark*, an account of the 2010 Chilean mine disaster and rescue. His work has appeared in the *New York Times*, the *New Yorker*, and *Best American Short Stories*. He is an associate professor at the University of California, Irvine.

Mai Der Vang is the author of *Afterland* (Graywolf Press, 2017), which recounts the Hmong exodus from Laos and the fate of thousands of refugees seeking asylum. The book received the Walt Whitman Award from the Academy of American Poets, was longlisted for the 2017 National Book Award in Poetry, and was a finalist for the 2018 Kate Tufts Discovery Award. Vang is a member of the Hmong American Writers' Circle where she co-edited *How Do I Begin: A Hmong American Literary Anthology*. Born and raised in Fresno, California, she earned degrees from the University of California, Berkeley, and Columbia University. In Fall 2019, Vang will join the Creative Writing MFA faculty at Fresno State as an Assistant Professor of English in Creative Writing.

Oscar Villalon is the managing editor at *ZYZZYVA*. His work has appeared in the *Virginia Quarterly Review*, the *Believer*, and *Zocalo*. He lives in San Francisco.

William T. Vollmann is the author of ten novels, including *Europe Central*, which won the National Book Award. He has also written four collections of stories, including *The Atlas*, which won the PEN Center USA West Award for Fiction; a memoir; and eight works of nonfiction, including *Rising Up and Rising Down: Some Thoughts on Violence, Freedom and Urgent Means* and *Imperial*, both of which were finalists for the National Book Critics Circle Award. His latest books are *No Good Alternative* and *No Immediate Danger*. He lives in Northern California.

Xuan Juliana Wang was born in Heilongjiang, China, and moved to Los Angeles when she was seven years old. She was a Wallace Stegner Fellow at Stanford University and received her MFA from Columbia University. Her work has appeared in the *Atlantic, Ploughshares, The Best American Nonrequired Reading*, and the Pushcart Prize anthology. She lives in California. Her debut collection of short stories, *Home Remedies* (Hogarth), was published in 2019.

Karen Tei Yamashita is the author of *Letters to Memory, Through the Arc of the Rain Forest, Brazil-Maru, Tropic of Orange, Circle K Cycles, I Hotel*, and *Anime Wong. I Hotel* was selected as a finalist for the National Book Award and received the California Book Award, the American Book Award, the Asian/Pacific American Librarians Association Award, and the Association for Asian American Studies Book Award. She is currently Professor Emeritus of Literature and Creative Writing at the University of California, Santa Cruz.

Javier Zamora was born in El Salvador and migrated to the United States when he was nine. He is a Radcliffe Fellow at Harvard University and has held fellowships from the Lannan Foundation, Poetry Foundation, and the National Endowment for the Arts, among other places. His first book, *Unaccompanied*, was published by Copper Canyon Press in September 2017.

About the Editor

John Freeman was the editor of *Granta* until 2013. His books include *How to Read a Novelist*, *Tales of Two Cities*, and *Tales of Two Americas*. *Maps*, his debut collection of poems, was published by Copper Canyon in 2017. He is the executive editor at *Literary Hub* and teaches at the New School and New York University. His work has appeared in the *New Yorker* and the *Paris Review* and has been translated into twenty languages.